THE EXTRAORDINARY LIFE OF AN ORDINARY MAN

'Newman at his best . . . Twice the book one could have dared to hope for, a narrative that is astute, introspective and surprisingly graceful.'
Wall Street Journal

'A stunning memoir . . . stuns with brutal honesty . . . smoulders with introspection.'
Daily Mail

'It is not your usual Hollywood celebrity memoir . . . this is an exercise in soul-searching, in public therapy.'
Mail on Sunday

'Utterly impossible to put down.'
Sunday Times Books of the Year

'It's never not psychologically fascinating.'
The Times

'Painfully honest and full of jaw-dropping revelations.'
Spectator

'A shocking posthumous memoir based on Paul Newman's brutally honest lost recordings.'
Express

THE EXTRAORDINARY LIFE
OF AN ORDINARY MAN

PAUL NEWMAN
THE EXTRAORDINARY LIFE
OF AN ORDINARY MAN

A MEMOIR

BASED ON INTERVIEWS AND ORAL HISTORIES CONDUCTED BY

Stewart Stern

COMPILED AND EDITED BY

David Rosenthal

FOREWORD BY

Melissa Newman

AFTERWORD BY

Clea Newman Soderlund

PENGUIN BOOKS

PENGUIN BOOKS

UK | USA | Canada | Ireland | Australia
India | New Zealand | South Africa

Penguin Books is part of the Penguin Random House group of companies
whose addresses can be found at global.penguinrandomhouse.com

First published in the US by Alfred A. Knopf, a division of
Penguin Random House LLC, New York, in 2022
First published in the UK by Century in 2022
Published in Penguin Books 2023

001

A select few names have been changed either due to inability to
confirm a memory or to protect them from a subjective observation.

Typeset by North Market Street Graphics, Lancaster, Pennsylvania
Printed and bound in Great Britain by Clays Ltd, Elcograf S.p.A.

Book design by Pei Loi Koay

The authorised representative in the EEA is Penguin Random House Ireland,
Morrison Chambers, 32 Nassau Street, Dublin DO2 YH68

A CIP catalogue record for this book is available from the British Library

ISBN: 978-1-804-94090-7

www.greenpenguin.co.uk

This book is dedicated to Stewart Henry Stern

March 22, 1922–February 2, 2015

Success is what determines the difference between vision and irresponsibility.

If I had to define "Newman" in the dictionary, I'd say: "One who tries too hard."

—PAUL NEWMAN, UNPUBLISHED INTERVIEWS, 1991

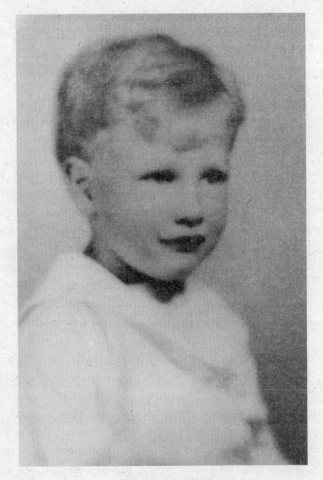
PAUL NEWMAN, CIRCA 1929

FOREWORD

In September of 1986, the year he embarked on this project, an article in *The New York Times* described Paul Newman as "a lean 5-foot-11."

A gossip columnist in the *New York Post* countered that "Anyone who has met Paul face to face says he has never hit 5-foot-11 except in heels" and offered a challenge: "$1,000 to Newman's favorite charity or political candidate for every inch he measures over 5-foot-8 . . . barefoot." Relishing the opportunity to stick it to Page Six, our dad matched it, upped the ante times a hundred and purchased some inversion boots so he could hang upside down for good measure. To our knowledge, the challenge was dropped.

In 1986 we can say with reasonable certainty he measured a solid 5-foot-10. Both papers were wrong.

He had integrity. He also had an abiding preference for privacy, and always felt awkward in interviews. The fact that our father ever considered the book you now hold in your hands seems completely weird to us, but he did keep at it for five years. An offering to the offspring is how he originally thought of it. That and maybe a way to "set the public record straight" after being dogged most of his life by the tabloids. Part confessional, part self-analysis, it's full of the kinds of revelations that, had they been shared with us sooner, might have made for some deeply meaningful conversations about relationships, identity, luck, and art, and, most likely, some pretty uncomfortable family dinners.

He decided the only possible choice of collaborator would be Stewart Stern, a dear friend, faithful keeper of family secrets, and a breathtaking writer. Probably best known for his screenplay of *Rebel Without a Cause,* he had also penned multiple screenplays for projects that involved both Paul and his second wife, Joanne.

Stewart's adoration of both of them, their collective children, and their children's children made him the kind of adopted relative who intertwined blissfully with the family DNA. Starting in 1986 he threw himself into this new project, passing along the subject's insistence that all the interviewees be as bluntly truthful as they could manage. Close friends and relatives were hired to transcribe. By 1991, however, he and our father seemed to have completely overwhelmed themselves out of it. They were up to their eyeballs in material.

Not much was said after that. After a year's illness (and almost one year exactly from his final win at Lime Rock race track), our father passed away in 2008. He was eighty-three. For us, for what seemed an eternity, the world stopped. There was the inevitable confusion and chaos to be dealt with, and the fog of grief.

Nearly a decade crawled by. Once in a while, the topic of the transcripts would come up. Details were hazy. There had been rumors of a bonfire. Stewart, who at ninety-two was now coming to the end of his own life journey, was desperate to know what happened to them. He wanted them archived at least for posterity. Before the mystery could be solved, he was gone.

We assumed the transcripts were floating around somewhere. Or perhaps not. We wanted to see them . . . or did we, really? In 2019 we stumbled upon some ancillary interviews in locked file cabinets that had migrated to the damp basement of the family house in Connecticut. Sometime later our friend, producer Emily Wachtel, found the entirety of our father's transcripts as she was archiving a family storage unit. A cursory peek turned into a year-long reading project, and what was revealed felt raw and personal. Fourteen thousand pages in, she suggested it might be interesting to try to finish what was started.

You can read about private jets and red carpets elsewhere. This is definitely not that. Instead, it's sort of a self-dissection, a picking apart of feelings, motives, and motivations, augmented by a Greek chorus of other voices and opinions, relatives, Navy buddies, and fellow artists. One overriding theme is the chronic insecurity which will be familiar to so many artists. Objectivity is fickle. It's difficult for some people to understand, given all that success, how that sense of doubt could be so relentless. Here was someone who suspected himself an impostor, an ordinary man with an extraordinary face and luck on his side, achieving far beyond what he'd set out to do. He always felt it was tenacity, not talent, that saw him through. There were some who dismissed him, but luckily there were also plenty who recognized something remarkable in him long before he did.

And finally, there is the public fairy tale of two Hollywood stars and their blissfully uncomplicated fifty-year marriage, which, besides being bogus, seems unfair to anyone, famous or not, who has ever committed to a romantic relationship. Acknowledge that there were two families, half siblings, and other collateral damage and suddenly the story becomes far more relatable. The mood in the house was unstable, stormy one minute, joyous the next. The truth ultimately gives more credit to the flesh-and-blood couple who weathered all of that drama and betrayal and came out on the other side, battle-scarred but still inexorably intertwined.

It's a cliché for fathers of a certain vintage to be distant or unknowable. Ours was the inevitable sequel to his own frustrated father and all the preceding generations that flailed away at parenting with little or no guidance. This book looks backward from a moment in time. To his lasting credit, our father continued to evolve after these interviews were conducted, contributing some of the best of himself, emotionally, artistically, and altruistically all the way to the end. To suddenly have at our fingertips this encyclopedia of his thoughts and motivations, his conflicts . . . his context, has been, shall we say, deep. That he speaks about wanting us to know everything is beyond moving.

Melissa Newman

L et's see if we can write a first chapter, then try that with a second chapter, then a third, then a fourth and a fifth . . . Let's see now: we've got *that* covered, we've got *this* covered—we've got the attitude down, the creation, the drinking and all of the humor and whatever the morality is.

The most ironic thing of all is that one could say at the beginning, like writers do in some biographies, "This is the boy who accomplished this and then that and then grew up to be the prime minister. And now we'll go back and look at the details of how that happened."

But it turns out that this book is just the story of a little boy who became a decoration for his mother, a decoration for her house, admired for his decorative nature. If he had been an ugly child, his mother would not have given him the time of day. If he had had a limp, or an eyelid that drooped, and she stopped to comfort that small invalid beside her, it would have been to satisfy her own sense of needing to comfort something—but nothing actually to do with the boy.

And the boy became so offended by the artificiality of it, and the fact that it did not relate or connect to him in any way, that the core of this kid finally said, "Jesus Christ, take it, it's yours! I'm going to save what's left of me over here."

Then the boy with the decoration just ran away with the football. He was getting everything. He was eating and living well, and he was leaving the the core—the orphan, if you will—in the dust.

But the orphan kept running to catch up with that decorative little shit he so despised, even as the decorative little shit was getting away with all the honors, doing all the plays, grabbing all the encomiums and the praise, and the orphan kept losing ground. He never did catch up until the last few years, and then he said, "Whoa. Wait a second. Let me at least look around and see if I can make any sense out of this."

I was my mother's Pinocchio, the one that went wrong.

And I'm still trying today to disentangle my own heart and wants from everyone else around me who are certain they know the answers.

This book came out of the struggle to try and explain it all to my kids. I was thought of as distant and reserved; well, that happened not because other people's arms were too long but because mine were too short. And as their arms became longer and longer, my own became shorter and shorter: it was a sense of suffocation that happened to me.

I want to leave some kind of record that sets things straight, pokes holes in the mythology that's sprung up around me, destroys some of the legends, and keeps the piranhas off. Something that documents the time I was on this planet with some kind of accuracy. Probably, in my dotage, I'll go over it and create an autobiography with some semblance of truth. Because what exists on the record now has no bearing at all on the truth.

That's all I really want to do.

THE EXTRAORDINARY LIFE
OF AN ORDINARY MAN

I'm in my Connecticut house, in the library, sitting by the fire on a formal little couch. I just smoked a joint and remembered with absolute clarity the whole map of my boyhood hometown, Shaker Heights, Ohio. It's all there to be remembered, things I thought were dead and buried, things I never thought I'd recall . . .

I was born there in 1925. Shaker Heights then was the Cleveland suburb that every other American suburb aspired to become. It was the standard by which other affluent places measured themselves. We lived in a spacious, three-story home on Brighton Road, which was far from the wealthiest stretch in the neighborhood, but we were certainly well-to-do. My father, Arthur, and his brother, Joe (known as J.S., and in his spare time a prolific author of popular doggerel), ran the Newman-Stern sporting-goods company from an imposing corner building downtown; in its category, it was second only to New York's original Abercrombie & Fitch.

Having grown up in Shaker Heights, I can still remember the horse-drawn carriages that pulled the milk wagons or the blocks of ice. Our public schools were considered the best in the United States. There were hundreds of acres of woods, and five little lakes where we'd fish and explore. Safety was never an issue; in summertime, you could spend four days in those woods and nothing would happen to harm you. The most raucous it got was when we kids had a "war"; we'd snatch people's tomato-plant stakes and throw them as spears, defending ourselves with garbage-can lids. It was like a ritual from Papua New Guinea.

All the families were lily white; no foreigners, no Black people, either, amid the quiet streets and estates. The Newmans may have been the first Jewish family to penetrate Brighton Road. But we were really just like anyone else; we'd hold makeshift circuses in our backyard, selling lemonade, doing fancy tricks on our swings. Young kids my age and that of my older brother, Art Jr., would come to my house and our father would entertain them by telling them made-up stories, starring his creations the ever-adventurous Terry Berry Boys. He'd recount them as a serial, a different chapter every night. And when he was finished, he'd make believe he was a scary animal, and all the neighborhood kids would jump on top of him and wrestle him. He'd cover up, like a boxer; then it would just be over. "That's the end, guys," he'd say, and the children would be ushered back to their own houses while Art and I headed to bed. Of course, Art would always find the time to kick the bejesus out of me, often in what we called "the club"—actually our home's third-floor "attic," where we shared a playroom.

He'd delight in sitting on my back, taking hold of my chin and seeing just how far he could bend back my neck. I think he felt I deserved it, because he thought I was getting all the attention from our mother, Tress, all of her devotion, and that he didn't get more than crumbs. The big difference between Arthur and me was that our different relationships with our mother didn't ultimately bother him. Arthur always thought that of the choices available to him, God had put him in a place where nothing could be better. My brother chose to remember the good things from our childhood, while I best recall the failures and the things that didn't go right.

We spent a lot of time up in our playroom; it's where we did our homework. Art practiced his drums there, too, while I played records on the Victrola and sat in a comfortable chair reading lots of comic books. Our "club" was more congenial than our family's fancy living room downstairs, where no one really did any living. You might say my sense of "decoration" began right there in that carefully furnished showplace. My mother took great pride in how that

PAUL AND ARTHUR JR., CIRCA 1929

living room looked; to me, her taste was chilly, sort of what today might be called "Bloomingdale's Modern." Everything was mani-cured; everything was designed for appearance, not comfort. Early on, she decided to lay down all-black carpeting—and then bought herself a white Spitz dog because it looked great on the carpet. Of course, whenever the dog moved, he left a trail of white fur.

Next to the living room was a proper dining room, where for years we ate virtually all our meals together; there was rarely any conversation, and the evenings at the table could be painful. Our dining table was inlaid, and always covered with a linen tablecloth. It would be set each night with wonderful china. We'd be sitting there, my father always the last to arrive. He often wore a jacket and tie, though if he'd had the time to change after work, sometimes a bathrobe. Although we had a maid, my mother would pass the plates around herself, often serving some very simply cooked meat, vegetables, and mashed potatoes. Before beginning, there'd usually be some sort of toast offered by my father; my brother and I would clink our water glasses.

My mother eventually decided she didn't want to keep ironing that linen tablecloth, so she had us move to the much smaller breakfast room off the kitchen for our meals. My father disagreed with that shift, so he continued to eat in the dining room, alone. Dessert would be pudding or cake—my mother was a fine baker—and after that Father would say "Excuse me" and go upstairs to read (he never tired of the *Encyclopaedia Britannica*, which he went through end to end more than once) or to take a nap. Art and I would help with the dishes, then go up to our playroom, cook a batch of popcorn, and drink iced tea or pop.

It was also in the dining room that Art and I would bang our heads against the wall. Literally. We did it in secret until the dent got big enough for my parents to notice. This was not some tippy-toe banging; this was a serious whacking that took down the plaster behind the wall covering. We must have knocked our fucking brains out. It was our own Wailing Wall. I couldn't take my rage out on anybody my size, so I took it out against the wall. Today, it makes me laugh to think of us—these two little guys tapping each other on the shoulder, saying: "My turn." . . . "Oh, after you!" Art was bigger, so he probably got the first shot. Since his head was about six inches higher than mine, we never banged at exactly the same spot. (Years later, when I came home after World War II, I checked on the wall and was amazed to see the huge ruptures.)

Our house contained the sounds of constant warfare. It could be

ARTHUR AND PAUL IN THE MID-1930S

a quiet war, like the chunking of knives in human flesh, as surreptitious and stalking as commandos moving silently through the night. It could also be explosive and noisy, which was usually my mother erupting. Or threatening to erupt. We'd sit there waiting for something to go wrong, for somebody to fall off the eggshells and run, waiting for a mistake and the explosion to follow. We'd be in bed, and we'd hear our parents fighting, hollering at each other. I'd hear things breaking. There was one fight where my mother took a picture down from the wall and broke it over the top of my father's head. It was a pastel of nymphs cavorting nude (which I had examined many times with a magnifying glass). It hung right over the sofa in the living room. My father must have been left walking around with the frame around his shoulders. I'm certain there'd been serious grief, but all I see in my head now are cartoon images of these things.

––––––––

When I was five years old, America entered its Great Depression. A full 85 percent of the sporting-goods stores in the country went bust in those years, and my father seemed in the depths of despair. We were a luxury store at a time when no one was buying luxury items. Newman-Stern would hold a sale, and whether it was successful or not would determine whether we'd stay open.

At one point, the brothers Newman ran out of cash; I remember my father going to Chicago and getting the Spalding and Wilson companies to extend him $250,000 worth of merchandise on consignment; my dad had such a fine reputation for integrity, the manufacturers knew they'd eventually get paid back for their goods. It was an extraordinary testament to my dad and my uncle Joe and their code of doing business that they survived the Depression financially intact.

All of us helped out. My father would never let my mother work, but she still let the maid go—and he was furious about this. My mother said, "I'll clean, and I'll take the money I was paying the maid and buy the kind of furniture I want." And she did. She took on all the washing, the mangling, the ironing, purchased new furnishings or reupholstered the old furniture herself, even sewed the drapes and valances. (It was a great source of pride, and a triumph of keeping up appearances, that my father never let our membership lapse at the Jewish country club, the Oakwood.)

I began working in the Newman-Stern stockroom, and as I got a little older, I was moved to the sales floor. I sold all kinds of things: binoculars, balls, tennis gear. I was a good salesman, an honest salesman. If I was selling a guy a bowling ball and he said, "Golly, I really don't know if I need a new bowling ball," I'd say, "If you don't need it, don't buy it." I enjoyed working there.

Following World War II, Newman-Stern also carried army surplus. A guy had dropped by peddling crates of leftover Norden bombsights, the futuristic, once-top-secret military device that allowed US planes to accurately drop their payloads on Germany and Japan. This guy couldn't unload his cumbersome inventory, understandably. You'd see these elaborate contraptions and think, "What can anyone use this thing for?" But Uncle Joe (who'd studied applied science while in college) and my father began taking the machines apart and figured out the puzzle. There was a segment of the bombsight where if you pushed a little button, a powerful electric motor turned on, and with a little improvisation you could have yourself a relatively inexpensive automatic garage-door opener. There were rheostats that could be repurposed for many critical household uses, and even an early analog computer was built in.

The brothers took a full-page ad in the Cleveland *Plain Dealer* describing how each of the bombsight's thirty-six separate components might be repurposed. For three or four days, you couldn't fight your way into our store. Cleveland's renowned Case School called and bought two entire units for $2,800 apiece—a tremendous amount of money then. It was bedlam—maybe $200,000 in revenue for a few days.

Uncle Joe and my father were ebullient. It wasn't so much the money, but that they had taken something that had been offered around everywhere and only they had the vision to see its possibilities. They'd invented a huge success. This was the romance of retailing. And the brothers Newman were romantics.

It hadn't started that way, certainly not for my father. When he was a young man, my father wanted to be a writer; it was really all he wanted to do. Not long after returning from his service in World

ARTHUR NEWMAN SR. AT HIS OFFICE IN 1938

War I, he became the youngest reporter ever hired by the *Cleve-land Press*. But brother Joe seduced him into joining his fledgling sporting-goods business, which originally had specialized in selling electrical-experiment kits for boys as well as more sophisticated microphones, transmitters, and telegraphs. (The big move to sporting goods came after the government banned private telegraphy equipment sales following America's declaration of war on the Kaiser in 1917.) Joe was the firm's president, my father the secretary-treasurer, and he fell under the shadow of my uncle. He couldn't find a way out—he was just starting a family, he had responsibilities, and he was an honorable man. He couldn't possibly place all the financial burden on his young wife, and Arthur Newman Sr. never believed in divorce.

He became a prisoner: imprisoned by the store, imprisoned by his dick, with no time to really think through his decisions.

I don't think his work ultimately pleased him. I don't think his castle pleased him. And I don't think his family pleased him, either.

Teresa Fetzko, my mother, was a beautiful young woman who immigrated here with her family from Eastern Europe (what was then the disintegrating Austro-Hungarian Empire, the part we now call Slovakia). She arrived not long after the turn of the twentieth century, practically a girl, practically in rags. Her family was very poor, and that contributed to my mother's everlasting fear of losing everything. She claimed her father was a professor, but in fact he was a bricklayer. Her own mother had died when she was still a child, and at sixteen she married a young guy, but divorced him shortly afterwards because, she claimed, he abused her.

When my father met her, she was working as a ticket taker at the Alhambra Theatre in Cleveland. Going out with my father, who was far more accomplished than she was, she decided to convert from Roman Catholicism to the relatively less fraught (and perhaps less familiar to her beau's Jewish family) Christian Science. She soon became pregnant by my father, and despite a great deal of pressure from his family, the baby (my brother, Art Jr.) was indeed born and Arthur Sr. and Tress married sometime later. My father did so under duress, and I suspect had he not been such an honorable man, he would have left her in a minute. I'm not sure if my mother simply loved him greatly, abhorred abortion, or had other reasons for wedlock, but the two of them managed to settle down together. I was born just about a year after Art Jr., a pending birth that apparently prompted considerable discussion about alternative options.

The Newman relatives, from the beginning, had an attitude about Tress for many reasons. Because she was a Gentile and they were Jews, even if mostly nonpracticing ones. Because she was gorgeous. Because they considered her a hussy ("Wasn't she a divorcée?"), a gold digger, and below their social and educational station (ironic, given that only one generation removed, the Newmans themselves were itinerant peddlers and tinkers). They viewed my mother's people as an embarrassment. How inferior that must have made her feel; how left out it must have made him feel!

My father was basically a shy man who never, in my memory, mingled with his wife's family. My mother took my brother and me every other week to visit our dour and silent grandfather (where we were fed his wife's wonderful chicken soup), but my father never came along; I think he met them only twice. I also think my father was angry at us for going, because we always visited our grandparents on a Sunday; my father worked six days a week, and our trips left him home alone. Sunday, in fact, was less happy for him than any other day of the week. Still, my father didn't want anything to do with them; I don't even know if he ever allowed them to set foot in our house. They were the poor relations.

It's probably not surprising, then, that my mother became a very private woman with only a few close friends. And while she was devoted to her house and her husband, she ultimately despised them both, and mistrusted all of her family. She was the most suspicious woman who ever lived, hysterical with the thought she'd never be accepted or get her fair share of anything. And those suspicions followed us throughout our lives.

What my mother did embrace was her own consuming passions—although never the objects that created the passion. She came to love opera, for example, and would drag me to five-hour Wagner performances at Severance Hall; the music would provoke a soaring response in her. As a child, I might do something cute or come

ARTHUR AND TRESS IN 1921

downstairs looking especially pretty, wearing little shorts and a sweater, and she reveled in the great flood of emotion that flowed through her, whether it was tears or joy. The child himself was not really seen, just as the opera was not really heard. What happened inside her head and heart had very little to do with the Wagner or with me, only with her own flood of ecstasy. You could only pray that she'd let go of you. And if the child managed to pull away or the music stopped, she wouldn't have missed either of them; her emotions would have continued, fed by their own size and scale, until they died of exhaustion. Only then might she have asked "Where is he?" or "Did someone turn off the music?"

Sexually you could probably have taken away her partner and the passion wouldn't have stopped until she came and asked "Where'd he go?" That's a terrible thing to say about your mother, I know, but I think it's terribly funny—and terribly sad.

There's an image I see in my mind's eye where I'm a child in some kind of pain with a splinter in my finger, and my mother surrounds me, cooing and grappling and groping until the life is squeezed out of this little wretch. And as she discovers the lifeless form in her arms, bewildered, she cries out, "But I was only trying to comfort the poor thing!"

I was like one of those poor fucking dogs of hers who became cancerous and so obese they could hardly move, and my mother would keep feeding them chocolates until she killed them with kindness. My mother was oblivious to the damage being done. Her need to bestow affection not only overwhelmed the object she bestowed affection upon, but had nothing to do with that object. My mother's dogs were an analog to her children, to that empty decoration running around loose grabbing all the affection while his orphaned core just tried to protect himself from being crushed by the decoration. It took fifty years before the core could sit down and begin to deal with it.

She never saw the dogs themselves, only her own kindness. And she was so flooded with and in love with her own kindness that she kept poisoning these squat, obese dogs till they melted like ice-cream cones and slithered down the side of the living room couch to join all those white hairs they'd shed on her black carpet.

LUCILLE NEWMAN WAS PAUL'S AUNT,
THE WIFE OF ARTHUR NEWMAN SR.'S BROTHER, JOE

Both of the Newman boys, Paul and Arthur Jr., have to realize that both their mother and father were sick people. Sick
in the sense that they had no peace, real peace, ever, and that
they were drowning.

If Art Sr. had tried to divorce Tress, given her temper, she
might have done something very irrational. She was a lonely
person, and some of the things she could do were plain cruel.

I really don't know what kind of life Art Sr. would have had
if he'd married someone else; there really was a tremendous
attraction there. And to Tress, he represented a kind of security. Whether she had real love for him, I don't know. But she
couldn't have really loved anything except that blind, fat dog
she fed the candy to.

One of the ways their marriage may have affected my father was
that he developed into a secret drinker, an alcoholic. I'd always
thought that when my father died, in 1950, the cause was cancer.
But it is only recently that we examined the results of his autopsy
and discovered that it was alcohol's effects on his pancreas that was
a major contributor to his untimely death at age fifty-six.

This was the routine: The Newman-Stern store would close each
evening at 5:30. It would take my father exactly twelve minutes to
walk from there to the Terminal Tower in downtown Cleveland to
catch the rapid-transit train to Shaker Heights. That would leave
him seven minutes to stop into Fred Harvey's, the bar where all
the businessmen went after work, and quickly down a couple of
drinks—two double bourbons with water chasers. He'd dash for his

train, and when he got home he'd head right upstairs, where he had a bourbon bottle stashed in his closet, and pour himself another double.

———————

BABETTE NEWMAN WAS ONE OF ARTHUR NEWMAN SR.'S
SISTERS-IN-LAW; SHE MARRIED HIS BROTHER AARON.
STEWART STERN WAS A HIGHLY REGARDED SCREENWRITER
AND HE WAS ONE OF PAUL NEWMAN'S CLOSEST FRIENDS.

LUCILLE NEWMAN: Tress told me Arthur would do things like this: Let's say it was a holiday, and the children were there, of course, and they were dressed for the occasion and she had prepared a nice dinner, set the table pretty and everything, and he'd go upstairs and put on the dirtiest old rotten clothes he could find and come down to the table looking a wreck.

BABETTE NEWMAN: Just a sad, sad thing. You want to cry.

LN: It's terrible.

STEWART STERN: But what was he protesting, I wonder? Her perfection? He wanted to dirty it up and make it liveable, do you think?

BN: Well, I know that I never saw Tress without being perfect. Her hair was beautifully—

LN: Right to the last minute of her life, and she was wearing wigs.

BN: He may have been protesting that.

———————

At the kiosks along the rapid transit line, there'd be ones where you could buy magazines, candy, bubble gum, and, at one point, 3.2 percent beer. It was called Fort Pitt beer; the label conjured up images of cowboys and Indians. One Sunday afternoon, Arthur and I, who were probably around eleven and twelve, talked our father into buying us a bottle. We brought it back to the house, and with great ceremony he opened it up and toasted us. I had my first taste and thought, "God, what affliction is this? Why would anyone drink something that tastes like that?" It was just awful.

My father didn't care. "You wanted it. We ordered it. You didn't like it. Now you better finish it."

I got it down the hatch and swore to myself that I'd never drink another glass of beer.

I don't think Art and I ever saw our father truly drunk. We knew he'd taken the edge off before dinner, and years later we'd find empty liquor bottles secreted in a crawl space near our basement. No wonder he went downstairs to check on the furnace so often. What we also later found were piles of secreted cigarette butts. Though Arthur and I were often berated for sneaking smokes up in our attic "club," it turns out our father was regularly having his own cigarettes—despite the fact he had sworn to my mother he wasn't smoking.

LUCILLE NEWMAN

When Paul went back with Arthur to see the house at the time of Tress's funeral, they wanted to see two things—one was if the dent in the wall was still there where they had banged their heads, and if the hole was still there in the third-floor screen where they had shoved their cigarettes for fear that they might be caught smoking them.

I didn't want generations of Newmans doing secret things in different rooms again. If my son, Scott, smoked pot, I'd smoke with him, too. I've wondered in recent years whether the serious problems I eventually had with booze, that Scott suffered so terribly with addiction, might have somehow been partly inherited—bad blood with the Newman men. And I also often wonder whether my father's drinking had anything to do with the difficulties the two of us had in communicating.

ARTHUR JR. AND PAUL IN SHAKER HEIGHTS, CIRCA 1928

The strongest recollection I have of my father (and that best describes our relationship) happened when I was about twelve. It was on a Sunday, and my father said to me, "Let's go take a walk." I was delighted, staggered by the opportunity. We walked and walked, but I could think of nothing to say that was of any interest to him. Nor could he find anything to say that provoked a response from me. The best we could do were rhetorical exchanges like "Isn't that a nice tree?" or "Isn't that a nice fire hydrant?" I'd walk sideways, half skipping, looking up at him, and he'd just keep nodding his head affirmatively. Not a single thought passed between us.

Kids find out about their parents only by asking questions. Unless, of course, their mothers and fathers are tellers and talkers, which I never was and never have been. My own kids were fascinated once I did start talking to them; but if you're a nontalker and your kids never ask, what then?

One afternoon, playing baseball, I was trying to catch a fly ball but missed it and landed on top of the ball; I badly hurt my ankle. It was right before dinner, and I started practically crawling home. My father, who'd just come from the rapid-transit station after work, passed by. I asked him to help me, and he replied, "Are you kidding?" and just walked on. He probably thought I was being a crybaby. The next morning, when my ankle blew up to the size of a grapefruit, I was taken to the hospital. It turned out to have been broken.

There was a sense of dissatisfaction around the house that I couldn't do anything right. My father was dismissive, disinterested; a note of sarcasm would always creep into his voice. I think he stopped trying to inspire me because he felt he was licked. I didn't try harder to be an educated man because in a strange way I knew I couldn't. When I read Schopenhauer in school, I didn't remember it, and I didn't even remember what I didn't get. Years later, when Joanne and I became good friends with Gore Vidal, it was difficult for me to be around a man who could speak so intelligently about so many things: American writers, the Greeks, the Romans, French playwrights, while I was just an illiterate. I've come to realize I have some kind of disability that makes it difficult for me to listen, to hear people, to read faster than I can speak, even to memorize. Whatever the reasons, I never did anything academic with distinction, never gave my father anything to be proud of.

The only way I could get any sense of accomplishment was through work, to make money. It may have been the only thing I did that really pleased my father, to show him I could be a self-starter, able to get jobs all by myself. I think I also had a desperate need to be independent, to get away from a sense of always being taken care of at home. And we were always being taken care of—I can't remember my brother and I ever having to clean up anything. I sure worked a lot. I was making deliveries for the florist and for the dry cleaner, carting pickle barrels and Coca-Cola cases up and down stairs for the delicatessen, and even did a stretch as a Fuller Brush man. I applied when I was thirteen, and became an undersized little towhead carting around this suitcase filled with samples that weighed more than, and was fully as big as, me.

I did have a perfect route, in a blue-collar neighborhood off Kinsman Road. My mother would pick me up after school, then drop me off there with my gear and collect me three hours later. Kinsman was where the working people lived, and they all needed what I was selling: garage brooms, hairbrushes, toothbrushes, whisk brooms—sixty different varieties, excellent quality, and much cheaper than they'd cost in a store. I didn't have much of a spiel, but I didn't have to walk far from house to house, either, and wound up making maybe forty dollars a week.

I remember ringing a doorbell to one house and this very good-looking young woman, maybe twenty-four, answered the door wearing just a slip with her breasts practically falling out; she seemed slightly wasted and degenerate to me. She said, "Come on in, little boy," and I instantly sensed this was highly irregular and had nothing to do with Fuller Brushes. Quickly calculating the odds of surviving this lady, I fled, dragging my suitcase flat on its side, with my samples falling out behind me as I ran.

The job I had that may have left the strongest impression was when I was delivering newspapers. I was a really good bike rider, and my paper route was near my house. On Shaker Heights Boulevard there were these huge houses—they'd be selling for millions of dollars now. They were right out of F. Scott Fitzgerald and *The Great Gatsby*, all the pretty women in their summer dresses, patrician elegance, and ease of grace and manner. I developed a real yearning to be rich. I mean *fiercely* rich. I got it, because I saw all these beautiful people to whom I was delivering my papers. And it seemed so far from anything I could ever reach toward, just out of sight.

ARTHUR NEWMAN JR.

Paul ended up with drive and energy and resourcefulness and maybe it came from being a boy who wants to pull himself out of his environment by his bootstraps. Maybe all the things he has in the back of his mind with respect to his youth and his mom's domineering were the seeds for all that drive, energy, and guts. He gets this self-starting built into him and what happens to him? He becomes a success.

Art and I had a friend, Dick Goss, whose family was very wealthy—we'd always heard that the father, Colonel Goss, had gotten rich developing chemical-warfare weapons in the First World War. Besides their Shaker Heights home, they also owned a plantation down south and summer places up north. One day after school, I was visiting, walking through their library, and saw their new Christmas tree was up, all covered with lights—and decked as well with five- and ten-dollar bills. When Mrs. Goss, a very dignified-looking woman, who was reading in the corner, saw me, she said,

"Good afternoon, Paul." And I replied, "Mrs. Goss, excuse me, but could you please explain to me why your Christmas tree has all these five- and ten-dollar bills on it?"

And this was her exact answer: "It's to prove to Dick that money does not in fact grow on trees—it is put there."

It left an impression.

STEWART STERN

What would make kids in that household bang their heads against a wall?

Paul never knew what was going to hit him because—though Tress was overwhelmingly proud of him, proud of his beauty, and dress him up like another part of her house—she would suddenly, without any reason Paul could think of, attack him savagely with a hairbrush then immediately smother him with love. He wouldn't know who she was or who she thought he was. How did he survive?

Paul has told me he so often feels anesthetized that he blacks out most of his childhood, doesn't remember most of it. What he's been looking for is the answer to the riddle of his being—why he has so much distance from his own emotions that, until recently, he could feel very, very little. A little sad, a little happy—but could never allow himself to feel all the way with either.

JEWELL FETZCO WAS A SISTER OF
PAUL'S MOTHER, TRESS.

Before Tress met Art Sr., she married a plumber named
Elmer. He was insanely jealous of her; if she just looked at
someone, there'd be hell to pay. He beat her terribly. I went
over to see her one Sunday, and her face was so disfigured
you couldn't even tell it was her. "Tress, what happened?" I
asked. She wouldn't say anything except, "Well, I just had
some trouble."

Elmer was a handsome devil, dark hair, a moustache, nicely
built. But he was as mean as the dickens. My sister Mae and
I told her she was going to get killed, that she needed to get
a divorce. She was embarrassed about the whole thing, but
she agreed to go down to the court with us so a judge and
an attorney could see for themselves what she looked like
all beaten. She went to live with Mae for about six months
while the divorce was getting finalized; she came home one
afternoon and everything she had, all her furniture, had
been taken, everything except a mattress to sleep on. She
screamed.

We took her back to see her attorney the next day, and he
got an order for Elmer to return it all. Not long afterward,
the divorce became official.

When she met Arthur, Tress fell madly in love with him.
That he was Jewish made no difference to her; she didn't care
whether his family or her family liked it or not.

I think Arthur was in love with her, too. Tress said: "I'll get
him."

And she did.

BABETTE NEWMAN

Arthur was going with a beautiful woman before he met Tress, and was very much in love with her. She turned him down and he married Tress on the rebound. Tress looked a great deal like the woman who turned him down.

JEWELL FETZCO

Tress was living alone in an apartment when Arthur Jr. was coming into this world. Our mother sent me to stay with her; I didn't know what was going on. "Where is Arthur?" I asked Tress. "Why do I have to be here with you all the time?"

I was a dumb kid. Then, after she started to show, she didn't discuss it. You didn't mention it. When she finally told me she was pregnant, she said Arthur's family didn't accept her and that's why he wouldn't come live with her. All I can remember is she cried a lot.

LUCILLE NEWMAN

Tress was pretty, she was bright, she was a talented person. But her sense of values was not an ordinary sense of values— she would rather sacrifice people before sacrificing her house or any piece of it. Tress had to leave home very early and all her life she wanted the security of a home. She was always so set on ensuring the security of their house that she would not even allow anyone to come in and clean or put up wallpaper or paint. Even after she sold the place many years later, she took the chandelier with her and substituted a different one because that chandelier was just a part of her. Once, she gave me a gift, six salad bowls. And a few days afterwards she called me and asked: "You really don't need six, do you?" and she took four of them back.

When Scott Newman was a little boy, he locked himself in one of the upstairs bathrooms and couldn't get out. Tress refused to let Paul break down the door. He ended up having to call the fire department to go in through the bathroom window to get Scott out.

I remember a lot more about grammar school and junior high than I do about high school. How the places looked. The class-rooms and auditoriums. What it was like to walk home. I felt very much a part of those schools and the life that went on around them. I felt accepted and involved.

I rode my bike well and dangerously, pretty daredevil stuff. We'd follow the rapid-transit tracks to where the streetcars stopped; there were kiosks there to buy ice cream and soda pop. We had yo-yo contests, too, and I was very good.

We'd play hockey in the winter; holes were dug in vacant lots, to get flooded and freeze; there was also a big pond for hockey or ice skating. Sometimes we'd take our car out for Sunday trips to the outer reaches of Shaker Heights, the end of civilization, and my father would teach Art and me how to drive our Studebaker. Other times we'd head over to Akron and get sandwiches at a great barbecued-beef joint. I remember these days with great affection; these were easygoing times.

Then, around when I started adolescence, something in me closed down. I don't know what it was, but I began to feel like an outcast. I began to sense I was on the outside looking in, and didn't even know what I was looking for inside. I got painfully shy. I tried to play football, and though I knew I was fast, everybody else seemed to have gotten five times bigger than me, and I couldn't be successful anymore.

I was so small, I had to get special dispensation from my school's principal to play on the ninth-grade team; at fourteen, I didn't even weigh a hundred pounds. I felt like a goddamn freak. I also didn't know how to deal with girls, because I was so short; they thought I was a joke, a happy buffoon. I was a lightweight—a description that permeated every area of my life.

I started to develop an awareness that certain other people were true originals, instinctive at whatever they did, and everyone could recognize that. Everyone could separate the natural football player from the ones that had to labor at what they were trying to be. Everyone could separate the great lovers—great because they were instinctive—from those who *studied* love. Some people were simply who they were, and the rest were scholars.

I wasn't naturally anything. I wasn't a lover. I wasn't an athlete. I wasn't a student. I wasn't a leader. I measured things by what I wasn't, not by anything I was. I felt that there was something lacking in me that I couldn't bridge, didn't know much about and couldn't fathom. I wasn't getting it. I wasn't getting the message.

So if I read stories today where people who knew me growing up say they saw me as some swaggering romantic, as a loner too confident to bother with their company, it comes as a real surprise. I was just too painfully shy to pursue friendships with the people I wanted to be friends with. I was afraid they'd recognize me as a fraud, just pat me on the head and say, "See you around."

All I was interested in was girls; they were all I could think of. And I just wasn't very successful with them.

Sex, in my youth, was seen in a different context than it is today. Back then, if a button on your pants was accidentally left open, and someone said, "Hey, your fly is open," my God, you'd walk around in paroxysms of embarrassment for a month. Talking about sex in the 1930s is like talking about people in the Stone Age, draped in furs and carrying clubs. If there'd been such a thing as *Playboy* magazine back then, I would have cut off my arm just for a peek. If I wanted to see a picture of a woman's breasts I had to sneak into our library's stack of *National Geographic*s and thumb through pages

PAUL AND FRIENDS IN SHAKER HEIGHTS, EARLY 1930S

that were already softened by wear. Either that, or ride my bike at dusk down to Hathaway Brown, the all-female boarding school in Shaker Heights, and try to spy a glimpse of some unsuspecting girl walking naked past the window on her way to the shower. Or scoot over to that new house on Eaton Road where the lady who moved in had mistakenly installed a two-way mirror in her bathroom. From a distance—until she and her husband figured out the problem and put up some blinds—she unknowingly serviced quite a few prepubescent neighborhood boys.

There were no adult movies. No dirty postcards. And no dirty girls, which made it hard to follow my mother's advice that any kind of sexual intemperance was to be exercised only with ladies of the lower caste, not the well-bred ones of Shaker Heights. My mother's highfalutin ideas were perhaps born of her feeling that she once had been the woman soiled and trampled on, forced to bear children out of wedlock—and her wonder at now being a part of the upper class herself made her resolve that Art and I must remain unsoiled.

The best Arthur and I could do was the old burlesque house on 9th Street in Cleveland. I don't know how we got in; I must have looked like I was nine years old; maybe I hid underneath someone's coat. Anyway, it was absolutely riveting. Though Arthur ran home and tried to sterilize himself afterwards.

From my earliest sexual memories, it seems I was getting the short end of the stick. When I was maybe six or seven, I went into the bushes with Dorothy Frances and her friend and said, "I'll show you mine if you show me yours." And I did show them mine—but they just giggled, clutched their panties, and wouldn't show me theirs.

Later, in junior high, I went to my first hayride and barn dance; I just knew I was finally going to have a serious sexual foray. What I didn't know was just how bad my hay fever was, and just as Mary Jane Phipps was about to lay back in the hay and enjoy my advances, I started sneezing. I was absolutely crippled. There'd be no lengthy kisses, because there was no way I could breathe through my nose.

It wasn't long afterwards that Mother fired Ruth, our longtime maid; I'd heard it was because she'd gotten pregnant by her boyfriend. She was promptly replaced with a seventeen-year-old girl who'd been the runner-up beauty queen at a Cleveland high school. My mother assigned her a bedroom right next to Art and me. My God, what could have been better than to be a fourteen-year-old boy with an attractive seventeen-year-old girl nearby that you could imagine banging? I would have been such a willing and anxious student! The delights that might have surfaced, the dalliances between two o'clock and four o'clock when she had a couple of hours off! But I was deprived of that experience. My mother, the harridan, was lurking everywhere, omnipotent, and it wasn't long before she caught me in the girl's room, where we were simply looking at each other provocatively. That new maid was packed up and gone the next day.

My losing streak continued even after I enrolled at Ohio University before being drafted. I auditioned for a part in a student production and actually got the role (probably because there were so few other men left on campus owing to the war). It didn't take long before I became infatuated with another cast member, a statuesque French beauty who was likely a full head taller than me; I loved to dance with her because I could just lay my head between her boobs. I think she was indifferent to me, but I did finally manage to get a real date with her. I had visions of, if not getting laid, then at least rubbing my lips across her neck. I brought her back to the dorm, and as I prayed for an invitation up to her room, she patted me on the head and affectionately said, "I like going out with you because you're so harmless!"

Sometime in the late fifties, I saw a poll in a popular magazine where they asked a lot of women which well-known personality they had sexual fantasies about. Whose picture did they use when they abused themselves? Well, the "winner" happened to be me. Which I guess is pretty funny, until you consider that had I been killed in my bomber during World War II, had I gone down in flames, that was as hot as things would have gotten for me—I'd been laid only twice. Which is a fact that likely would have both elated and displeased my mother. The young woman who took my virginity (which I dispensed with quick charity) was a lady whom I'd picked up in a disreputable part of town. My second encounter, for the record, was with a lady of very lofty birth in Jacksonville, Florida, where I would undergo part of my naval training. Needless to say, neither of these breakthroughs occurred until I was out of my home and safely heading to the South Pacific on my way to fight the Japanese.

PAUL, TRESS, AND ARTHUR JR. ON VACATION AT
PIKES PEAK IN THE LATE 1930S

A strong sense of otherness also emerged pertaining to religion. When I was young, being half Jewish—or simply thinking of myself as Jewish—got in the way of sitting at the "A" table, which was important to me.

Nothing in my childhood gave me the instructions that would have made me proud or knowledgeable about my Jewish heritage. I only knew that if you were Jewish, some avenues were shut to you, avenues you might have liked to walk on. That hurt me and my brother a great deal. And I think there was a period in my life when I tried to make up for it.

One way was to deflect pain with humor. The attacks came not just because I was Jewish, but because I was so small. (After you've been punched and been sat on a couple of times, you learn ways to avoid punishment.) I started to do Yiddish voices for laughs, volunteering to do an imitation of Schlepperman, a popular recurring character on Jack Benny's radio show, voiced by Sam Hearn with a thick Yiddish accent.

When I was fifteen or so, I began to realize there was exclusion. I was applying to a high-school fraternity—they were very popular then—when Arthur told me, "I wouldn't expect very much. You'll get blackballed because you're half Jewish." And I thought to myself, "No, that could never possibly be true." But then my friend Roger came back from his frat meeting and told me the news: "God," he said to me, "I'm really sorry, but there are things in our bylaws that say we can't have Jewish brothers."

I'm ashamed of the fact that I was vulnerable enough to be deceptive, or at least not a hundred percent open, on my original Kenyon College application after my time in the Navy. The application asked for my religion. I didn't just write in "Preference: None" or "Half Catholic, Half Jewish." I wrote in my mother's adopted faith, claiming I was a Christian Scientist. Other than that, I never hid my background from anyone; nobody had to dig it out of me, and I certainly didn't deny it.

It's probably not a coincidence that when I served in World War II the only bloody fight I got into involved an anti-Semitic taunt. I was based in Hawaii on my way out to the Pacific theater. There was a beer garden there for the sailors, though you weren't supposed to take the beer off premises. I figured a way to smuggle out the bottles, by wearing a denim jacket under which I could hide four or five brews inside my belt. The trick was you'd go over a back wall, then right back to your barracks with the contraband. One of the sailors there looked up from his bunk and said to me that I owed him a beer.

"For what?" I replied.

"You kike, you owe me a beer."

I charged the guy and a big brawl ensued. Though I wasn't much of a puncher, I had practiced wrestling at Ohio University; I had an extraordinary sense of balance and could throw down an opponent, get on top of him in midair and fall on him. When I landed on this guy, he had his arm underneath his hip and tore everything out of his elbow. When he got off the floor, he could only move one hand. The fight was called off and no one bothered me again.

Years later, when my acting career started gaining momentum, I was given the opportunity to pass, to change my name and become a Tony Curtis (born Bernard Schwartz) or Kirk Douglas (aka Issur Danielovich). Broadway and Hollywood suggested I become Buck Something-or-Other, a really WASPy identity; and I could have eliminated my Jewish roots, simply obliterated the thing that had caused so much discomfort. But it seemed more of a challenge to me to keep my real name, to insist upon it as a badge.

In 1953, the famed, ruthless producer Sam Spiegel, who went by the pseudonym S. P. Eagle for over two decades, was briefly considering me for the Terry Malloy role in *On the Waterfront*; he asked me to get rid of "Paul Newman." "What do you want me to change it to?" I asked him. "S. P. Ewman?"

My father, unlike some of his relatives, was always a nonpracticing Jew. Nevertheless, he held on to two seats at our local synagogue, which he paid for every year. One weekend, my mother told him, "I'd like to go over to that synagogue, see what it's like in there." And so they went: the husband and the wife he routinely took out late on Saturday nights so she wouldn't have the energy to wake up on time to attend her Christian Science service on Sunday morning. The only problem was that when they got inside the synagogue, my father's seats were occupied. So my father went right to the business office, where it was explained to him that they'd indeed sold his seats, twice; since he never did attend services, what harm would it do? After some back-and-forth my father ended up keeping those seats for the rest of his life, to guarantee that he and my mother, the Gentile, could one day be buried side by side in the Jewish cemetery administered by the synagogue. And so they were.

Other than the pew he rented, my father displayed no outward symbols of Judaism. We celebrated Christmas with caroling and a generous pile of beautifully wrapped gifts under an impressive tree (which, to my chagrin, my mother insisted on buying, and she embraced a metallic one with the awful artificiality that conveyed). In our home, my father (though he received a daily copy of Cleveland's Jewish newspaper) didn't own so much as a menorah. Still, he was anything but naive about the bigotry Jews faced in the world.

Though we rarely took family vacations, one year we got in the car and took a summer outing to Maine. Though this was in the midst of the Depression, my father insisted that we travel in style, and he booked a cabin at the Black Point Inn on Prouts Neck. It was grand, on the sea, surrounded by blueberry bushes, and was unquestionably stuffy, ritzy, and very Gentile—a point not lost on my father who decided to register us under an assumed, very non-Jewish name. Honestly, I think the only reason they let us check in was because we were driving a classy Studebaker Commander.

BUSH KEELER WAS A CLOSE CHILDHOOD
FRIEND OF PAUL'S.

The Jewish stigma in Shaker Heights was very strong. I know that my mother had a certain reluctance about me seeing a lot of Paul because he was partly Jewish. She was dissatisfied with our companionship. Although her true self liked Paul, her socially conditioned self made her ambivalent.

She just wanted me to be involved with that damn private-school crowd. Paul didn't seem Jewish at all, but he paid a price, he had a rough time. There used to be a lot of ethnic quips about Jews that would go around the high school.

Paul was a funny guy, and he could find humor in almost everything. And that's how he bounced back from the prejudice. Do you know the Schlepperman character from the old Jack Benny show? Paul was the master impersonator, and he'd get everyone howling. I think he did it to tell them they were hurting him. Somebody used to pick on him, but he would always come back laughing.

———

JIM MARTIN WAS ONE OF PAUL'S CLOSEST FRIENDS IN SHAKER HEIGHTS AND THROUGH COLLEGE.

I always found the younger Paul quite frivolous. I always felt he was very happy, with nothing to hide. And Paul's mother, Tress, was an absolutely wonderful person. She'd normally have a big strawberry cake baked for us after school.

But I also was troubled that Paul's household seemed somehow sad. The place was immaculate, always. We'd have to remove our shoes before we came inside. There were always sheets covering the furniture in the living room—the lamps, the sofas, everything. It didn't feel like anybody lived there.

———

≡ III ≡

My one recurring nightmare is only sound, and it has never gone away.

It's very impressionistic, benign at the beginning, just a sense of clouds with a kind of ease about them. And then it's as though these clouds are accompanied by a noise that is not really definable. Rustling leaves, maybe, the sound of water, maybe, but always closer and closer.

There's a great sense of roiling, nothing distinguishable, until it can't get any closer, can't get any louder. But it does get closer and louder and closer and louder and closer and louder. It's wind and sea and sound but never identifiable.

I've had this nightmare since my memory begins. Never more specific, but ominous somehow.

When that nightmare first started, I had never flown, nor did I know what it was like to be in an airplane during a thunderstorm. In my dream, there's something of that same threat.

It terrifies me.

My father went out for a Sunday stroll on December 7, 1941, and came back to our house by the side door. He was white as a sheet and he told us the Japanese had just bombed Pearl Harbor.

For all that it meant to me, he might as well have said that Mickey Mouse and Minnie Mouse had just given birth to four dogs. I hadn't the slightest idea where Pearl Harbor was. I didn't know what a war was or what constituted a war. I didn't even know what cancer was. These were years of my illiterateness of the most shallow kind. I was just living inside my head. I was occupied creating an imaginary, exciting world in which I was the White Knight who vanquished all enemies, a world where I was seven and a half feet tall and only did important things.

———

I always tell people—and I know it has been written about—that I was thrown out of the Navy's pilot-training program because it was discovered I was color-blind. But it's a little more complicated than that; looking back, it wasn't just my color blindness but a combination of issues. I couldn't do the mathematical things that being a pilot requires. I don't really understand hard science. It does not penetrate. This doesn't mean I am unwilling to learn it, but the more I'm involved in the pursuit of *how* to understand something rather than actually understanding it, we appear to be in trouble. Physics, trigonometry, and chemistry—they were too complex for me. I got discouraged and just gave up.

I hadn't yet finished high school when the war began. And after graduating in June 1942, when I was still seventeen, I had, as usual, absolutely no solid plan for what I wanted to do. But I did know that if you didn't pursue your education, you'd be drafted as soon as you came of age and end up swabbing decks on a battleship. This was a big reason I enrolled at Ohio University—attending college was the way I might eventually get to make some choices for myself, at least as far as the military was concerned. So when I began college at Ohio U, in Athens, I also enlisted—knowing that my official call to duty was set to occur no sooner than my eighteenth birthday, on January 26 (and likely later); I took the written aptitude tests and applied for pilot training.

To my surprise, just after my birthday, I was summoned from school and directed to Detroit for a physical. And I was stunned, because I flunked; the medical examiners discovered I was color-

TRESS AND PAUL AT OHIO UNIVERSITY IN ATHENS, OHIO, IN 1943

blind. (I should have had a tip-off a few months earlier when my brother, Arthur, wrote me that he'd been rejected for pilot training because—guess what?—the doctors found out he was color-blind.)

So my choice was to continue with my officer enlistment protocols or just withdraw and head back to Ohio U and wait for my draft number to come up. But, I thought, to what end? I'd enjoyed the drama classes I'd tried in my first semester, but Ohio U really was nothing but a lot of beer drinking and dating. The only thing that distinguished me there was that I was a great chug-a-lugger. And since it was taking forever for my Navy paperwork to get reprocessed and have me officially thrown out of the pilot program, I was still sent to deck officers' training school, which was held on Yale University's campus. With the luck of the draw, I got billeted in a structure that was actually an old annex to the finest dormitory there. I had a big living room with a bedroom off to one side, even a wood-burning fireplace. I guess if I'd been a good student in New Haven, my color blindness might have been overlooked entirely; but pretty soon I was ordered off the campus and back to square one to attend enlisted men's boot camp, basic training, in Newport, Rhode Island.

Hundreds of sailors-to-be lived in my barracks, and like me they were not even given a bunk bed but assigned to a hammock—I didn't get a decent night's sleep for four months. We were roused at four thirty or five each morning—and it was cold there. The first order of business was calisthenics, and then we'd have to run a couple of miles. I was not in very good shape and was smoking cigarettes, so these were hard times.

When at Newport, I was required to undergo another physical. One of the corpsmen administering the exams was a guy I'd met during my brief time at Yale; he'd been thrown out of medical school there, and ended up in my boot camp, too, as a pharmacist's mate, third class. And when he gave me the color-chart test, I was, bewilderingly, not color-blind anymore.

What it meant was I could now apply for the Naval Air Corps, at least as an enlisted man. No, I likely couldn't be a pilot, but I applied for training as an aviation radioman and was accepted. So I was assigned to radio school in Jacksonville; I finished that course and volunteered to fly on torpedo bomber planes. These TPM Avenger bombers, manufactured by the thousands by General Motors, were slow, lumbering, single-propeller aircraft, carrying just three-man crews—a pilot, a machine gunner based in a "bubble" just above the cockpit, and a radioman/gunner based in a turret under the plane's belly. The cruising speed was only about 150 miles per hour. The TPM's primary mission was to spot enemy submarines and torpedo them from the skies. We'd see a sub, lock in the gyroscopic aiming device on our target, and then drop down to between six feet and fifteen feet over the water and hold a steady position before firing. That made the TPMs sitting ducks for enemy planes, perfect for the enemy's target practice.

My next stop was Miami for gunnery classes (Robert Stack was my instructor), and to tell you the truth, I wasn't an especially talented machine gunner. Then it was off to Oxnard Air Base in Southern California and finally to Pearl Harbor as part of a squadron of six TPMs.

I became pals with two sailors during my Florida training: Milt Dance, whom we called Danny and who came from the Maryland shore, and Tommy Brady, a tough little guy from Boston. What first drew us together was that the three of us were all roughly the same size; we were also good-time Charlies who discovered we liked to laugh a lot. When we were asked for our preferred assignments, Danny, like me, volunteered for torpedo-bomber duty, while Brady somehow got himself attached to a dive-bomber squad.

A few days later, on Brady's very first exercise flight off the Florida coast, he was killed when a wing on his plane got clipped by another dive bomber's wing and went down in a midair crash. I remember being stunned by the news, but I somehow didn't connect it to myself. I don't even recall getting edgy about getting in an airplane afterwards. Back then, there must have been a strange, wonderful sense of immortality. And my own evolving type of emotional anesthesia.

It never entered my head that there was a chance we wouldn't come back alive.

———

MILTON DANCE WAS A TORPEDO PLANE CREWMATE
OF PAUL'S THROUGHOUT WWII.

When we had to qualify for gunnery, they flew a towed sleeve behind a plane and you'd have to hit it with your anti-aircraft gun. Each sailor was given a belt of ammunition that was painted a certain color, so when you shot through the sleeve, it was easy to tell whose bullets hit and went through.

As a gunner, Paul couldn't hit beans, couldn't hit that towed sleeve with the turret gun to qualify as our plane's gunner. But someone else on another crew had hit it, putting fifty

PAUL IN HIS NAVY UNIFORM, 1944

rounds with red on their casings through that sleeve. When we landed, we told the Navy trainers: "Paul was shooting those red ones, that's him!"

We lied so Paul could qualify—but I don't think that son of a bitch ever hit the sleeve.

———

We stayed in Hawaii while our squadron awaited orders to be assigned to some battle-bound aircraft carrier. Each morning I'd report for duty to the flight shack, a little makeshift wooden structure attached to one of the hangars. Sometimes we'd have to take off for flight exercises, but we generally did absolutely nothing all day, sitting around, just playing Hearts and drinking a little beer (after five o'clock, of course). I did use a lot of the down time to read a tremendous amount, mainly philosophy by the likes of Spinoza and Nietzsche; I was trying to get an education, and was probably also trying, I suppose, to impress people. There was also an enormous number of letters from my family to go through; I was receiving more mail, it seemed, than anyone else in our flight group. Arthur would regularly write me from his base in England, and my father corresponded just about every day I was in the service. My father's letters were very unemotional, often focused on bringing me up-to-date about what was happening at Newman-Stern.

And my responses were anything but candid. I lied to my brother, I lied to my mother, I lied to my father. Gross, personal deceptions. I can't think of any true thing that came out of my letters, except maybe "I stood watch last night." But there wasn't a single adroit perception in any of them; I think I resent that the most about myself.

To be honest, though, I was much more interested in getting letters from a couple of ladies I'd left behind. The one I remember best was Joan Gloeckler. She was exceptionally good looking, with a sensational figure; we were in the same class at Shaker Heights High. I don't think it was anything steady, but just as I left for the war, there was some sense that we were suddenly romantic. I wouldn't call it a hot love affair, maybe it was just wishful thinking, but it was comforting to have someone back home you thought was your girlfriend. She wrote to me for a long time while I was in the Navy. But about a year before the war ended, she sent me another letter saying that she had found some other guy; I was history. It broke my heart; I don't know why, because it had never been very serious.

Sometimes a bunch of us would get a pass and go out to a place just north of Barbers Point, about sixty miles from Honolulu. There was an extraordinary beach there with very soft sand, and the water was pleasantly warm. You'd spend a couple of hours just running into these five- or six-foot waves that would break against an angled falloff point close to the shore, and get bowled ass over teakettle without any movement or restriction. Again and again you'd be washed up on the beach, like a frog. Our whole squadron would head out there and the Hawaiians would throw a luau for us, cook a whole pig outdoors.

On many days, Danny and I would get in some flight exercises and practice antisubmarine attacks, strafing targets towed by target planes or dropping depth charges. Then we'd just head back to barracks, where we'd hang out with the other crews; it was pure boredom.

The most exciting thing that happened to me—and the most harrowing—came when Danny and I agreed to participate in a little "experiment."

The Navy was concerned about the possibility of our planes that were attacking the Japanese mainland getting shot down by coastal batteries and ditching into Tokyo Bay. What needed to be tested was a method by which the survivors in those downed planes' life rafts could be saved by Allied submarines. The idea was that our subs might somehow grab hold of the lifeboats and drag them into deeper water unseen by the Japanese; there, the airmen could actually be taken on board by the sub—all hands safely out of the range of the Japanese solid shore armaments.

Danny and I thought it would be a diversion and no big deal. So off we headed to a staging area, where our test raft launching had to be abandoned because the water was infested with sharks. So we were ferried to an alternative site, where each of us was put in a one-man raft tethered to each other by a rope—then abandoned together in the Pacific Ocean to await our underwater ride back home.

We'd taken a bunch of contraceptives with us which we used to hold our keys and keep our cigarettes and some cookies dry. As instructed, we released green-dye markers around us, to make us more visible to our planes. Dive bombers would be sent out, spot us, and then radio our position to nearby subs. It was really a hoot. At first.

And so we waited. And waited and waited some more. The sea was coming up, the air was starting to get cold, and all we had on were sweatshirts and shorts. We were alone in the ocean and there was still no sign of any aircraft.

Suddenly into view came a big amphibious transport boat that had no connection to our experiment but had noticed our dye markers. They signaled us they were heading our way, but we signaled back "Go away, go away!" They ignored that, and pretty soon, they launched a smaller craft and pulled alongside our rafts. The commanding officer said, "Get on board," but he finally got the message when we said, "We can't—we're doing a test." I could swear the waist gunner on the ship was so angry at us that he unlatched his safety and considered pulling the trigger. At any rate, they took off and we continued to watch the sky for our rescue dive bombers.

Late that afternoon they finally appeared. And a half hour behind them was a Navy submarine. It was weird seeing a submarine coming right at you at water level; it had about eight feet of periscope pinpointing us, but when it tried to snag our tether to haul us from danger, it missed completely. It could only spot us at a specific angle. The sub sailed about 150 feet past us before it realized we weren't attached. We were hysterical until the sub made another run at us, caught us, and started to pull. No one had anticipated that with our hookup at the top of the rafts, a sub would not only pull us forward but under the surface; we were dragged for about two miles and held on for dear life. Then the submarine started to surface. I didn't know what the hell was happening. It's hard to describe what it's like being on a tiny raft when this huge thing starts blowing its tanks, rising out of the sea. The noise was unbelievable; this was the only time I was really scared. Even worse, the sub's antenna poked right through the bottom of Danny's raft and practically impaled him in his butt.

We were safe, but there's a postscript here, too. The skipper welcomed us aboard his sub, and noticed we looked blue.

"God, you guys must be frozen!" he said.

So we were very appreciative when the skipper disappeared for a moment and came back with an old and very good bottle of Canadian rye. He poured the three of us a couple of fingers, we slammed them down, then he poured another round.

"Well," the skipper said, "now I'm supposed to ask you some questions about the rescue. Please tell me your names, ranks, and serial numbers."

"My name is Paul Newman, sir. I'm not an officer. I have no rank. I'm an aviation mate, third class."

"You're an enlisted man?"

"Yes," I replied. And with that, he took away our whiskey and poured it right back into the bottle.

Booze would play an interesting role in my war. Danny and I got teamed with a pilot named Pat Filippi, an ensign. Like the other officers, Pat would receive a booze ration every month. Since Pat didn't drink, he'd often give his bottles to Danny and me.

If we didn't drink it ourselves, we'd sell the booze to other enlisted men for anywhere from fifty to a hundred bucks a pop, whatever the going price was that week. I had more than adequate money to start with, since my pay was seventy-eight dollars a month for being a third-class mate, plus a 50 percent bonus for flight duty. Problem was, I was a terrible gambler. Between poker, shooting craps, and blackjack, I'd lose my whole check within an hour of getting it. So I had to earn it back somehow, which I did by playing bridge for money against the pilots and selling the booze I got from Pat. And what did I use this money for? To buy beer, of course. If I couldn't steal it.

Right after we were finally ordered off Hawaii, my TPM crew (and our plane) sailed much closer to the war zone, dropping anchor off Guam. The first night we disembarked to the island, all of us got pissed off because there was no beer rationing. But it didn't take long before we discovered where the beer and liquor cache was stored.

Everything was kept under a big supply tent and was protected by a couple of marine guards. We sent a couple of decoys over to the sentries to ask directions to the infirmary and distract them while the rest of us snuck under the canvas to where the beer cases were stacked. It wasn't like we planned on rifling thousands of dollars' worth of alcohol; we just wanted to grab a few for ourselves and sneak back to our bunks. But instead, we all ended up just sitting down under the tent, finally back on dry land, just bullshitting with one another until we heard taps and the lights went out.

"Let's go," said one of my companions, while another guy suggested, "Well, why don't we just wait until things quiet down a little bit." Which we did. Until we heard shots fired. Turns out one of the marine sentries caught a couple of other soldiers sneaking under the tent and shot them both. I don't know whether they lived or died, though word was they were hurt pretty bad. Needless to say, my crew soon got out and decided not to try that stunt again.

We'd traveled to Guam on a CVE, which everyone called a "jeep carrier." These were converted troop transports or freighters, and they became our floating home until the end of the war. The CVEs were like miniature aircraft carriers, complete with a flight deck, though their runways were much, much shorter and thus scarier. This made for many a white-knuckle landing, especially in rough weather, when the nose of the CVE was constantly rising and falling in the swells.

One afternoon we had a routine patrol flight with a pilot I didn't know who was filling in for Pat. We came in for a landing and as we were close to touching down, the deck controller gave us a wave-off, which meant we had to climb and come around again. It made me a bit nervous, because this was usually done only if a plane came in improperly aligned with the runway. We made another descent, and again we were waved off; I was getting more uncomfortable, especially since I was in the turret with my back to the cockpit and couldn't really see what was going on.

So around we went one more time, and I got pretty unsettled when yet again we weren't allowed to land. This time, though, our pilot turned to the right of the bridge when he was waved off, which was unheard of, because it was truly dangerous—if you misjudged your turn, you'd hit the carrier. Next time we approached, we were finally permitted to touch down, and as soon as we came to a stop, our pilot jumped out of our plane and started yelling angrily at the sailor who'd been waving us off. What we found out later was that there had been nothing wrong with our pilot's flying, only that on board our CVE was a photographer from one of the big weekly magazines taking pictures of planes touching down on a flattop. He wanted the perfect shot, and the Navy was just helping him out by giving him some extra material for his pictorial.

We were honestly very fortunate. A few months before, when we were still in Hawaii, the six planes in our original TPM group were assigned to report to the USS *Bunker Hill*, one of the most powerful carriers in the Seventh Fleet. But our pilot took ill that morning, and we were grounded; we never went there, and we became an unaffiliated plane waiting to become a replacement on one of the other big ships—something pretty unlikely for an unattached aircraft, as entire squadrons tended to be assigned together. Late in the war, off Okinawa, the *Bunker Hill* was attacked by two kamikazes, each carrying a 550-pound bomb. One of the suicide pilots penetrated the flight tower and the pilot's ready room, setting off huge fires and killing close to 400 sailors—including ten of the fifteen crew members from the squadron to which we'd originally belonged.

We sailed from Guam to Saipan, where we disembarked in the aftermath of one of the war's most ferocious battles. Even though our commanders told us to be on our guard for Japanese army stragglers raiding our camp at night for food, I don't think it was actually very dangerous by the time we got there. In fact, eight or ten of us marched ourselves into the mountains one day looking for

PAUL SHOWING OFF HIS NEW NAVY DUDS
TO HIS MOTHER IN 1944

souvenirs—discarded helmets, uniforms, or ammunition belts; we didn't see any sign of Japanese survivors. The worst thing that happened is that we hiked through a thicket and I was attacked by a swarm of yellow jackets; I think I got bit twenty-four times.

Most of our time, really, was spent on our jeep-carrier ship. Everybody was talking about our anticipated invasion of Japan, how we were really grouping for a final attack, and how the potential for huge losses in that invasion was very high.

Our ship was about seventy-five miles off the Japanese mainland when we heard about the A-bomb, and then the surrender. There was a tremendous sense of elation that this whole thing was over. Just a few days after Nagasaki, our CVE was ordered back to Pearl Harbor. My first thought was "Here we go again—we'll all get stuck there for another year before we're discharged." But as we got close to Hawaii, new orders came down that basically said "Keep going." And so, without stopping, we just headed straight for San Francisco. We docked and were given a two-week leave, with orders to report afterwards up in Seattle.

But before that happened, there was celebrating to do. Some pilots I had met on board rented a big room at the renowned Mark Hopkins Hotel, and a couple dozen of us sailors stayed at that party for about three days. There wasn't an orgy, but it got pretty wild. The pilots would head down to the Mark Hopkins bar, pick up some girls, and bring them upstairs to the party. I remember a lot of guys from the flight crews running around in their boxer shorts; the girls seemed to think we were all officers. You'd wake up and start drinking beer again in the morning. Remember, the war had only been over about three weeks then; we were all behaving badly.

The five months I ended up spending in Seattle were equally "productive." I was assigned to an airplane hangar, where they had me doing mechanical work I was in no way equipped to do. That, or helping to pull old generators out of Hellcat planes.

Since I was still losing money gambling, I needed cash to keep from going broke. To that end, I got guys who were being discharged to give me a piece of ID and their booze coupons, which entitled the bearer to buy liquor on the cheap. Another sailor I met, Joe Beeler from Kansas, had gotten $1,300 from his father to buy a used car, and he picked up a four-door Pontiac. Out of spare wood and scrap metal, I fashioned a bar that we slung over the back seat; I covered it with carpet, and cut holes in the plywood for bottles, glasses, and even an ice chest. In 1946, there wasn't another limousine out there that looked anything like that.

We essentially used the Pontiac for three things. On weekends, we'd take a couple of girls we met, students at the University of Washington, up to Mount Rainier to go skiing. It was an expensive proposition; so during the week we ran a car service from the base to the mountains, and we'd take pilots and other officers along for a price. Beeler and I would do some work waxing skis, then go skiing ourselves—and still get back to the parking area in time to ferry our customers back to town. Our finest work came when we would drive to the downtown Seattle dance halls, which closed about midnight. There were all these guys there who had picked up girls but now had no place to drink. So Beeler and I would pull up and just stand there holding these unmarked pints and quarts of liquor. We'd charge them fifteen or twenty-five bucks each, and that would finance our next week's ski trips with the girls, with enough left over to buy them dinner.

I was honorably discharged in April 1946, went home to Shaker Heights, and by June 1, was enrolled at Kenyon College. Perhaps the most notable thing that came out of my years in the service was that I really shot up. When I went in, I barely made the height minimum of five foot five. I left at least five inches taller.

———

For all the effect the war had on me, it was probably the same thing as being in a touring company of *The Taming of the Shrew* going through Schenectady, Poughkeepsie, and upstate New York. There was no sense of amazement. No sense of survival. There was very little sense of danger, very little sense of growing up or developing some maturity as a result of it. It was like going through a shower, that's all.

———

Sometime in the mid-1950s, Joanne and I snuck off for a weekend together and we ended up on Cape Cod. I pulled into this little dock area and saw a guy coming out of a shack at the end of the pier. And I yelled out to him, "Hey, where can I get a sport-fishing boat out here?" He didn't answer but started walking over toward me, so I asked him again: "Do you know where I can get a sport-fishing boat?"

I got a good look at him and noticed a tear trickling down the side of his nose. He comes over, throws his arms around me, and starts crying. I didn't know what the hell was going on. Joanne was hopeless, too.

"Martin. Randy Martin," he said. I had no idea who Randy Martin was, but he seemed to know a great deal about me.

"Do you remember Kathy Anne?" he went on. "I married her, we got two kids . . ." And this all started to ring a bell. "Come on over to our place and have some dinner."

Joanne and I got in our Volkswagen, and I said to her, "I know who that is; he's a guy who I was in the Navy with, he was in our squadron." He'd made some reference to the beach at Barbers Point, and I finally remembered—he was a gunner. We went to his home, ate dinner with his family, and learned a lot about lobsters.

I ended up going out on his boat with him the next day, and it was the most exciting time. It was like being in Vegas, pulling up lobster pots, seeing if there was anything in them. I'd start jumping up and down when we got a big one, a fifteen-pounder, but Randy would turn it on its belly to see if there were eggs; if there were, he threw it right back in the water.

Pretty soon, there were lobsters crawling all over our deck and we'd chase them around and try to put these wooden plugs in their claws. And coming back to Chatham at low tide, there was a narrow channel into the inlet, and Randy just waited for a wave and rode it to the dock like we were on a surfboard. What a wonderful skipper! In fact, in years to come, I'd take my kids up to visit, and it was great seeing them so excited, trying to grab the clacking lobsters on the deck and put rubber bands around them.

But Randy turned into a terrible drunk, a bad alcoholic. He lost his family, he lost his boat, and one day he turned up on our doorstep in Connecticut. So I took him over to the rehab center near Westport, where they admitted him and dried him out. When he was discharged, he had a girlfriend from AA come to pick him up and take him back to the Cape. I arranged a loan for him so he could get a new boat.

But Randy went off the wagon, crashed his car, broke his shoulder, and ultimately sank his boat.

I haven't heard from him since.

PAT FILIPPI

Newman always cocked his hat, and I used to chew his ass out. "Get that thing on right!" He'd tilt it back properly in front and the next thing you knew, it was angled on the back of his head again.

From a thousand yards away, I could tell it was Newman coming because of the way he walked. He had a certain stride about him; he was a confident kid even then as a nineteen-year-old. Hell, I was only three years older, but he impressed me that way.

Paul was a one-liner. Whenever he expressed himself, he said it in one sentence. When I hear him now in an interview I say to myself, "Jesus Christ, this kid hasn't changed one bit."

IV

T he incredibly stupid mistake I made coming out of the war, having not been shot down in the Pacific, was signing up for a non-coed school like Kenyon College. I thought what I wanted, even more than women, was a good education. I was something of a rake, and having women on campus, as I found at Ohio University, could cause a deflection in my concentration; going coed would be a great detriment to me. In an all-male school, I could really buckle down and study. Problem was, without women there, women became the obsession. Your every waking hour was spent figuring how you could get yourself a Gambier, Ohio, town girl. So instead of having girls on campus and kind of basking in their company, being able to pick and choose, their absence became the preoccupation.

I had also neglected to research Kenyon College's reputation as a party school.

The very day I arrived there, dropped off by my parents on a Sunday afternoon in June at about three, I got distracted by a beer keg. By six o'clock, I was crocked. That was how long it took me to get in with the wrong crowd at Kenyon. So much for discipline. By the time I left Kenyon, I had no real education but owned the school's beer-chugalug record. The caption under my yearbook photo said: "Prone to getting out of hand on long tiring evenings."

Unfortunately, I wasn't really a student of anything. I did start out by signing up to be an economics major. Maybe I'd been thinking that I could end up working for my father at Newman-Stern (I even mentioned that as a possibility on my Kenyon application). I liked the store—and as I said, I was a good salesman—but the idea of a career there bored me. And while I got through my economics classes, even through accounting, I switched my major to poli sci. To tell you the truth, though, aided by the new stature I'd attained in the Navy, what I most enjoyed was being on the college's football squad.

Of course, when I found myself in disciplinary trouble, my plans had to change. Here's how that happened, and it had everything to do with attending an all-male school.

About ten miles east of Kenyon is Mount Vernon, Ohio, where many of us would hang out. There was a club there, the Bluebird Club, that sometimes had live dance bands or popular canned music. On the weekends, it was where you went to try and pick up

PAUL (IN WHITE T-SHIRT) WITH FRATERNITY BROTHERS AT
KENYON COLLEGE IN THE LATE 1940S

single girls from town. And on this particular night, a bunch of us from the football team decided to visit together.

There was a lot of antipathy between the local town boys and us. The townies were about our age, but they weren't in school, many of them working for a living with their hands. We were the outsider college kids, so the antagonism was natural. It wasn't unusual for fights to break out. What precipitated things was that we Kenyon guys were regularly trying to take their girls away from them. The townies would go to the john and when they came back, we'd be dancing with their dates.

Usually these fights were really more pushing matches than anything else. Maybe some bloody noses or black eyes. But nobody ever kicked anyone when they were on the ground, and no one hid anything in their pockets. In fact in the days after these typical altercations, you might be walking down the street and see one of the townies you fought walking just across the way. You'd wave at each other and say, "I'm going to get you next week," and the other kid would reply, "I'm around," and that's all there was to it.

One night though, things might have gone a little extra over the line; there'd been more of a real fight, though it quickly had simmered down. But the bartender at the club called the cops, and two plainclothesmen came through the door. Before they could fish out their badges, Bert Forman, our quarterback, decked one of them. Bert went out into the middle of the dance floor and said, "Come and get me!" One cop now flashes his badge and Bert responds, "I'm right here, where do you want me to go?"

The other plainclothesman turns to the bartender and asks, "Who started all of it?" and the barman pointed to three or four of our guys, who were promptly marched outside and put into police cars. Just as they were about to be driven away, one of the guys flipped me his keys and said, "Bring my car into town."

So forty-five minutes later I take his car to the police station and I find the sergeant and tell him, "One of the guys you've got in the slammer asked me to drop his keys off." And the sergeant answers,

"Let me see your knuckles." And, of course, my knuckles were pretty cut up from the fight. Before I knew it, the sergeant said, "Well, you're in, too," and they threw me in the slammer with our other guys.

When I looked outside through the bars, I saw the whole court-yard next to the station house loaded with Kenyon kids who'd come out to support us. Someone had gotten a keg of beer, and everyone was sitting on the ground singing old college songs until about three a.m., when the cops dispersed them. There was a great sense of fun about the whole thing.

The next day, the story appeared in the newspapers, including the Cleveland *Plain Dealer*—Kenyon's football team was in hot water. My name was listed among those arrested, and my father saw the article—it was, to him, a reaffirmation that I was screwing up, which I was. Three or four kids were thrown out of Kenyon right away, and another three or four, including me, were placed on probation. For good measure, I was also kicked off the football squad.

With all this extra time suddenly on my hands, I went down to the speech department and read for a play. I was going to try out for the theater.

It made sense. I had done some drama at Ohio U and liked the experience. Plays were less problematic for me than taking traditional classes; I had always had a terrible time studying from books. Part of the reason was that I had never learned how to study. I still maintain I have a learning disability, and even today I don't read right. In fact, I still have difficulty memorizing scripts.

I'd actually started early onstage; in grammar school, we put on a show about Robin Hood, and I played the court jester. I sang a song my uncle Joe (who besides being my father's business partner was a published author of light verse and even the lyricist of the song "Black Cross," recorded by both Lord Buckley and Bob Dylan) had written for me about Robin's bow and arrow: "Robin Hood he saw a flea / And knocked the fuzz right off its knee / In merry England isle-o"—and then I yodeled. (I was a very good yodeler before my testicles descended. I yodeled until my thirty-eighth year, waiting, hoping. Well, not really that long, but my body did grow up late—late growing hair, late growing taller, late growing testicles. A close friend of mine, steeped in psychoanalytic theory, once suggested that I subconsciously caused the delay in my testicular descent as a way of prolonging my mother's babying me. "Boy," I replied, "that would be one incredible act of will!")

Some people thought "Isn't he cute?" and after a few more stage turns, my mother decided to get me into the theater, regardless of what I wanted to do. My mother had hated football, and didn't want me to play a game that was inherently dangerous. She was always fluttering around trying to put on my eyelashes and straighten my lipstick when I escaped to football practice.

JOANNE WOODWARD

I remember Paul used to say to me, "For God's sake, she treated me like a girl, she wanted me to be a girl!" He was her doll.

My mother wanted me to sing, to go to dancing school, to do something arty like be an actor. So she brought me down to the Cleveland Play House, where the legendary K. Elmo Lowe, a good friend of Uncle Joe's, was the artistic director. The Play House was an acclaimed regional theater, and also ran a highly-regarded program for youngsters, called the Curtain Pullers, to which I was admitted. One play we put on was *St. George and the Dragon,* a kids' version, where at age nine I got to be St. George. I didn't slay the dragon, but I did pour salt on its tail, put my foot on its chest, and make a fiery gesture with my wooden sword. The poor dragon went through a terrible fit of writhing. It even resulted in my first professional stage photo. We did a few performances, apparently successful, and most of the moms and dads came to see us.

———————

At Kenyon, we would put on a full schedule, between eight and ten productions a year, at the Hill Theater. Jim Michael, who was my instructor, director, and ultimately good friend, gave me a great deal of confidence by casting me all the time. Did I reach that moment of understanding or perception that someone instills in you, plugs you in, and all of a sudden the light goes on? It certainly wasn't that. I never got the sense that anything I did on stage there was spectacular, or even something very exciting. It may have been workmanlike or okay, but I was really a highly, highly unknowledgeable actor. I was a kid with an attractive exterior, had a tremendous amount of energy and a lot of personality. But was I someone who instinctively knew how to do Shakespeare or naturalistic roles? My stage work at Kenyon was just an average college performance; it would have been recognized as a product of a university and a lot of phonetics classes.

In my own mind, certainly, there was nothing special going on. Everybody shakes their heads and says, "Couldn't you read the signals that people thought you were really something?" To which I say, "No."

Take someone whose experience at almost everything has been mediocre and who then finds something that at least is the best of whatever it is that they can do—it's not great, it's not even all that rewarding, but it is their best. They know that they wouldn't be a good mechanic, they wouldn't be a good football coach, they couldn't teach history or algebra. They could still sell bowling balls— but they don't want to sell bowling balls. So the next best thing they *can* do is to somehow be connected to the theater. And it's not a triumphal thing, but it is, again, the best they can do.

If I think back at the work I did early in my career ages ago, I can't even look at it. That doesn't make me a bad person, it doesn't mean I aspired to something unreasonable. And even though that may not be okay for you, it's okay for me. I just get so pissed off when everyone imposes their standards and evaluations and their remembrances of what they worked on, what they did, and they assume that's the way it happened for me, too.

I never enjoyed acting, never enjoyed going out there and doing it. I enjoyed all the preliminary work—the detail, the observation, putting things together. Every once in a while I'd do a scene that might come together in some unusual way and I would be astonished. But that was a tiny percentage of the time I actually spent doing it.

It's probably a reason I drank as much as I did. The exuberance, the danger, the exultation of performing was multiplied by a factor of eighty. If I got it just from acting, I wouldn't have had to go out and get bombed.

But I'm getting ahead of myself here.

The first big show I starred in was *The Front Page,* playing the fast-talking, wiseass tabloid editor Hildy Johnson. There's not much I recall about our production itself, but it was clearly well received by the audiences, and Jim Michael came to believe I had a real flair for comedic roles. I did everything from Captain Shotover in George Bernard Shaw's *Heartbreak House* (in which I was actually a last-minute replacement for another actor and had to learn the script in ten days—not a memory I'm comfortable with) and the drag role of Lord Fancourt Babberley in the Victorian farce *Charley's Aunt* to Čapek's modern science-fiction classic *R.U.R.* to Petruchio in Shakespeare's *Taming of the Shrew.*

I know there were some people in the drama department who seemed startled by some of the stage business I did with Katherina in *Shrew,* especially when I grabbed her, forced her to the ground, and straddled her. Even trying it unprompted in rehearsal was pretty courageous, they thought. But I never felt it was some great step forward. "Want my tongue in your ass, Kate?" is what Petruchio is basically saying. It's a pretty bawdy scene when they get together. All you need to do is go back and look at the lines.

Reminds me of the response to *R.U.R.* Lots of praise, but when I think back on my attack, it was really just highly oratorical. It was way out of style with what actors were doing in New York back then. (When I eventually got to New York and read for my first stage play with Anne Jackson, she just looked at me afterwards and said, "Don't work so hard. Don't act.")

Performing in Jean Anouilh's *Antigone* was most memorable in

PAUL IN A PRODUCTION AT KENYON COLLEGE

that it brought on one of the worst cases of the giggles I've ever had. I played the First Guard, which is a pretty substantial role; he has to keep an eye on the doomed princess, Antigone, and then report to King Creon the news that "the sergeant found the shovel," which was the key evidence that Antigone herself had illicitly tried to inter her brother's corpse. For some reason, I found it ridiculous that someone would think their life had been changed by finding a shovel, and that line, "The sergeant found the shovel," just started me laughing. And every time I entered during rehearsal to say the line, I just laughed uncontrollably. The cast became infuriated, and no one could do anything to help me. The company took a break, but we had to work until three a.m. before I could enter stage left and proclaim "The sergeant found the shovel" with a straight face.

It reminds me of a similar situation years later when we were filming *Butch Cassidy and the Sundance Kid*. I wrote a line for myself: When Sundance and I get off the train in Bolivia and there's nothing there but hovels and pigsties, Butch puts on a brave face and tries to bolster Sundance's sagging morale. I just look at Redford and say, "It's hard to believe that just fifty years ago, there was absolutely nothing here." I thought it was a great line, hysterical, and it just broke me up. They had to back up the antique train we were riding for a retake, but as soon as the cameras rolled again, I just started laughing. That train kept backing up, and George Roy Hill, the director, tried everything—long shots, medium shots, whatever, but he finally called a wrap in surrender. The line never made it into the film; I'm still looking for someplace to use it.

Anyway, as much attention as I was getting for my onstage work at Kenyon, I never regarded my performances as real successes; they were just something that was done, nothing more important than someone working hard and getting an A in political science. I was doing the same thing other people were doing in class or on the tennis or football team. I didn't attach any glamour or celebrity status to it, nothing like that.

I don't remember the success of those plays, I only remember the work on them. I remember being there, being onstage, the rehearsals, making the sets, more than I remember anything about being in school. And I realize now that the most barometric incident in my college life was entrepreneurial, not theatrical: it was my laundry business.

Newman's Laundry started from absolutely nothing, but it had invention, it approached things in a revolutionary way. Though a lot of people predicted doom and dire consequences for me, it was almost bulletproof, and became the biggest triumph of my school days.

Picture Main Street, Gambier, a nineteenth-century group of storefronts, a barber, some tiny grocery shops, each maybe twelve feet across and forty feet deep, like railroad flats. I noticed one place was vacant, and it struck me that this would be a great spot for a laundry collection agency—if I could only get the Kenyon kids to use it. And I imagined that the one thing that might entice students was free beer: bring in your clothes, we'll give you a beer.

I approached the venerable Licking Laundry Company in Newark, Ohio, and asked if they'd consider a deal with me. They told me if I could make $200 a week gross in laundry, they would do the actual washing and folding. I could practically guarantee it, I said, and they offered me 25 percent of the profit—and they'd even do the pickup and deliveries. I agreed, but said I needed them to give me enough money up front so I could paint the place, buy bins, and build a counter—and they did. I distributed hundreds of flyers that said, "Free beer if you bring down your laundry!" The first weekend alone, we got $300 worth of wash. And in the middle of a beautiful Saturday afternoon, a lot of my customers left the shop really intoxicated. I even took an ad in *The Kenyon Collegian* with the line: "Yep, the only studunt entaprize on main-street!" On the receipt slips it said: "If your clothes aren't becoming to you, you should be coming to me." By the time I graduated, I knocked out all the student laundry competition, and I was even able to sell the business when I left Gambier. That was my real success story at college.

———

C. RAY SMITH WAS A CLASSMATE AT KENYON
WHO WAS ACTIVE IN THE THEATER.

Late one night we were finishing building the set for *Charley's Aunt* (which I had designed); Paul often stayed late to help work on sets. The smell of paint got to be too much and he said, "Let's go take a ride!"

So out we went in an open jeep, and we had wonderful views of the valleys, the dogwoods, and the moon.

"Look at that moon!" he said.

"That's terrific," I said. "I wonder why the moon affects us the way it does. It makes us romantic, questioning . . ."

And there I was, in the middle of this great cosmic question, when Paul says, "Oh, why worry about it? Why not just enjoy it?"

———

After rehearsals, performances, or spending my evenings constructing sets or painting flats for our theater, I'd head over to a place called Dorothy's. It was in the ground floor of a farmhouse on the outskirts of town, and it held Gambier's only beer license. It was where everyone would congregate at night. Dorothy Rattray was a plump, jovial, blond-haired lady who ran the place with her partner, a fellow who called himself Jean Valjean. Dorothy loved her Kenyon boys and it was mutual.

The bar itself was situated right off the front door, with maybe eight or ten stools, and there was a room in the back with some old wooden kitchen tables and booths. There was one small bathroom.

There were other places you could go around Gambier, but you didn't bother. Dorothy's didn't serve hard liquor, though you could order some not very sophisticated sandwiches with your beers. If you were going to drink too much, there was no other place you went, even though Dorothy's closed at eleven o'clock. You couldn't get into trouble, it was the same as being home.

And, I guess, I was making a second home out of Dorothy's. Because I didn't belong to a frat, I was living in a dorm called the T-Barracks with a bunch of other "independents." The rooms were tiny, each with a pair of single beds, a couple of small desks and dresser drawers. No space even to turn around. I liked most of my classmates—Jonathan Winters, also just back from the war in the Pacific, was in my dorm that first year; you could see the beginnings of his diabolical wit, but his head was on the other side of the moon—and I had a good time with them; but what stopped me from having an *unbelievably* good time was that I just wasn't becoming a good student. I couldn't enjoy the good things I had. We were all loose and drank too much beer. Most of the time I had not done my assignments, or I turned them in late.

It likely didn't help that I sometimes acted a bit out of control. My first roommate was a kid named Charlie. He was very studious and thought that I partied too much; I didn't think ours was going to be a wonderful marriage. I came home one night after Dorothy's closed carrying a pint of cheap muscatel someone had given me. Well, Charlie was just lying there, snoring away with his mouth open, and little by little I poured about half a pint down his throat before he coughed and woke up. He packed his bags the next day and was gone. (Charlie later got even: he drained all the water out of the radiator on my Ford and filled it with muscatel.)

I did work very hard at the theater, but that just meant that when I played, I played as hard as anybody. And I played a lot. I think the first panty raid ever organized at Kenyon was staged by my class. There was a very well-off student named Nicholson—I think he was part of one of the big Ohio tire-company families—who had a pilot's license. One Saturday, he chartered a plane that took off from Mount Vernon while a bunch of us drove the twenty-five miles down from Gambier to Denison University in Granville.

We plotted it all out and it worked like a charm. Nicholson flew above the girls' dormitories doing aerial acrobatics. He also dropped leaflets overhead urging the girls to "Ditch Those Wimps at Denison." Of course, all the girls ran out on the lawn to see what was going on up in the sky. When they did, we ran into the girls' rooms and rifled their panty drawers. They came back in and discovered they had no brassieres, shorts, or anything. We took the trophies and attached them to our cars' antennas and drove around the campus honking our horns; we thought this was the cat's pajamas! It was considered very daring. And to do it in conjunction with another student doing airplane stunts? Well, that was classic 1948.

———

Long after I graduated, Dorothy got old and sold her place. I went back to visit her and talked over times past, and I ended up buying one of the bar's tables where each student over the years had carved his initials; I paid a lot of money for it. I didn't have room for it in Connecticut, so I gave it to either the Williamstown Theatre or to one of my children's camps. I wish I could remember exactly where, because I'd take it right back home with me. Sentiment, I suppose.

———

BOB CONNOLLY WAS A FRIEND AND CLASSMATE
OF PAUL'S AT KENYON.

Paul was wild, lascivious, dangerous. He was probably the most well-known guy on campus. He drank more. He screwed more. He was tough and cold—it turned on the girls. They liked him because he was the devil.

Paul would run around stark naked, sloshed out of his mind. Everybody drank, but he drank more than anybody else. At Dorothy's, he once pissed in an empty beer stein and put it back on the bar. Paul would mistake my room for his, and he'd come in and pass out on the bunk on top of mine.

This was an ambitious guy; Paul knew what he wanted to get and he got there.

———

On the last weekend of February 1949, I'd been to a party in the Deke wing of the dorms. Like each of the frats, they had what we called a bull's-eye room on the fourth floor, which had common areas where the socializing and drinking went on. It had been a long Saturday evening, and a bunch of us decided to sack out or just pass out there. Kenyon was wonderful that way; you spent weekends sleeping in different places. Nobody paid much attention to the overnight boarders.

I couldn't smell any smoke, but a fire marshal was running around, banging on doors, waking everybody up and yelling, "Fire! Get out of the building!" We couldn't see any flames, but we got up and started down the stairs. I was just wearing my boxers and a T-shirt, so I ran back up and grabbed my Navy flight jacket and began running down again. With a buddy of mine, I also grabbed a keg of beer that we had just tapped at the party before falling asleep. We carried that keg from the building, passed around some glasses, and a bunch of us drank beer outside while we watched the flames.

From where were standing, we had no idea at first that there had been injuries; we were in the front of the large building, and the worst of the fire turned out to be in the back structure, known as Middle Kenyon. We watched it go up in flames, but assumed everyone had gotten out. We didn't know there had been anybody left in there and that the fire had actually sped through the floors so quickly.

We tried to collect ourselves, huddled together in the night. No one went around the back, because the ambulances had probably left by then. There was no communication about what was going on. Then word began to filter out little by little that some kids had been hurt.

It wasn't until dawn that we heard that at least six kids had died and there were others in the hospital. By the next day, the death toll had risen to nine students.

I did know some of the kids who were killed. The grief on campus was just so powerful. No one really was able to take in what had happened. A couple of days later, classes resumed, and many of the kids didn't have any books or coats they could wear; they'd been burned.

The fire was on the front page of every big newspaper in the country. A mass was offered for the dead. And at the Hill Theater, the cast and the speech department decided we would finish rehearsals for *Charley's Aunt* and perform it the next week as originally scheduled. I have no recollection of how the decision was reached. We didn't want to give the play, we didn't want *not* to give the play. We wanted life to go on, but we didn't want to make the performances formal. Anybody who wanted to come was invited. I've read that it was the first time laughter was heard at Kenyon since the night of the fire.

I'm not sure who first had the idea, but heading into senior year I became determined to put on a satiric revue show before graduation. The conceit was that a well-to-do kid comes to Kenyon to be shown around as a prospective student. He meets the dean. He meets the dietician. He gets introduced to all the campus characters. He even tours T-Barracks and greets the football team. A classmate named C. Ray Smith choreographed the dances to Gilbert & Sullivan music and did the orchestrations. I wrote the lyrics and the book and directed. Perhaps our greatest accomplishment was convincing a bunch of intensely macho, painfully shy, gorilla-size football players to squeeze into tutus and waltz onstage like they were in *The Nutcracker.*

The whole show was a howl; it was raucous, hysterical, and became a very hot ticket. Since no one at Kenyon seemed familiar with the annual club spoofs performed at Harvard and Yale, this truly broke new ground. I remember some of the songs even today; they were pretty damn good:

> For fifteen years we've lived up here,
> Like any early pioneer,
> And filled with joy and kegs of beer
> Our only happy moments.
>
> At last we have a legal chance
> To put some ants in babies' pants,
> And nurse them with a song and dance
> Discouraging enrollments.
>
> But wait a moment, change the pace,
> Don't hack the nose despite the face
> Nor pull a tricky coup de grace,
> Contented we'll appear.
>
> Forget the ants for babies' pants,
> We'll have another drink perchance
> To chip in for the beer.

When I first thought of putting this show together, I tried collaborating with C. Ray. I even invited him to my house in Shaker Heights—something I rarely did with anyone—so we could spend a weekend writing. We ended up staying just one night.

I know C. Ray felt my father was treating him very badly. He was a guest in our house. At the dinner table, my father picked on him, wondered why he wasn't on the football team or going to dances, even suggesting C. Ray should visit a psychiatrist. C. Ray was shaken by his behavior, and I was badly embarrassed by the whole thing. I suspect what actually happened was my old man had a couple of drinks, because he wouldn't have done that if he'd been sober.

Maybe he thought C. Ray was gay, but thinking about it, I don't think that would have offended him—he knew actors from his associations with the Cleveland Play House. I do recollect some other occasions when I brought home a visitor, and my father gave him the silent treatment. A buddy of mine once said that at my home, it seemed like I needed an appointment just to talk with my father.

After that dinner, C. Ray was very upset, frozen with humiliation. And when we sat down to try and get back to work, he couldn't write a thing. I knew it would be best if we returned to Kenyon early. And he suggested to me that the show would be better off if I tried working with another classmate, Doug Downey, rather than him. When the winter break started in 1948, Doug and I stayed behind from December 17th until Christmas Day at T-Barracks, alone in an empty building, on an empty campus, trying to finish the revue. Which, with a good deal of help from Budweiser, we did.

I decided to show the script to my father. He read it and said, "Well, I suppose there are some funny things in there, and some funny lines of poetry. But it's not what I would give. It isn't the kind of show that pokes fun at national or international foibles or that kind of thing. It's really a very local script." What he was saying, I suppose, is that if I wrote it, it was probably not very good. I guess I was disappointed. But it was expected, too. Though I can look back at it and say, "Yes, I concur without any kind of rancor or acrimony. It's probably true." The show was very funny to the guys at Kenyon, but they hadn't had a musical performed there in fifty years.

At the end of our first performance, we were taking curtain calls. We took our first one, and were about to do our second one when the whole cast jumped in back of me and pushed me out in front. I was embarrassed, I ran off the stage, and they did the next curtain call without me at all. I hated being singled out. The fact was, I worked hard in the theater or whatever, and when that was over went out and drank a lot of beer and drank hard. I suppose that was something about me, doing things hard. I don't know if it was an affectation, but that's what I did.

I was never sure what I thought of the *Kenyon College Revue* when I was doing it, but what mattered was that when you are committed to something, you go ahead and finish it. If I made up my mind to do something, then it would get completed and it would get done. I don't know any other way to attack things.

A BRIEF BIOGRAPHICAL ENCOMIUM

by Paul Newman

PUBLISHED IN *THE KENYON COLLEGIAN*, MAY 4, 1949, PAGE 1

Checking through *Life* magazine a few weeks ago, I was not surprised to find myself listed as an unmistakeable highbrow. This discovery, however, was noted without the aid of *Life* as early as 1946 and was basically responsible for my enroll-ment at Kenyon. After three hell-raising years in the Navy, I was ready to forsake previous attachments to co-eds, frat clubs and beer mugs in order to pursue the contents of the *Encyclopaedia Britannica* and a Phi Beta Kappa key. (How else but to isolate oneself at Kenyon?) With this in mind I packed a four-year overnight bag in a trunk and shipped myself first class to Gambier. As Hamlet said, "Alas" (Act VII, Scene 1), in one way or another, my lofty intellectual goal was thwarted. My first contact was not with Aristotle's *Poetics* or even a reasonable facsimile, but with a roommate who was cleverly disguised by the Dean's Office as a cocktail shaker. Intro-ducing myself as an Old Fashioned glass, we poured through many interesting things together, none of which I presently recall. And so it continued, nip and sip. . . .

Suddenly, I found myself a Junior, much to the surprise of my father whose only report of me for two years had been when a Cleveland *Plain Dealer* reporter called up home to tell him that I was in jail with five other Gambierians, one of whom had kicked five teeth loose from the face of a local constable. The people at home began to wonder what kind of company I was keeping. And people who were keeping company with me began to wonder what type of company they were keeping with.

No longer able to show my face (or what have you) in Ascension Hall, I found refuge beneath the skirt of Dona Lucia d'Alvadorez [impersonated by Newman in *Charley's Aunt*] where the nuts come from. (It was here that I departed entirely from the pursuit of Phi Beta Kappa by developing the unique philosophy that I would not let my studies interfere with my extracurricular activities.) I modestly nicknamed myself "Barrymore." The directors modestly recognized my talents and set me to work—painting flats. I may say without fear of contradiction that painting flats is a filthy job. The result was obvious. I attached myself to a laundry business. Every Monday night I would trudge around the barracks area collecting shirts with dirty collars. Every Friday afternoon I would trudge back through the barracks area returning shirts without any collars. Sometimes not even returning the shirts. The business grew and grew until now the laundry is, as one Gambier citizen put it: Yep, the only studunt entaprize on main-street . . .

Finally, in my senior year, I became adjusted mentally. Professors tore out *mit der hair und trousers*. Why? "Barrymore" made the merit list, right between Moorman and Nugent.

Merit List! My dream come true.

V

I graduated from Kenyon at two o'clock on Monday, June 13, 1949, and by four o'clock that same afternoon I was on the train to Chicago, headed for Williams Bay, Wisconsin. A summer-stock theater there, the Belfry Players, offered me a "scholarship" for its upcoming season. Of course, a scholarship to the Belfry meant you acted for nothing and built sets for nothing—but you had the opportunity to earn honor. Plus free room and board.

My father's lack of expertise in the going rate for summer-stock theater employment made him insistent that I should be paid for my labors or reject the Belfry's offer. What he didn't understand was how many other young theater people were waiting to take your place if your demands were too high—or you made any demands at all. I was as much a professional actor as any of the other kids in the company, and they weren't professional, either. Belfry did employ (with pay) some recent drama-school graduates, who formed a sort of resident company, and they also managed to engage some people who were not of the highest echelon to direct our shows. But theaters like the Belfry really didn't have much to recommend them except the chance to do a lot of plays in a very short time.

The Belfry Players leased a lovely old wooden house at nearby Lake Geneva. It was connected to the Yerkes Observatory, a nineteenth-century scientific landmark (and tourist attraction) that was run by the University of Chicago and housed what was once the world's largest telescope. There were six tourist-cabin-type structures around back, and that was where all the apprentices lived, including myself and a beautiful, local Wisconsin drama student I met named Jackie Witte.

We'd go out in the evenings and talk at one of the local bars, and when the bars closed, we'd sit together in the moonlight on the doorstep of the residence house and talk some more about our futures. Jackie was still in college and wanted to be an actor, too; I spoke with her about the play we were both in, *John Loves Mary*, about my aspirations, probably in a very unrealistic, poetic way— and I remember her responding in kind. We were two provincial yokels thinking that what they had to say was terribly important because it was the first time they'd said it out loud to anyone. We didn't know about Freud. We didn't know anything about the Constitution of the United States or anything else remotely adult. I didn't know who any of the great actors were; if you asked me who Olivier was, I couldn't have told you. (I probably would have recognized Van Johnson.) I could not have named one play on Broadway. We wanted to do big things. I don't remember what they were, I only remember that they were big.

To have a friend in the theater that you saw not only working during the day but even at night, someone who didn't have to dart back to her family, someone who after a hard day of building sets together, of rehearsing together, would share the privilege of going out for a beer together, too, well, that was an almost unspeakable ecstasy.

I'd never been with a woman I could talk to; I'd never even had the opportunity. There was my mother, of course, and then, at seventeen, the war. After the Pacific, an all-male college with Dorothy down at her Gambier tavern. There were the faculty wives and their daughters who acted with us in the plays. Then no one else until Jackie.

She was the first and best I'd ever seen.

JACKIE WITTE IN 1949

Jackie's folks lived in Beloit, though they also owned a waterfront summer cabin not far from Lake Geneva; it was a great refuge and a great place to hide. Jackie introduced me to them early on but I didn't really know what to make of them. Her mother was a nervous woman who never looked you in the eye and darted around like a ferret. She was perfectly pleasant, but somehow very evasive, always bustling about, busy organizing bridge parties. The dad was a nice, decent man, thin and not very talkative, but with an occasional burst of dry humor. I thought he must be miserable. Occasionally, I went out fishing with him in his rowboat. These were idyllic days.

I suppose marrying Jackie—which I did just a few months after meeting her—was like the *Kenyon College Revue*. I'm not sure what I thought when I was writing the revue, but once you were committed to doing something, you simply went ahead and it would be done. With Jackie, I made the first real contact I had made with anyone, and I thought that having made that initial contact with a woman, the next thing you did was get married and have lots of kids.

I wish someone, a priest or a social worker or a psychiatrist, had just sat the two of us down for a minute and said, "Think this out, just follow it through and create a script for yourselves." I probably would have looked at Jackie and said, "Well, I'm not really sure. How do you feel?" And Jackie would have said, "I'm not really sure, either." It was the first experience with a relationship either of us had with the luxury of time, the first we'd ever experienced in an atmosphere of freedom. But we simply followed a set of half-learned things that we thought were rules. There was some book we were playing this by, some music we were singing all the songs to. It was as if it had all been decided and decreed, with no choice but to perform things as written. You're supposed to graduate from college, you're supposed to find a profession, you're supposed to get married, you're supposed to have children, you're supposed to protect and provide for those children. There was very little I understood beyond that. Neither Jackie nor I had a clue of our own, not an inkling. We never thought of using contraceptives, never asked. We had no philosophy about raising kids, we'd never even had a discussion about having children or not. Things just happened because they happened.

Looking back on it now, from a more sophisticated vantage point, I ask myself how I could have been so irresponsible as to take the first girl with whom I had a speaking relationship, marry her, and impregnate her right away. Then, it felt appropriate. There was a sense of fatality about it, that it was somehow all predestined, pre-ordained. You finished what you began.

I had no awareness that I could shape things myself.

After we became engaged that summer, I'd sometimes spend nights at Jackie's parents' house. Jackie's room was downstairs, and her folks' room was up. I was petrified that her parents would come down and surprise us.

We waited until our wedding night.

I don't remember a thing about our actual wedding, at an Episcopal church near Jackie's folks' home, only about leaving the reception afterwards. We borrowed her father's old Nash, and ended up driving five or six hours through a snowstorm. By the time we got to our hotel, we were completely exhausted. If we'd had any sense, we would have said, "Why don't we just rest up now?"

But I think our son, Scott, was conceived that night.

The next morning, we just got up, got into the car, and drove around in a big circle. Eventually, we pointed the car down toward Woodstock, Illinois, where we both were scheduled to start work at a winter theater company. We arrived there very quickly.

———————

Though Jackie and I were both promised jobs at Woodstock, when we got there the shady guy who managed the theater said there was no room for Jackie in the company. He promised her a couple of parts, but instead hired her for the box office at ten dollars a week. I got forty-five as an actor and got cast in a stage adaptation of *Ethan Frome* and as Christian in *Cyrano de Bergerac;* our company's Cyrano had a southern accent, and we nearly lost our Roxane one night when her balcony started to collapse.

We rehearsed those plays in only six days and it was all pretty hysterical. Though the company had completed one successful season and the local community was supportive of the performances, which took place in a beautiful old opera house, the theater started going bankrupt and couldn't pay its bills. Our sleight-of-hand manager absconded with the money and the Woodstock Players went under. Still, Jackie and I had this four-room furnished apartment on the upper floor of some grand home in town that we rented for just a few dollars a month. We got what we paid for—for that price, we had no running water.

I wrote to my father that it would likely take me another month to find another regular job, and that I was applying for unemployment insurance. The letter he wrote back to me was absolutely scathing. Lethal. Welfare was for people, he wrote, who couldn't earn a living; it would be a blight on the Newman family name to admit that one of his sons had gone out and collected unemployment.

So I took a job at a nearby farm run by a guy named Tilley. I had to clean the sheep pen in the barn. The sheep would pee and shit and you'd cover it with clean hay. Then they'd pee and shit some more and you'd cover it again. After it got to be about six feet deep and practically up to the eaves, you'd finally clean the whole thing out. That was my job. With my allergies, every day by two or three in the afternoon I couldn't breathe. I stayed there though for about six or seven weeks.

It was my father's illness that brought me back home. He had exploratory surgery in January 1950, but I don't think they ended up doing anything to him. The surgeons said his illness was too far along. He'd be in and out of the hospital for the rest of his life.

I went to visit a couple of times while he was recuperating from the operation. He would still go to his sporting-goods store sporadically. But with me having no job, and with my father's health rapidly declining, Jackie and I headed to Cleveland.

Jackie, my brother, Arthur, and I moved into my parents' house. Jackie was pregnant while my father was wasting away. It was the toughest time I ever spent. My mother hated Jackie, who tried to be as nice and sweet as she could, but she took a tremendous shellacking. There were two main things, I think, that turned my mother against her. First, because she was my wife; my mother lived this terrible illness of jealousy that isolated her so. And second, because Jackie's father was a butcher and my mother expected me to marry better than that. She treated Jackie as an inferior.

Jackie was a stoic. She was not a whiner or a crybaby. If my mother was a monster to her, well, that's the way things were. Jackie had come from a home where there wasn't much joy, and so our household was not really a change. The horrors of being left alone with Tress Newman all day? An absolute nightmare. My mother, with her sweet, perfectly modulated voice, was like a steamroller over Jackie. The only option Jackie had to protect herself was to learn exactly what it was my mother did and follow what she was told exactly. My mother was doing to Jackie what she had always done to me. I don't even remember talking with Jackie about it. I was away at Newman-Stern, pitching in twelve-hour days at the family store. All I could get was hearsay.

Ours was a big house, and it could have been a wonderful sanctuary. It's too bad the time for Jackie had to be so miserable. I don't think I even realized then how bad it was.

After dinner there each evening, we'd get out of the house as quickly as we could, and come back as late as we could.

———

While he was failing, my father still seemed to greatly worry about his appearance—not surprising, perhaps, as this was one of the last gentlemen to regularly wear spats. He didn't have the strength to shave himself, and he hated not being shaved. Arthur would shave him almost every day, but one afternoon, though Arthur was there, my father asked me to do it. I remember a combination of wanting to be at his service and at the same time drawing back. He was so frail, and I was afraid I would cut him; we had almost never touched. Not long after, as Arthur and I both sat together near his hospital bed, I heard my father say, "Paul is the better shaver of you two." I can still remember the disappointment on Arthur's face.

Before he died, my father made it clear to Arthur and me that there'd be nothing for us in his will. We had no expectation, so no disappointment. "I figure I owed it to both of you to clothe you, feed you, comfort you, and give you a decent education," he'd always said. "But when you reach your maturity, you're on your own."

As he realized he was dying, my father wanted to put all his money into a trust for my mother, to protect her—he did it that way because he was afraid that otherwise she'd lose everything playing the stock market. He felt she was unstable. What he didn't realize was how suspicious she was, even suspicious enough to think he might be plotting to deny her the inheritance.

Tress was convinced my father had a girlfriend stashed away somewhere, and that he was scheming to take away her home and the control of Newman-Stern from her and bestow it to the "mistress." As he lay there ill in the hospital, he just needed to get her agreement to his estate plan, but she refused to sign anything. Tress kept yelling at him on his deathbed, accusing him, vilifying him. She wouldn't let him fucking die!

When my father finally passed that spring, Tress's hysterical response had more to do with her fear of what might be stolen from her than the fact that she had lost a husband. A man had died, but what was important was not that a flame had gone out of a human being who would never see the sunset again, or read another book, or make people laugh. What was important to my mother was that his family was going to rob her.

At the time of my father's death in May 1950, my mother hadn't spoken with her own family in three years. She asked them all to the funeral. What did she do that for except to show the Newman side that she had friends, too? By inviting her people to our house and immediately herding them up the stairs, though both families were at our home together to pay respects—and never even going back downstairs to offer the Newmans a cup of tea—was she declaring her separateness? Was it a punishment? Was it like the child squeezed to death in her embrace, or her dog poisoned by chocolate? Emotions triggered with no sense of the consequences?

My father was a battleground during his marriage and a battleground while he was dying. Did her fight with my father's brother, my uncle Joe, about her share of Newman-Stern, her mistrust of my father's intentions for his estate, and now the sudden inclusion of her own relatives (and the exclusion of his) in the mourning period define the sheet of steel that existed between the two families?

I wonder whether it wasn't also true of their marriage itself. I've tried to understand what they meant to each other. My mother had always said to me: "Your father and I argued a lot, but we were great together in bed." Maybe that's what it was, the glue, that passion. Maybe it was that she was the student and my father the willing teacher?

I think she could never be aware of the carnage she created.

After he died, my mother keened over my father. I didn't know why. A week before his death, she'd been kicking the bejesus out of him, accusing him of keeping another woman. Things had become very unpleasant in our household. Arthur wouldn't speak to her. Things were bad between her and Uncle Joe over her stake in the store; it was hard to convince her Joe was an honorable man. But when the will was finally read, Tress was, to say the least, surprised. My father had left her all his interest in Newman-Stern, the house, everything. Arthur and I had kept telling her, "Mother, Dad always told us it is all going to you, and nothing is coming to us." She never forgave my brother and me for being right about the will.

———————

My father was a highly moral, deeply unhappy man who got what joy he had from observing his own ethics; he certainly never got that joy at home. I see him as a funny little clown of a man who's off doing a jig someplace, behaving very much like me.

One of my great regrets about my father's early death (he was only fifty-six) is that the two of us never really connected. His response to the recognition that eventually came to me would have filled him with wonder and relish. There was a lot we could have shared—a sense of accomplishment for one. He would have been proud of our association in a way that wasn't simply the reflection on him of me, his puppet, a possession. He would have honored me and recognized me. Whereas my mother thought I was simply a weapon of her Catholicism to be paraded in front of my father's people as the royal vindication of her own family, her smartness, her genes. My satisfaction with my success has always been tempered with a great sadness that my mother could never truly feel a part of the enjoyment.

Most people who have experienced themselves fully have in common that they remember some person—a teacher, a religious figure, a parent, uncle, grandfather—someone about whom they can say, "That was my mentor. That was my rock. That's who pointed me in the direction I followed, who inspired me, who gave me the example to learn from and emulate."

I never had that.

I've always wondered that I was never able to find a mentor. I never had anyone in my childhood I can look back on as an adult and say, "Boy, I never realized what a foundation that was, how I leaned on that." I did get little bits of morality from my father; I don't know what I got from my mother. I don't know that any teachers gave me anything or any understanding of myself. No scout leader or camp person. Nobody in a church. Nothing.

As far as I can tell, I got no emotional support from anyone.

ARTHUR NEWMAN

If Paul had accepted my advice and gone into business he still would have been successful because he was loveable, had a great personality, and made people instantly like him. Furthermore, he was smart and he was perceptive and he had all the ingredients no matter what he did.

I wasn't very happy with the Newman-Stern Co. I was making about seventy-five dollars a week, but I couldn't find any thrust to my life there. I don't know whether it would have been offered to me, but I had no interest in one day running the store. By the following May, the Newman-Stern Co. was sold, and I went to work at a golf range run by Newman-Stern's new owners. I stayed there until the end of July, but I stole money out of the driving range's cash register. It came to maybe $175 over a three- or four-month period; I kept a record of it (and when I later took a part-time job in graduate school, I reimbursed the golf range). I don't know why I did it—beer money or something?

I guess I also needed the extra cash. By the time Scott was born, in September 1950, Jackie and I had moved into a new home in Bedford, a Cleveland suburb close to Shaker Heights. I think the way I was able to buy it—for $11,700!—was that just before he passed, my father signed a note guaranteeing a loan.

My new house was one story, on a tiny corner lot, with a tiny living room, a tiny kitchen, a tiny garage, and two tiny bedrooms. It was all brand-new. There were no furnishings or appliances. There was no front lawn, no hedges, no shrubs or landscaping. I had to put them all in. I went to work, came home, we went across the street and had dinner with one of the neighbors, or sometimes over to Horrigan's, downtown, a long, narrow old Irish bar where I liked to loosen up (and the very amiable proprietor would delight us by sitting down at a piano and singing "H-O-double R-I-G-A-N spells Horrigan!"). Not every day in Bedford was a delight; nor was every day a disaster.

What Jackie and I were mostly doing was expecting our first child. I don't think, as per usual, we made a lot of plans. We were having a baby, and it was going to grow like tulips on the new lawn or whatever else we stuck in the ground, that's all. We were two very young people trying to act grown up.

I know I've told people that if I had one plan in life, it was to apply to the Yale School of Drama and get a master's degree in directing so I could always teach if I couldn't get jobs as an actor. (And I never thought I would be in the movies.) But if I had actually thought through going to Yale in 1951, why did I buy this new house in fall 1950, with all that interest to pay? I wasn't thinking far ahead, or else I just figured I could root or uproot my family at will, make plans, cancel plans, and never have any of it be a big deal. Adventurous? Whimsical? Uncaring?

Going to Yale was not exactly a rational decision. My GI Bill education benefits were getting set to expire; I suspect I'd had a couple of beers, gone off inside my head someplace, pounded my fist, jumped up and down and said, "Let's go to Yale!"

I guess I thought of Yale as running away from something that wasn't providing any sense of growth or advancement. I know I didn't have a real sense of running hysterically toward the affirmation of theater, because I had no expectation of achieving anything professionally. Still, I was starting to get known in Cleveland with a couple of small jobs on radio and TV. I did a few commercials for a local bank—kind of ironic, since I was advising people to put money away for their kids when I had never saved a nickel in my life. I did late-night TV weather, too. I was scared to death when I had to deliver lines right into the camera. Television was brand-new then (though my mother had one of the first sets), and I'd never done that before; I still can't talk to anything that doesn't talk back—it's pretty frightening. I have no idea why they hired me.

I don't think I ever had a real discussion with Jackie about going to New Haven. I sent in an application. I'm accepted. I remember it as a fait accompli. Let's pack up the car and go.

The period between my father's death and our driving the Chevy to Connecticut is really just a hodgepodge of impressions for me; no single, strong, lasting memory. Except, really, for becoming a father with Scott's arrival. I remember a great sense of physical connection with Scott. Holding him and bouncing him, working his legs, taking him up and down the street in his perambulator.

But the connectedness was more brotherly than paternal, because I somehow didn't think of myself as a father. I have a great sense of omission now about this, of things unfinished or never started. A sense of screwing up. What should have been a strong father-and-son attachment was failing, a marriage was coming apart, and I didn't even realize it. I didn't know enough about my own feelings to start examining them or take any real actions; I had a real sense of disgust with the fact I was being so ineffective.

For all the hard work and joy of immersion that came at Yale, my time there was a kind of purgatory, just a resting place. I see that period in my life as the beginning of a great failure: failure to provide relief for Jackie at the home she lived in, failure as a husband, a lover, as an actor, as a father. I don't deny anything. I'm not trying to allay anything. I do, though, have a predisposition to look at the negative of things.

JACKIE WITTE

I actually don't remember when or how we became engaged.

That summer at the Belfry was the first time I'd lived independently. (At the start of the season, I'd been driving back to my parents' home each night, but I soon decided to move with another girl into one of the converted chicken coops that served as housing for the company.) I was still in college, and all these people who I looked at as being a lot more than I was professionally were accepting me.

Paul and I spent a lot of time together. We probably both had hidden needs to escape whatever was holding us back. We must have decided we were each other's salvation. I think I was very, very infatuated, and in my experience that was love.

I'm not sure whether Paul had an overwhelming desire to become an actor. I'm not sure what kind of commitment he really had to theater, but he had a stage presence, a magnetism. He played the Gentleman Caller in *The Glass Menagerie* that summer, and I think he was quite good. I'm sure he was very good-looking, too. But I would have been much better off if there'd been at least a part of me worrying more about what Jackie was going to do rather than what Paul was going to do—with Jackie just tagging along.

What Paul did have, though, was a real desire not to work at his family's Newman-Stern Co. Paul's father didn't envision him in a theatrical career; that was not Arthur Sr.'s wish, and he made no pretense about it. I think this probably bothered Paul a whole lot more than I realized then.

When we went to visit my parents to tell them we were engaged, my mother was charmed by Paul; neither of my parents gave us any protest over our plans. Paul had written to his family to tell them about the engagement, too; and while we were staying at my home, he received a letter back from his father. Paul read it aloud to everyone under the guise of "Isn't my father a witty, clever man?" Later on I thought, "Yeah, but what a letter to write your son when he tells you he's getting married!" There was no affection, no concern for his future, no fatherly anything—just a very clever, calculated exercise in wit. Of course, at the time, I took the letter at face value; I honestly don't know how Paul really felt.

By the end of that summer, both sets of parents were exchanging letters and phone calls, and Paul took me to Cleveland to meet everyone. We went to dinner at their country club, and I ate my first lobster there that night. I'd put on a new dress, all little knife pleats of taffeta, and Tress—accidentally, I'm sure—spilled melted lobster butter all over me. My pleats were never the same.

I thought the Newmans' house was quite lovely, and they seemed to live in a very affluent neighborhood (or at least Tress told me it was affluent). I met quite a few of Paul's relatives, and liked them. The way I grew up, somebody would have had to take me by the hand and tell me, "This is a Jewish family." This was all totally out of my ken.

We eventually moved into the Newman house. After Paul's father died, Tress was undone, a poor, distraught woman who was at loose ends and didn't know how to cope with anyone or anything. Tress also had the most irritating voice I ever encountered in a human being. That's probably unfair, because the voice wasn't her fault, but it just grated on the ear.

Tress had always been a well-groomed woman, but now she often wore a certain housedress that I thought she never changed. She never went anyplace. Paul and his brother, Arthur, were at the store all day, and I was in this big home with a woman I didn't even know; it was weird. I didn't know a bloody soul in Cleveland; there was no car for me to drive; I was just stuck inside with Tress as we rattled around the house all day.

With Paul and Arthur now living at home, Tress had her two sons back—and I was just somebody there. I think she had absolutely no concept that Paul and I were husband and wife, an entity of our own. It always struck me that she gave us a bedroom with a pair of twin beds—to a newly married couple!—which to me was very reflective about her attitude. I thought we would never get away from the presence of Mommy.

Paul was very, very upset by his father's death. He loathed being at Newman-Stern, of having to fit into the mold of that company. He probably did it because of pressure from Tress and guilt—and after a long day at the store, he must have thought, "What an awful household to come home to! There's Tress with a list of complaints, my pregnant wife, who's certainly got her list, too." And Paul's upset showed by him becoming even more closed up.

Somewhere along the line, we came to a point where Paul finally said: "I'm not going to do this anymore. Enough of this already. I'm going to enroll at Yale." Tress was not happy about our plan to move all the way to New Haven. For us, it was a great sense of relief.

Scott was born before we left Cleveland. I just went about my business, doing all those things you were supposed to do: cook the meals, wash the clothes, tote that barge. I hadn't known anything about pregnancy; I didn't know what any of the risks were, didn't know anything you were supposed to be careful about. I did whatever I did, including smoking.

Paul was very much the proud father. I'm not saying he did it consistently—the diapering and whatnot—but he certainly helped with Scott; he wasn't one of those husbands who said, "That's woman's work." Scott was born into a household where the mother and father knew absolutely nothing about parenting. As time went along, I honestly felt my instincts were probably better than Paul's, but these were instincts I grew into.

Scott was an incredibly sensitive child. And I don't think incredibly sensitive people fare well in this world.

VI

What I remember more than anything else about Yale was the work. I started at nine in the morning, went on until dinner, and then continued with rehearsals till maybe eleven p.m. You'd be doing two or three plays at the same time, as well as one-act plays on Saturday mornings that the Yale playwrights' group asked the student actors and directors to perform.

This was total theater immersion; yet there seemed to be no pressure. Hard work, but fun. There were so many compatible people at Yale that you had a real sense of community and ease.

I decided to major in directing, but it was really a subterfuge. The idea was to shine a little dignity on what I was studying. I was convinced the nameplate that said "Director" on your door was better than one that said "Actor." As I mentioned, I had no real plan; but with directing, what I had was a parachute.

A longtime faculty member named Frank McMullan taught acting and phonetics at Yale, and he was in charge of our directing studies. I thought he was kind of pedantic; in fact, Yale's whole approach to theater was very academic—we even were required to learn fencing. At one point in the semester, I'd gone down to Manhattan to try and meet some agents; I was really affected by the personality, haste, tension, and urgency in their offices. Young actors were being shoveled in and out of doors, new ones hustled in and then hustled out. When I got back to campus, I created a scene for McMullan's directing class based on that experience. I got a garbage can and had a kid upstage beating on it with a stick; meanwhile, a typist was typing away in a different rhythm downstage with seven or eight actors hurrying around in time to the beats. My class loved it. But when it was done, Frank McMullan looked at me and said, "Why don't we do this in a more realistic way? Let's take that beat out of it." Of course, the actors did what he said. It was so funny that what I had seen as the heart of the exercise was the very thing he excised. But that is my memory of Yale.

What I most remember about Connie Welch, my primary acting teacher at Yale, was everything I don't remember about later studying at the Actors Studio in New York. Her classes seemed orchestrated, technical, planned, and, again, academic. They were not, to me, very inspired.

Strangely, the course at Yale that helped me the most was the History of Theater, taught by a German refugee named Alois Nagler. It ran all the way from the Greeks through the classic French playwrights like Racine. Even with my terrible work schedule—besides classes and rehearsals at the drama school, I was also selling encyclopedias for extra cash—I had to read all kinds of plays. Which resulted in my getting a much better sense of what constituted a good play and a bad play.

And ultimately, recognizing the difference between a good script and a bad one.

———

I'd found my family a place to live on New Haven's Chapel Street. It was three rooms on the third floor of a building with a furrier's shop at street level, and where the second floor had been condemned. There was a kitchen, a bedroom and a screened porch; we gave Scott the bedroom, while Jackie and I took the porch, which the landlord had glassed in so he could charge for another room.

A lady by the name of Mrs. Dupuy lived there, too. The first time we met, she had rapped on our door and introduced herself; as she did so, we noticed she was scratching the side of her head with a .45 Colt revolver. Mrs. Dupuy told us she was a widow, but was doing just fine, because she kept this gun at her side in case her apartment was invaded. She also shared that what she best recalled about her marriage was that she gave off so much body heat that it drove her late husband crazy, since he could never get their bed cool enough for him to sleep.

We had parties at our place all the time. We cooked in the tiny kitchen, and also did barbecues in the backyards of some of the other married students nearby. I'd make a special dish, like open-faced grilled-cheese sandwiches with garlic butter, bacon, and mozzarella. People thought they were wonderful, and whenever they heard I was cooking them, they'd show up in droves. (I recently tried making them again and they actually tasted pretty bad.) We never had much money, so all of us bought food in a communal way to save.

In warm weather, each Sunday, we'd have picnics in a wonderful little spot next to the Merritt Parkway. Scott was nifty, sort of the center of attention. Everyone would bring their own young kids, and we'd play with them beside a little stream that ran nearby.

I liked having a lot of people around. We had good times in New Haven. Probably the best of all our family times, the best times for Jackie and me.

I don't remember much about the Yale production of *Beethoven* except that I wore a red jacket while everyone else on stage seemed to be dressed in black; my costume was so bright it was like a flashbulb going off in the dark. What I actually do recall is the name of the playwright, another graduate student at the drama school named Dorothy Bland. The title role was performed by Sorrell Booke; though he was just twenty-one, he was already going bald. He was the Yale drama class's resident intellectual, who hoped to one day shake the very foundations of American theater and become the reigning Shakespearean actor of our time. (His career didn't work out quite that way; Sorrell often appeared on Broadway, and spent years as a successful character actor, best known, perhaps, as one of the stars of *The Dukes of Hazzard,* playing the comically corrupt politician Boss Hogg.)

I was Karl Beethoven, the composer's conniving nephew, who sold his famous uncle's latest music for the money to buy himself clothes—thus the bright-red jacket, which was supposed to show, I guess, what a bastard he was. Frank McMullan directed and cast me in the part that first got me recognized onstage. It was pretty unusual for a first-year student to get a leading role in what was considered one of the year's major productions.

ANNE KNOLL NIXON WAS A FRIEND OF JACKIE WITTE FROM BELOIT, WHO ATTENDED THE YALE SCHOOL OF DRAMA WITH PAUL.

Every actor at the drama school wanted to play Karl Beethoven; it was a juicy part, very dominant and sexy. The competition for the role was extraordinary. Paul got it because he was by far the most magnetic and attractive of all the actors there.

Karl wasn't even Paul's kind of part; it wasn't in him, really, to do Shaw or Shakespeare; he's not a classical actor, he doesn't have that sort of language or presence. What Paul did have was personal presence. He looked wonderfully handsome. He plunged in; he may not have done it right, but he didn't hang back. It was a chance to make an impression on his peers, and also on the theater people who'd come up from New York to see the main Yale productions.

Was it luck he got the part in *Beethoven?* No. He got Beethoven because he made sure he got it.

In those days—and still today—theatrical agents took the train up from Grand Central Station to New Haven to scout the new talent at the drama school. There was apparently at least one in attendance for one of Yale's four performances of *Beethoven*, a fellow from the Liebling-Wood Agency, Jim Merrick. He came backstage afterwards, gave me his card, and suggested I come see him sometime in Manhattan.

The Liebling-Wood Agency was a powerhouse on Broadway. It represented many of the era's leading playwrights—such as Tennessee Williams, William Inge, Yip Harburg—as well as some of the hottest stage talent, including Marlon Brando and Montgomery Clift.

So I began making day trips to the city during the rest of the semester, just to test the waters, maybe three or four times, on those days when I didn't have classes. I read a theatrical trade paper called *Actor's Cues* to find out about open casting calls, and went to many of them at CBS and NBC. They were airing a lot of live television dramas then being shot and broadcast from New York, but I never got any jobs from these open calls. I did meet some casting people who said, "Well, come back another time and maybe we can find a part for you," but that was about it.

Jim Merrick wanted to sign me to the Liebling-Wood Agency, but his bosses didn't want to make a commitment to me. Why they didn't want me to actually sign was bewildering; they'd send me around without any contract with them, and made it clear they'd be pissed if I got work through anyone else. In the meantime, unbeknownst to Liebling-Wood, I'd also been seen by another talent agent, Maynard Morris, from the big MCA operation—but again with no commitment or obligation.

One afternoon, Maynard sent me out to see a theater producer that the Liebling-Wood Agency had already had me visit. I told Maynard I felt peculiar about it, especially given what might happen if I actually got the job and had to pay commission to one side or the other. "Well," he said, "we can't have you going around any-more until you make up your mind about who you belong to."

That's when I decided to leave Liebling-Wood.

That summer, I told Jackie I wanted to give New York a real try. For the time being, she would remain in New Haven with Scott, while I moved into a tiny apartment on the corner of Spring Street and Sixth Avenue, what's now considered SoHo. It was incredibly tiny and I stayed there with two other people—a Yale-connected young woman named Joan Szell and her boyfriend, who were sum-mer housesitting for the actual tenants.

Even when I decided not to return to Yale, to take a leave begin-ning in September, it was an extremely speculative choice, with no sense of any surety. I'd only studied at Yale for around eight months, and despite all the open calls I went to during the summer, I'd gotten no speaking roles, nothing. Maybe there was a walk-on in *The March of Time*. The thought of an acting career was all really just a hunch.

What eventually made the whole move easier was that Jackie had an aunt who lived on Staten Island. By the summer's end, the aunt gave us a place to stay, plus free babysitting for Scott. Plus, while we were there, someone we met suggested I might be able to get a job as a model.

I was broke. I owned only one suit. And when I got offered a cover shoot for a detective magazine, I took it. I was posed with a girl in a brassiere, and I was supposed to be grabbing her arm. I was really embarrassed—but they paid me $150, which was quite a bit of money then. And they paid in cash. Well, I walked out of that studio thinking, "Boy, I can go out now and buy me a new suit for $39.95!"

Just as I hit the street, some guy rolled up in a panel truck and said, "Hey, buddy, you wanna buy a suit?" I thought: "How did he know that?" I got into the truck and he showed me these bolts of fabric he ordered for some of his Park Avenue customers. "I thought you sold suits," I said. "No," he replied, "all I've got are these bolts, but they're worth eight hundred dollars each. How much have you got on you?" I answered, "Only a hundred and fifty." To which he replied, "Okay, that'll do." Ten minutes later, I hopped out of that truck with two bolts of cloth that I didn't even have the money to have turned into suits.

Flash forward a year or so. There was a tailor's shop in the theater district, at the corner of Eighth Avenue and Forty-Fifth Street, that I walked past every day on my way to work. I had some money, and took one of those fabric bolts to the tailor and got myself measured with great fanfare. I chose a style, picked out a lining, and in a week or so it was finished. I had a new suit and it looked great. On the second day I wore it, I spilled something on it and carried it to the dry cleaners. I knew the owner, and when I came by to pick it up four days later, he said to me, "Tell me about this suit."

"I just had it made," I said. "What's the problem?"

"With the lining," he said, "nothing. But as for the rest of it . . ."

PAUL AND JOANNE READ A DRAFT OF *BABY WANT A KISS* WITH PLAYWRIGHT JAMES COSTIGAN IN 1964. PHOTO BY PHILIPPE HALSMAN

And then he carried out the rest of my suit. It had absolutely shrunk into itself. All that remained really was an outsized, perfect lining attached to a tiny outfit that seemed to have melted down.

I never did anything with that second bolt I bought. God, I can't believe I was ever that naive. Actually, yes I can.

I left the ranks of the bourgeoisie and became a member of the Actors Studio, the extraordinary acting study group headed by Lee Strasberg and famous for preaching the Method—the art of using your own memories and feelings to inhabit a role. How, I still wonder, did I ever pass that audition?

They didn't, and couldn't, have responded to my acting. I'm sure the other actors there wondered, "How did this son of a bitch get in here?" But when I mixed my confidence and energy with my real emotions—terror and fright (which came out as rage)—something genuine was going on, even if just by accident. I felt the Actors Studio members were the real actors, the bohemians, and they saw this kid from Shaker Heights wearing his seersucker suit and, well—I was *in* their world but definitely not a part of it. There were people there like Geraldine Page and Kim Stanley and Ben Gazzara, Frank Corsaro, Julie Harris, Jimmy Dean, Eli Wallach, and Annie Jackson; Brando was basically emeritus by the time I joined, but he did come around once in a while, especially if Elia Kazan, the director, had a scene he wanted him to look at.

STEWART STERN

For many years, Paul's favorite short story has been *Tonio Kröger* by Thomas Mann. It's about a boy in nineteenth-century Germany who adored an older boy with blue eyes who came from the north like his father. Tonio's mother came from the south and gave him her brown eyes. All his life he envied the blue-eyed people. When he grew up and became an artist, the conventional, blue-eyed part of his nature—successful, socially acceptable, was always criticizing his brown-eyed part—the sensitive, poetic, creative persona.

From the time he's been conscious, Paul has felt split down the middle of his soul. He can't permit himself to be blue-eyed or brown-eyed, because when he moves toward one side, the other pulls him back.

———

In high school I felt unaccepted by the people I wanted to be associated with, the socially acceptable people, the beautiful people at the Christian country club. I really just wanted to be social. I didn't want to be academic, and I didn't want to be a poet.

Ultimately, I thought talent would be a measurable explosion, an incredible sense of bohemia, somehow, a scarf that wrapped around your neck that disconnected you from any predisposition to the conventional. To be the innovator, a person who discovered things, new modes and new styles. I never felt that. I never had a sense of talent because I was always a follower, following someone else with stuff that I basically interpreted and did not really create.

I was sure none of these people at the Actors Studio actually considered me an actor. I was a pretty boy, a real conventional kid who somehow had staggered into this melange. I wasn't even a Yalie anymore. Also, I'd arrived there just as I was starting to work on Broadway. I now had a family settled in Staten Island. I couldn't really socialize, participate in what the Actors Studio folks did at night, and it was difficult to get into Manhattan early enough to attend classes and exercises. Everyone else seemed to have an extracurricular life that didn't involve me.

I did very few scenes myself, but I learned from osmosis and observation, watching these people, seeing how they did it. They had the pursuit of intentions, the impetus of active verbs, and just the simple act of moving. Successful actors really don't have to do anything more than that; of course, it took me thirty years to figure that out for myself.

When I first got the job in *Picnic*, I had a wife and child (with another one on the way) and only $250 in the bank. I don't know how long I would have been able to stay afloat without some financial cushion or if the play didn't run. I'd even applied for a job at the Hillside Avenue branch of the US Post Office in Queens.

I always could have gone and sold encyclopedias again. I wasn't actually worried about starving and going on welfare. If some opportunity had arisen that was secure but was away from the theater, I might have done it; I don't know.

———

So this bright-eyed yokel in his seersucker suit comes to New York via Yale, gets a few TV walk-ons, graduates to three- or four-line

PAUL AND JOANNE IN THE BROADWAY PRODUCTION
OF *BABY WANT A KISS* IN 1964

parts. He's introduced to the director Josh Logan, who's putting together a production of a new play called *Picnic* by William Inge. I get cast in the small part of the newsboy, with about ten or twelve lines in the first act. I'm also the understudy for Hal, the seductive drifter, and for the main supporting role of Alan, his hapless rival. Pretty soon, before the opening, I'm promoted to play Alan full-time, whose part seems exactly what the bright-eyed yokel was: a kid from Shaker Heights in a tan linen suit, who has to compete for the girl against the star, Ralph Meeker, who was Mr. Animal, and not having a clue physically or mentally about what that involved. The Shaker Heights kid, already married with a wife and child, runs into a sensational twenty-three-year-old girl named Joanne, who herself is understudying the play's female lead and some other parts. *Picnic*, memorably, has a long dance scene that triggers the primary onstage romance. The kid has no physical grace, so back in the wings Joanne, pearly of skin and sensitive to touch, teaches him how to dance. I was nursing an ailing marriage and this thing I carried around in my trousers every time we danced backstage together. Every day.

And still, after the play was a hit, and Ralph Meeker was set to take a two-week vacation, and I asked Josh Logan whether I could take over the part, Logan patted me in a fatherly way on top of my head and said, "I'd like to, kid, but you don't have any sex threat."

JOSH LOGAN, PULITIZER PRIZE WINNER AND DIRECTOR
OF WILLIAM INGE'S *PICNIC* ON BROADWAY IN 1953

Paul was introduced to me by William Liebling, husband of Audrey Wood, who was the agent for the play. I met Paul just to please him. My first impression of Paul Newman was that he was way too much of a gentleman to be a good actor, and that it would take too much effort to break down all his politeness to get to the real core of the man. But when we were casting the show, Paul's good looks made him right for the part of the one-line character, Bomber, who makes a pass at Madge after the picnic.

We also made Paul the understudy to the play's rich boy, Alan, and he soon proved to be better than the man he was understudying. So I asked Bill Inge if he could rewrite the part of Alan for a younger man and we recast Paul. He immediately fell into the part of the rich boy, and made the play stronger. In fact, it was Paul who made the play a hit.

I also ended up making Paul the understudy for the lead role of Hal. I noticed Paul had a good build and if he would work out and learn to dance, he could play the part. We did one rehearsal with Paul as Hal, and I said he'd be fine if he could wiggle his ass a little bit when he danced.

Sometime between the opening of *Picnic* in February 1953 and filming *The Long, Hot Summer* four years later, I went from being not much of a sexual threat to something else entirely that people recognized. I never thought it was really genuine, any more than I felt my anger on screen was genuine—I well remember Ben Gazzara criticizing my stage anger during a scene at the Actors Studio as "phony . . . it's just yelling"—but I guess it fooled enough of the people enough of the time to seem convincing. Something had rubbed off on me. It was the introduction of Joanne and her sexuality into my life. The years of dreaming and longing were suddenly a possible reality.

Joanne gave birth to a sexual creature. She taught him, she encouraged him, she delighted in the experimental. I was in pursuit of lust. I'm simply a creature of her invention.

STEWART STERN

Joanne relates with her heart, spontaneously and unmistakably. I mean she is a lady whose emotions come right out of her skin. She is sudden, and she cannot be false: it is not in her system.

You know how it's decided some luminary deserves a special evening, an honor night? If I ever deserve an evening tribute, it should be for the invention of that sex symbol that was created by Joanne. And it shouldn't be done at the American Film Institute or the Oscars—it should be a parade right before the Orange Bowl or the Rose Bowl. There could be a float with flag waving. There could be interviews with women who remember the French soft-core porn film *Emmanuelle,* where the heroine opens a magazine to a photo of me. I thought that was really the moment of my arrival.

In my marriage, Jackie was available, but there was always a gauze, a veil, over our responses to each other. At the core of my marital problems was a deep-seated sense of responsibility gone wrong, starting out with the delusion that we were building on a firm foundation. And when it wasn't that firm, neither of us had enough courage to say, "Let's stop here." You determine to hold the thing together, to churn your way through with pure stamina.

I suspect Jackie and I were doing that from our first moments of marriage. I know I couldn't be personal with anybody. And she probably wanted just that more than I gave her credit for.

We were deluded: blue skies—no need to deal with black clouds. Everything is terrific! I never realized how shallow I made the waters.

She had a tough go of it, Jackie did.

PAUL IN THE LATE 1950S

Still, I knew there had to be something else down the pike. There were a couple of quick diversions here and there; you couldn't even call them one-nighters. And they were always followed by terrible pangs of recrimination and guilt.

My ethical self was overwhelmed by the discovery of much more powerful appetites. Betraying my marital vows to Jackie seemed insignificant against that discovery. All my desperate fantasies and years of being turned down disappeared with Joanne. I suddenly found the door of opportunity flung open right before my eyes. Joanne made me feel sexy.

Orphans do have big appetites, and Joanne and I seemed like a couple of orphans. She first knew I was one because of that problem in my pants each time we danced, and I knew that she was an orphan because I couldn't see the definition of her personality other than her sexuality. It took one to know one, and we just banged it together. We made a point during *Picnic* and afterwards to let the lusty aspects of ourselves have time to function without interruption or distraction; I think we were pretty good about that, we left a trail of lust all over the place. Hotels and motels and public parks and bathrooms and swimming pools and ocean beaches and rumble seats and Hertz rental cars.

I don't know that Joanne and I sat around questioning our morals. There was passion in what we had. Something had happened to us and we had no idea where it was going. One day I'd determine to commit to her, and the next day, faced with having to do it, I'd find I couldn't bring myself to break away from Jackie.

I remember a night when everything exploded on me. I was leaving our house for the theater, the kids were carrying on, there was food all over the floor. I just wanted to drop down on my knees and tell Joanne that I really loved her, and I had to get out of this mess that I was in. Then, all of a sudden, I realized I couldn't do that; I didn't have enough money and just couldn't desert Jackie—God, it was horrible.

My indecision and judiciousness, constantly weighing all the elements, was paralleled by Joanne's unpredictability. There was a wonderful joining in that, too. We were constantly keeping each other off balance; I think that was great, because there was no commitment in that, and I don't know that either of us really wanted a commitment. Yes, we did want all the movie-star shit and the lust and the scuttling around—I know we said we didn't, but that was part of the allure. Because it was naughty and somewhere, some-where, there was sacrifice involved. I don't know when exactly that became clear, but there was also the most incredible, unforgivable brutality in that. Brutal in my detachment from my family. There was no signal given to Jackie, no chance for her to regroup.

Each time there'd be an evening of great passion and affection with Joanne, I'd change my mind again about a divorce. My vacilla-tions went on for years.

JOANNE WOODWARD

I was already having a hard time because there was something so amazing about living this fantasy, even for someone who had lived her entire life in fantasy, as one long movie script, there were just things coming in that I couldn't grasp onto.

There were also times that Joanne felt guilty, that she was betray-ing a family and children. But we'd always come back to the point that what bound us together was irresistible.

ED LEVY, A CLOSE FRIEND OF PAUL'S AT KENYON AND OF BOTH PAUL'S AND JACKIE'S IN NEW YORK.

Paul invited my parents and my aunt to see *Picnic,* and he set up to meet us for a drink after the show. He brought Joanne. She was eager to be there, eager to please. She was just wait-ing for things to happen, euphoric because she was starting to fall in love with Paul.

As we were leaving, Joanne said she was afraid to walk home alone, it was dangerous; Paul said he would see her home, and they left. My aunt said to me, "She's kinda sweet on him."

"No, nothing to it," I said.

I refused to believe it was anything; I'd never easily suspect Paul of having an affair, because he was kind of straight—the way people were back then who were recently married.

Not long after that evening, when I saw Paul and Jackie together, I said to him, "Oh, tell me about Joanne Woodward. I have a feeling she might be living with someone." And what I meant was: might she be available to date me? Then Jackie said, "I have that feeling, too, about her living with someone." But she said it with an edge.

Paul kind of slid down in his chair, because he obviously hadn't clued me in. I think he'd been throwing out hints to me, but I refused to take them, because I didn't want to give up my image of Paul. The two of us would go out drinking and he'd say, "You know, I met this girl in a bar . . ." I couldn't believe it was anything more than him making conversation.

A couple years later—Paul was still married then, and I think he'd just had a third child with Jackie—and I ran into Joanne and him in Detroit, where Joanne was doing a play, *The Lovers*. I felt loyal to Paul, always. I wrote him that I didn't think he was a bastard, that I understood what he saw in Joanne and that I could tell where things weren't right with Jackie. Paul wrote a note back to me.

"You're the only one," he said, "who doesn't think I'm a shit."

———

Around the time *Picnic* opened, Jackie and I decided to move from Staten Island to a rental in Fresh Meadows, near the Queens/

Nassau County border. By then, I was regularly going out at night after our performances to one of our show bars with actors from the cast, including Meeker, Janice Rule, and Kim Stanley. But really, in my mind, it was mainly Joanne and me. There would also often be some college buddies of mine or friends of hers, TV folks—each night, a lot of people around us. Joanne had a fourth-floor walkup studio over on the East Side, it was just one room with a built-in kitchenette, so we'd often end up nearby, like at Costi's. Was Jackie suspicious about what was happening? I don't know; Jackie was the only person more naive than I was.

As the *Picnic* run came to an end, I wasn't sure what to do next; there'd been talk of starring in some TV productions, and some other Broadway shows, and Hollywood also came calling. Josh Logan told me not to sign up for movies. And my agent, Maynard Morris, said, "Well, listen. If you don't want to go to LA, it's okay. Just remember, though—people wait around and they wait around and they knock on your door, then they knock on your door again, and one day there's no more knocking. You never know when that last knock is going to be." And the knock I finally picked up on was for *The Silver Chalice*. Years later, when my career was a lot farther along, I was widely quoted as saying it was "the worst movie produced in the fifties": it was not an inaccurate quote.

———

My time in California didn't have an auspicious start. I drove there from New York, alone, and literally didn't know where I was going. I was booked for a room in Hollywood, at the Roosevelt Hotel, but I got off at the wrong exit on one of the freeways—I'm not even sure whether it was the Ventura or the Pasadena; I must have cut all the way through Kansas. Anyway, I don't really remember ever coming into Los Angeles itself, but I ended up exiting at Santa Monica Boulevard. I later, of course, found out there was a much easier way to get where I was headed, but I had to drive a long way on local roads along Sunset. It took forever until I found the Roosevelt.

The Silver Chalice was being shot at the Warner Bros. lot in Burbank, but early on I also had a meeting at MGM at the other end of the city. Some lady with a baby carriage had been coming across the street and I nearly ran her over. I started yelling, "You dumb shit!" A cop pulled me over and started railing: "You almost ran over that woman in a crosswalk!"

"What was wrong about that?"

"Well, in LA, pedestrians have the right of way. Where are you from, anyway?"

And before I could answer he noticed my New York plates and asked for my license.

"It's being sent out from New York; I just got here but I left my wallet at home."

Somehow, I wasn't locked up.

———

The Silver Chalice was a big-budget biblical toga epic about a young silversmith—played by me—who was asked to create the Holy Grail after Jesus's death. The director was Victor Saville, whose movies went back to the silent era and who had spent years getting the financing together to make this movie. During the few rehearsals we actually held, I realized that I wasn't going to get any help from Victor, whom I must have been driving crazy.

———

ARTHUR PARK BECAME PAUL'S PRIMARY MOVIE
AGENT AT MCA.

He was totally unlike himself when he was doing *The Silver Chalice*. Because he hated it. He hated the part, hated the way they were making it, hated the fact that he'd fallen into what he considered a trap. It was painful for him, and he was kicking himself in his own shin for letting himself get into this mess.

JOHN FOREMAN, PAUL'S AGENT AND LATER BUSINESS PARTNER

After Paul opened in *Picnic,* every studio wanted him. He was the hot guy. And the reason "coast" (what we called our LA office) made the decision in favor of Warner Bros. was that Paul had the chance to be the star of his first picture—plus they offered the best terms. Everyone went into *The Silver Chalice* with their eyes wide open, including Paul Newman, who at the time of the deal was thanking the heavens above for an opportunity to make some real money. He'd go from making around $350 or $400 a week on Broadway, to $1,750 a week to start at Warners.

MEADE ROBERTS, A SCREENWRITER BEST KNOWN FOR HIS COLLABORATIONS WITH TENNESSEE WILLIAMS ON *THE FUGITIVE KIND* AND *SUMMER AND SMOKE*, WAS CLOSE TO BOTH JOANNE AND PAUL IN THE 1950S.

Before he headed out to Hollywood, Paul told me he was very nervous about the *Silver Chalice* part. Paul said Maynard Morris had told him, "No Bible movie is ever a flop. Look what *The Robe* did for Richard Burton!"

To which Paul replied: "I don't think *The Silver Chalice* is *The Robe.*"

Someone I met there suggested I smooth my path by trying a Hollywood acting coach. To which I replied, "Are you some kind of freak?" But the more I thought about it, I began to see I was in trouble, and had to get on my feet with the part. So I ended up working with a little Hungarian lady named Elsa Schreiber. She wasn't attached to Warners, she was an independent coach, and always wore a bandanna around her head. She had me rehearse with one of her other students, doing some of the scenes from the film's script. It wasn't the same, of course, as working with the actual actress you'd be working with, and that didn't make much sense to me. But I'd practice the scenes and Elsa would stop me.

"You're not thinking," she told me. "You're just *thinking* that you're thinking."

And here I was, someone who'd already been on Broadway and had a year at the Actors Studio, and it finally occurred to me what the hell she was saying. There were a lot of other people who probably would have gotten that instantaneously, and here I was, someone who was already a couple of years into being a reasonably professional actor in New York. And this was the first time anybody said that to me in a way that made sense—and I listened.

Just when I began working with Elsa, I was at the lot and ran into Jimmy Dean, whom I knew from the Actors Studio. He was getting ready to start filming *East of Eden,* and we went to the commissary.

"Hey, I read your script," he said.

"What do you think of it?"

"Well," he answered, "it's just endless pages of exposition."

Here was Jimmy launching his movie career in a film directed by Elia Kazan, and I was about to work with Victor Saville. Somehow, it seemed appropriate.

MEADE ROBERTS

A few months after *Chalice* was released, I met up with Paul at a tavern we liked at Fifty-Fourth Street and Sixth, right across from the old Ziegfeld. And sitting right inside was Jimmy Dean.

The word was already out about Dean's upcoming picture.

Jimmy said: "Oh Paul, you poor guy! Look what you're in! Have you heard how great *East of Eden* is?" He got very snide and just awful.

Paul took it with a great deal of dignity. I'd have hit him. I was itching to.

VII

For me, the experience of making *The Silver Chalice* became a metaphor for the whole movie junk, the failure of it, the hollowness, the superficiality. I guess that made it appropriate that it would be the first film I would do and that it would fall flat on its ass. And it would be appropriate that I, sensing the disaster of it, sensing the amateurness of it before the movie was even finished shooting, would already be negotiating to go back to New York and do another Broadway play. Thus began the struggle to extricate myself from this image I couldn't escape. But like a great many other things in my life, to paraphrase Theodore Roosevelt, on the one hand I would stomp it underfoot, but on the other hand, not so fast.

I'm not talking about success (or lack thereof) but about my appearance. It isn't uncomplicated. It was my appearance that got me in the door. Where the hell would I have been if I looked like Golda Meir? Probably no place; it was like being a guy with a trust fund who doesn't have to work. I always had that trust fund of appearance. I could get by on that. But I realized that to survive, I needed something else.

Especially because my life seemed to be changing again.

MARY HARA, NICKNAMED BLATZ, A FRIEND OF PAUL'S
FROM YALE'S DIRECTING PROGRAM

Paul had just come back to the city from making *The Silver Chalice* and he took me to see *Gate of Hell,* a samurai film from Japan.

"What was it like in Hollywood?" I asked. "Did you enjoy doing it?"

"Blatz," Paul answered, "they'll do anything for money out there. They'll do anything for money, they'll kill for money. It's just awful."

When I left Hollywood after *Silver Chalice* wrapped, Joanne (who'd also been working there) and I had this terrible fight. It was over, all finished between us. We decided we'd never see each other again. I decided to drive back to New York; my mother had been visiting, and I figured I would drop her off in Cleveland. (We even stopped off in Vegas, where we had a great all-you-can-eat dinner for one dollar.)

It was a miserable situation for Joanne; she was a backstreet wife and I wouldn't get a divorce. I didn't know how I'd do it, but I wanted to try and straighten out my marriage and be with my family. That idea permeated my thinking, and after I left California, Joanne and I didn't talk or communicate for what must have been months.

I began rehearsals for the Broadway version of *The Desperate Hours*—I played an escaped convict who takes Karl Malden and his family hostage. It became a hit play, and Jackie and I decided to rent a house in Sea Girt, New Jersey, only an hour and fifteen minutes from Manhattan. There were a lot of Grosse Pointe/Shaker Heights-type homes just a block away from the ocean, and in the middle of them all was a Charles Addams house that was unfinished on the inside, and had everything falling down on the outside. It was sensational.

The surf at Sea Girt was big and delicious. I'd drive there every night after the theater, and I'd swim at midnight in the breakers. I felt at home in those enveloping waves that knocked you right down, the wonderful comfort of being engulfed in that tumultuous water.

Strange, but I never was frightened by water despite almost drowning as a kid. I don't remember exactly how old I was, but I was in the town pool and I couldn't yet swim. A counselor was there, and maybe a hundred and fifty kids in the big pool with him. Six of us would jump on his back at once, and he'd go wading out into the water up to his shoulders—and over my head. One afternoon, I just dropped off and sank. Absolutely gone. Another counselor came swimming by—I remember the flash of his bathing suit—and I grabbed hold of his waist and would not let go. I was underwater around his belt, but the counselor thought I was just screwing around; so whenever I managed to surface, he dunked me. I was beginning to drown and he finally got it, pulling me to the side of the pool. I couldn't have lasted much longer. With all that bedlam, I would simply have sunk to the bottom, and much later someone would have said, "Well, isn't that funny? Some little fellow's down there looking for pennies at the bottom of the pool!"

Jackie and I had very good times in Sea Girt. Scott must have been four or five then, and our first daughter, Susan, was still a toddler; it was a good time for them, too. We'd always bring people to visit on my weekend—which was Sunday to Monday, since we did no Sunday matinees back then—and I'd do cookouts and everyone would go down to the beach for swims.

Then one day back in the city, I went to a script reading at some producer's place, and bingo, there's Joanne coming out of a neighboring office. We both just stood there, looking at each other, and it was on again.

And then it was off again.

There were more separations, breakups, lots of times we were not together. Terrible fights. But again, after some time passed, I had to go out to Warners in California for meetings. Joanne was already in Hollywood doing some TV shoot for 20th Century–Fox. There's a long boulevard within the Warner Bros. lot that passes by dressing rooms, parking lots, an administration building, an executive dining room, and the commissary, which one afternoon Joanne was just leaving. From the equivalent of four blocks away, we somehow saw each other and hollered; then, just like in some old movie, we began running toward each other, arms outstretched. It was amazing.

There came a point when I was really leading two lives. I was living my life with Jackie and I was living my life with Joanne. These were impossible times. Till then, I'd never had a sense of consequences, never suffered from them. I volunteered for a torpedo bomber and survived. I graduated college without working. I drove cars off cliffs after having too much beer. But now, with Jackie and Joanne, consequences began to weigh heavily on me. I was a failure as an adulterer.

My private turmoil was not interfering with my career. I was cast in *The Battler,* an hour-long TV drama, telecast live, based on one of Hemingway's Nick Adams stories and directed by Arthur Penn, about a punch-drunk ex-boxing champion who tragically chooses the glory of the arena over the love of a loyal woman. Jimmy Dean was cast as the lead, while I got the main supporting role. Two weeks before the show was to be broadcast, Jimmy was killed when he crashed his Porsche on a small highway in California. The decision was made to go ahead, and I took over Jimmy's part as the fighter.

It was exhausting. There were three rehearsals a day, from eight a.m. to ten o'clock at night. A run-through. A dress rehearsal with wardrobe changes and makeup—my character had to go from beat-up to handsome to beat-up again during the course of a live sixty-minute show; I was having prosthetics glued on and taken off my face at a crazy pace. When we finally got done preparing the night

JOANNE AND PAUL IN THE LATE 1960S.
PHOTO BY KAS HEPPNER

before, I went out with an executive from our show's sponsor, Pontiac, and with our producer, Fred Coe. I had two glasses of beer and I got really wobbly. And as we came out of this restaurant on Sunset Strip and waited for the valet to bring our car, Coe and the adman noticed a fancy sedan just sitting there idling—and they decided to have a little fun and fill one of its hubcaps with gravel. Some kid, the owner, came out of the restaurant, got into that car, and drove off—and it immediately sounded like the whole transmission was falling out.

He jumped out of the car, ran at us, and screamed: "Who did that?" Fred Coe pointed at me. The kid comes right over, punches me in my face, then gets back in his car and drives away. I made it back to my room at the Chateau Marmont, where Joanne had been staying with me, and I'm laughing. "I'm supposed to be a middle-weight champ and I'm standing there with both hands in my pockets and a kid crawls up on an orange crate and belts me in the eye. I never even knew what hit me." Over the next couple of days, everyone wanted to know how I got the terrible whack on my face. I made up a story that my costar Frederick O'Neal hit me too hard with his shoe in an action sequence; thank God, I said, it didn't blossom until we'd finished airing the show. I can't tell you how impressed they all were that I'd been wounded in the line of duty.

The Battler won a lot of positive attention, including from Bob Wise, the director who was getting ready to make the big Rocky Graziano biography picture, *Somebody Up There Likes Me*. Graziano was a true American sports star and folk hero, a tough New York kid who fought his way up from the slums and juvenile prisons to become a champion, a world title holder. Word was that the film was to be Jimmy Dean's next project, and his sudden death obviously scrambled things; Wise and the producers cast me, probably on the strength of my handling the part in *The Battler*.

I know there are some people who attribute my career breakthroughs to Jimmy's death. Yes, there were elements of luck—and a lot of my success has indeed involved what I call Newman's luck. Newman's luck began in 1925 when I was born white in America. Appearance is the second luck. Cognitive skills in inventing is the third luck. And I had the luck to overcome the fact that people always said about me "Isn't he darling!" or "Isn't he so cute!" by having enough drive to see I wasn't ever going to survive just on that. I'd been in contact with indifference and stupidity and my own lack of perception. But I'd never really come in contact with true adversity. Luck recognized me.

If Jimmy hadn't been killed, half of me says, "You could have done it anyway. It would have been a hair slower, but it would have happened."

ROBERT WISE WAS THE DIRECTOR OF
SOMEBODY UP THERE LIKES ME.

James Dean had agreed to the film. But before the script was done, he was killed in that unfortunate accident. The only other actor we considered was John Cassavetes; I had lunch with him at the MGM commissary and I told him I believed he was too slight, especially stripped down, to be convincing in the role. He was a little pissed off and said any real actor can act anything—including his size.

Paul had been on the lot, had just finished *The Rack,* and the studio recommended I watch some sequences. He was excellent and so it was agreed he'd be the one.

Paul and I agreed that since Rocky was very much alive, and Paul was very much of the same school as me—that you should dig and research as much as you can about a character—that we should spend time in New York with Rocky. We didn't want it to be just a copy of Rocky with any kind of falseness around the edges, but whatever of Rocky Paul could get for himself.

Rocky took us to visit all his old haunts on the Lower East Side, the pigeon keepers on the roofs, his neighborhood candy store. Sometimes Rocky would walk on ahead of us, and Paul would study his gait, and just notice he had rounded heels on his shoes that gave him a certain shift. The way he held his hands in his pockets. His phrasing, his lingo, his cadence, the pattern of speech—Paul brought those out to the coast with him for the shoot.

I think Paul felt secure in the fact that he had met the man he was going to portray and that he'd be able to draw on him, in the physical and internal sense. It gave Paul confidence.

Before making *Somebody Up There Likes Me,* I drove up to the
Catskills with Jackie, to one of the big resorts, to observe and spend
time with Graziano. He had to cancel at the last minute, but I did
meet a guy there, a practicing psychiatrist, whom I spoke with at
length before dinner at the bar on my first night. Later that evening,
I went down to his room, knocked, and asked him whether I could
have his business card, and if I could call him sometime. He'd just
been sitting in his room, drinking brandy by himself and quietly getting loaded.

The doctor was a soft-spoken, burly, bullet-headed, football-
necked Freudian in his late fifties from New York, and I wound
up entering into therapy with him. Did it help with my situation
between Jackie and Joanne? Marginally, it might have been instruc-
tive, but in terms of specifics I would have to say no. As much as
I must have needed the help, I wasn't in the frame of mind to be
helped. Not that I necessarily resisted, but I really didn't have
enough information to give him. In fact, it is only in recent years
that the information I could give any psychiatrist would be compe-
tent.

About three years into our sessions, the doctor got a tumor in
his head and died from it not long afterwards. I wanted to do something in his memory. I had once met his wife, a beautiful woman;
she and his associates at NYU got together and suggested I endow
a chair in psychiatry at the college in his honor; in those days, they
told me, that would cost about $150,000 (nowadays, probably more
like a million). Well, when I was doing *Somebody Up There Likes Me,* I
made $12,000 and was already in the 91 percent income-tax bracket.
I don't know where they thought I was going to get my hands on the
kind of money they wanted. I worried that everyone would think I
was very disloyal, so I just fled. I didn't know what to say to anybody.

Around the time we started actually filming the Graziano movie,
Jackie and I were not doing very well. I was also drinking up a storm.

Which was amazing, because the work on Graziano was really difficult. It was a tough show to do, and the last eight or nine days of production were reserved to shoot the climactic fight scenes in a boxing ring. Graziano actually fought Tony Zale for the championship three times, only winning the last one. Our script decided to dramatize just that final fight; off camera, our stunt guy would be calling out instructions to me and the real Tony Zale, who was playing himself on screen. The problem was Zale would get so pissed off re-creating his loss, he couldn't fake it, doctor it, or pull his punches. I took a terrible swipe from him, cracked a bone in my hand, and went down. The production had to be stopped for maybe four days. The crew finally built some plastic thing that went over the edge of my knuckles and was taped to the back of my forearm to absorb the shocks.

After my accident, Zale was replaced by our stunt guy for me to "fight" against. By the end of the first day back, we were both wrecks. I mentioned to my agent that I couldn't believe we had to do this for four or five more days straight.

"Ever heard of Miltown?" he asked. "Take one, and give one to your stunt man, about an hour and a half before you film, then take another every four hours." We did that and the stunt guy and I suddenly became the palsiest guys in the ring: "Go ahead, hit me harder, harder, hit me!" We got to be real happy fellows all the way until we finished the picture.

When the Graziano was finally ready to open about a year or so later, I got into another fight. My friend from Ohio Jim Martin was visiting, and I decided to take him and his wife out to dinner, driving my brand-new Volkswagen. I'd been connected to the VW dealer through a friend of Rudy Vallee's, who also suggested a dinner place I should try not too far from our rental in Fresh Meadows.

This seafood restaurant was on a very quiet, narrow street, the kind that customers would park on by driving up on the sidewalk and settling two wheels there. That's what I did, and there was nothing weird about it. Past midnight, as we walked out of the place, I told

Jim that maybe I'd had too much beer: "Why don't you drive?"—and I flipped him the keys. Jim got in, put the VW into first instead of reverse, and tapped a fireplug. I mean, *literally* tapped it—there was not a mark on my bumper or on the plug. As a point of information, in those days, Volkswagens had about fourteen horsepower and maybe a top speed of sixty miles per hour.

I realized this wasn't going to work, so I took the keys back from Jim and took the wheel to drive home. I thought I was driving pretty slowly when I heard a siren in back of me. I couldn't tell what kind of vehicle it was, but to get out of the way I pulled off to the right, apparently through a red light. At which point the squad car pulls up next to me and tells me I both ran a light and hit a fire hydrant.

I made them take me back to the restaurant to look at my bumper and the hydrant up close. And there was not a mark on either.

"So what are you guys complaining about?" I asked the cops.

"You're coming to the station," one of them replied.

"On what charge?"

And right then, I apparently took a swing at the cops. Next thing I knew, the cops took me in custody to the Mineola courthouse and I was thrown into the county slammer.

These cops were grandstanding. It was all a setup. They knew arresting me would be a big deal. By the time this happened, I'd been in enough television shows that the cops recognized who I was. It also didn't hurt that the first name of one of the cops was Rocky—it could make for a good story. The cops also knew something I didn't: that the courthouse that morning would be surrounded by newspaper photographers because a different case, a kidnapping, was going on and being covered in all the tabloids. Sure enough, in the next day's papers there were photos of me looking like a criminal being led into jail. It wasn't like I was trying to escape. I may have been unruly, and it is possible my behavior was a bit boorish—and though I don't know whether anyone will agree with me, my heart was in the right place.

I was brought before a judge the following day, charged with driving under the influence. The judge asked for my license, looked it over, then handed it right back to me.

"Dismissed," he ordered. And except for the lousy publicity—though the cop named Rocky got lots of positive tabloid attention—that was the end of that.

———

ALAN WRIGHT WAS ONE OF PAUL'S CLOSEST
FRIENDS IN COLLEGE AND, LATER, IN CLEVELAND; HE WAS
A GUEST AT PAUL AND JACKIE'S WEDDING AS WELL AS AT
SCOTT NEWMAN'S CHRISTENING.

I think Jackie was riddled with ambition, but she wasn't mature enough to recognize that this handsome young actor she married had the ingredients and the drive to be a big success—and she was either going to have to go along with that and be a wife and mother rather than a showbiz girl, or not. Paul once told me she had taken extensive dancing lessons, but I surmised she had nothing more than local-community-theater talent. She'd often talk all about her experiences at the Woodstock theater.

One time another friend of ours, Jim Rice, and I went to New York to visit Paul. We saw them in Staten Island and Paul and Jackie made a cookout for us on the little barbecue they had on their concrete patio. I could see there were tensions, and it seemed obvious Jackie was frustrated with her own life. That night, we went with Paul to Broadway and saw him in *Picnic*. It was a performance where the understudy, Joanne Woodward, happened to substitute for one of the stars, Janice Rule. Afterward, Paul took us out to a place near and dear to his heart, an all-night kind of place. Some members of the cast joined us, including Joanne.

We really tied one on. Joanne was very reserved. She told

me she was from Georgia, but she wasn't especially interested in these two characters from Cleveland who were old pals of Paul's. Still, there was an intimacy in the way she and Paul sat together, but I attributed that closeness to their being in a show together. There was a big jukebox in this joint, and I believe Paul and Joanne danced together once or twice.

Our conversation was not just with Paul so much as with the two of them. I must say, it was almost as if they were husband and wife.

Joanne may have fulfilled a lot of needs Paul had for companionship and professional discussion even as a friend. He was having fun with Joanne; he was glad to be with her. There was a well-rounded rapport. It was like turning on a light switch.

I didn't know that night there was a big love affair going on and that his marriage was going down the tubes. But I could tell that Paul and Joanne were gaga. They weren't trying to conceal it or show it off, either. That's just the way it was.

———

You might wonder: how, given the state of disrepair of my marriage to Jackie, could the two of us create a third child?

Stephanie Newman was probably conceived because of a misplaced sense of trying to make things right that you couldn't make right. I always had a sense that things just happened, that you didn't have much control over them.

To the extent that one is capable, or able, to change the course of events, then you do have to accept responsibility, and I don't know how you'd ever allocate that. If I had failed as an actor and made it easier for my children to believe that they could achieve more than I did, what would that have done? It's always *if* Jackie and I had stuck it out, no matter what, what would that have done? *If* I hadn't been a nomad? *If* I hadn't been involved in a business that meant being away from home so much, what would that have done?

Somewhere in all of this is the imponderable of being a human being.

There soon came a point when my family—Jackie, me, and our three kids—really split up. I hadn't gotten a divorce yet, but Jackie and I were now openly separated. And after long negotiations, Jackie agreed to a settlement. I think for the first year, she was guaranteed a certain income, around $200,000. I earned $225,000 that year, so I only kept $25,000 of that. If I had started drinking too much or made three or four bad pictures in a row, I'd have been in a very tough position.

I flew alone to Mexico City from New York to get the final legal documents. I'd never been to Mexico before, and I certainly didn't know the language. I arrived at night and the first thing I noticed was that all the drivers were crazed, the cars were of questionable sturdiness, and no one paid any attention to stop signs. It was arranged by my lawyers in LA that I would meet a local attorney there that evening, whose junky little office turned out to be the size of a closet but who needed to rubber-stamp all our Spanish paperwork. I was up most of the night trying to track that goddamn lawyer down.

The plan was that after I was done in Mexico City, I'd head to Las Vegas, where Joanne was waiting, and we'd get married at the El Rancho Hotel. Everything was set up, but I still didn't have the final papers for my divorce in hand. Though I did finally connect with the lawyer the next day, I'm honestly still not sure whether Joanne's and my marriage is legally valid, I mean, maybe it'll get thrown out of court someday.

———

In life, in relationships, the person who is inconstant does not see that as a flaw. He sees himself as someone who has the ability to be fluid, to see both sides of every question.

THE NEWMAN–WOODWARD WEDDING PARTY IN 1958: *LEFT TO RIGHT,*
ROBERT CARTER, ELINOR WOODWARD CARTER, JOANNE, PAUL, TERESA NEWMAN,
ARTHUR NEWMAN JR., FRANCES WOODWARD, WADE WOODWARD

Was it hurtful to others? I never recognized things from somebody else's point of view. I couldn't see what happened from Scott's,
from Susan's, I couldn't see it from Stephanie's. All I could do was
see it from my own, which was: "My God, look at these parents who
desert their kids. Look at them." I saw myself as somewhere in the
middle. A little of bad, a lot of good—and I provided.

But what I did just didn't have any class.

I didn't take them aside and give them comfort by explanation,
certainly not in a way that they would understand. Not because I
wouldn't do it, but because I didn't really get it.

You can't really say, "Oh, I must be understanding about this" when you haven't been understanding about anything for your whole life.

When you've given everything up to chance, the only thing left to have faith in is luck.

Joanne, in this regard, was no help. She was just as adolescent as I was. Orphans grow up late. At least these two did.

———

JANICE RULE WAS A MEMBER OF THE ORIGINAL
BROADWAY CAST OF WILLIAM INGE'S *PICNIC*.

I don't know if I was aware of Paul and Joanne. To me, Joanne was a pretty young girl who was at all the parties with a lot of different men for a while.

I was far more aware of Paul and Jackie. They seemed like a perfectly lovely suburban couple. Maybe jujubes were dancing in our heads with sugarplum fairies, but I have the most vivid sense of Paul and Jackie as a family.

Actually, I was not that observant.

———

JOANNE WOODWARD

I was in fear and awe of Janice Rule. As an understudy, I felt invisible and was hardly ever spoken to. I remember an horrendous evening when we were previewing *Picnic* out of town; a party was given for the whole cast except for the understudies—Tony Eisley, Moe Miller, and me.

———

KARL MALDEN WAS A MEMBER OF THE ACTORS STUDIO
WHO COSTARRED WITH NEWMAN IN THE BROADWAY STAGE
VERSION OF *THE DESPERATE HOURS*.

When *On the Waterfront* was being cast, there was a long
period when Marlon wasn't going to do it. This was during
the McCarthy era, and Marlon felt our director, Elia Kazan,
was a squealer. He didn't want to work for a man who had
named names.

Marlon and I knew each other well from doing *A Streetcar
Named Desire,* and the studio turned to me to try and convince him to change his mind about Kazan. I told him, "Marlon, you're judging who is right and who is wrong . . . don't
try to play God because it's going to hit you." He remained
adamantly against doing the picture.

So Kazan phoned and told me that he had to find someone
else.

"Will you do me a favor?" he asked. "I think Paul Newman
would be good as the boy."

I agreed with Kazan. Newman had a boxer's build and was
pretty athletic.

Kazan continued: "I'll tell him to find a scene and pick a
girl he wants to play it with. You work with him for a week,
and then we'll bring in Sam Spiegel [the producer] to see
him."

I agreed to help.

Joanne Woodward was the girl Newman chose.

They picked the park-bench scene and we rehearsed for a
week. It was beautiful. That's when I first realized that there
was something going on there. I couldn't quite put my finger
on it, but I think it was the way they'd come to the rehearsal
together and then leave together, too.

Joanne had a kind of innocence, and she was damn good. But my concentration was on Paul, because he's the one we'd have to sell.

We'd improvise a little, and I didn't give him any instructions except to titillate him about Joanne, something very vulgar, because that's what the scene is about—is he or isn't he going to lay her in the bushes? She would like it, yet doesn't know what to do about it, and he, being the kind of guy he is, he's for anything at all, at any time! I wanted to give him that freeness.

Well, Paul would get so excited he couldn't stand still. "Let me do it! Let me try," he said, and the more he did of that, the more I titillated him. Different kinds of sex. Tonight's the night, because she won't be here tomorrow.

I thought, "Gee, this is great, the way he can get himself worked up." There was a childlike excitement about him, a completely emotional thing that comes from the inside. He just goes all out.

That's the way I felt about Paul in his young days. I wasn't the director, I was only helping a friend, but Paul accepted me as the director. He accepted me as someone who could help him. And I admit, I liked that fact. Newman could have said, "Who the hell is Karl Malden? He's not Kazan—Kazan should be doing this himself!" No, what I loved was that he gave of himself completely to what I said.

After about five days of work, Sam Spiegel came and saw it. He said, "Good, fine," and left.

A couple of days later, Marlon agreed to do the part.

ELIA KAZAN DIRECTED ON THE WATERFRONT (WITH MARLON
BRANDO) AND SWEET BIRD OF YOUTH (WITH PAUL NEWMAN).
THE FOLLOWING IS AN EXCERPT FROM A LETTER KAZAN WROTE
TO BUDD SCHULBERG, SCREENWRITER OF ON THE WATERFRONT:

If we don't get Brando, I'm for Paul Newman. This boy will
definitely be a film star. I have absolutely no doubt. He's
just as good looking as Brando and his masculinity, which
is strong, is also more actual. He's not as good an actor as
Brando yet, probably will never be. But he's a darn good
actor with plenty of power, plenty of insides, plenty of sex.

VIII

P opularity can be divided into a couple of factors. There's the aspect that is intrusive and offends the private part of your life—what happens in the *New York Post* and the junk magazines. It's those people out in front of a theater calling attention to the fact you're there when you don't want any attention called. The people who follow you into libraries, into the lobby of your apartment building, fellows with flashbulbs, the people who are rude.

There are people who believe that somehow if they've bought a ticket to your motion picture it gives them voting stock in your corporation. And they don't understand why they can't just come to the back door of your house and say "Get me a job!" or "You're so big and I'm so little, why don't you make me big, too!" These are the people that can only discuss the blue eyes and the externals. Those are the elements of popularity that are disagreeable to me and a constant interference.

But another aspect of popularity, which is terribly important, is how it creates a kind of power that is transferable to business and thus gives the leverage to do the kind of projects you want to do. And as your popularity quotient goes down, so does your ability to exert the kind of pressure you need to make the kind of films you'd like to be a part of.

I would like to get rid of one part of my popularity, but if you get rid of one half, you get rid of the other, too.

LUCILLE NEWMAN

My own very special doctor took care of Tress at the end, and he was helping us get Paul into the hospital secretly. I said, "This country is ridiculous. This man is doing a job that he likes. Why does he have to be pestered so? Why can't he live a normal life? It's only in this country." And the doctor said, "Lucille, I was in Spain and I saw a five- or six-story building with a picture of him on the side. It's not just in this country."

Smiling for the cameras is a smile that doesn't come from anywhere except a command; there's no mirth in it. When Joanne and I have been at Cannes, for example, walking up this flight of stairs with a fifteen-foot-wide red carpet and having that music from *Star Wars* or whatever the hell it is at decibels that fry your eardrums . . . well, you get a sense of what the kings of England must have felt at their coronations. And then you start to think, "They should do this for me once a day, hustle me in, get the trumpets, cue the cameras and the applause and the band," just to get your confidence back. Between the bathroom and the breakfast room, every day when you come down from your shower, you could start your day with the fucking fanfares and flashbulbs going off. The dichotomy is that it is a dream and a nightmare at the same time.

When Joanne and I went to Paris to shoot a few scenes of *Mr. and Mrs. Bridge* there were photographers at the airport, and Joanne said to me: "Don't be a jerk. Pose for them and then they'll leave us alone." So you agree to stand there and smile for a minute or two, hold your wife's arm, etc. and you tell them, "I'll see you, goodbye." Then you walk to your car and about two-thirds of them follow and do exactly what you thought you were getting away from. They honor nothing, and they even chase the car.

We pull up to the Ritz, and the same bunch of photographers are there. What was the advantage of my posing at the airport? I'm now in an absolute fury and I head into the hotel manager's office and say, "You've got to give us some way to get in and out of here. I need a back door that we can use in the morning." Especially because once I actually get away from the Ritz, I can put on a baseball cap and no one will know me; Joanne and I can go wherever we want. By now I'm using foul language with the Ritz staff: "You make those fucking guys leave us alone!"

They finally showed us an old service elevator that had a sort of French-doors-type window that you can get out of that lands you in a backstreet behind the hotel. We were game. So Joanne and I get up the next day, ready to escape, and we noticed there wasn't a single photographer in sight at the entrance. So after my terrible outburst, I felt like such a schmuck.

One reason I always thought Brando was interesting was that in the world of actors, he initiated an attitude that in no way catered to the hierarchy of the Hollywood studios. The bosses, the gossip columnists, the publicity folks: he was the first who broke away from what everybody had considered a necessity—the interviews, the ass kissing, the "movie etiquette." Marlon took a stand that these rules did not apply to him, that they were foolish, sappy rules. And he ended up leading the parade of other actors who felt the same way.

MICHAEL BROCKMAN WAS A CLOSE FRIEND OF PAUL'S. HE WAS A HIGHLY REGARDED RACE CAR DRIVER WHO ALSO LATER BECAME AN ACTOR AND STUNTMAN.

Once we were having dinner—Paul, Bob Sharp, and his race crew, probably sixteen of us, all sitting there having a great time—when this lady leans over, grabs Paul, turns his head towards hers, and tries to kiss him on the lips. He stood up ready to attack her, and caught himself and sat down. "Jesus. What would *you* do?" he said. It was just like deflating a balloon. It ruined the night for him.

———

You work what you consider pretty hard at your craft and develop in a slow and painful way, and you're getting to the point where you're just starting to feel kind of good about yourself—and not just the way you look—and then somebody says, "Oh, God, take off your sunglasses so I can see your baby blue eyes!" All the self-esteem you've managed to build up goes right out the window. If I walked up to someone and said, "Let me see your brassiere," they'd be really offended.

The dark glasses are not *just* because I want to hide myself—it's far more complicated. I really have no tolerance for light, and I've made my eyes worse from wearing them. There's also an accumulation of Budweiser as well as damage from my early days making movies; in those days, the slower film exposures often required an actor to keep looking straight into an arc light. We always had to put ice on our eyes and insert irritating drops to keep them bright and white for the cameras. It isn't something you want to constantly do, especially with light-colored eyes.

I know some people resent that I won't sign autographs or pose for them—or even offer a stock answer besides no. But do you have to manufacture a response to their silliness and repeat that response on every occasion it happens? Doesn't a person run out of patience after four or five times of this?

It would make my life a lot easier if whenever someone stopped me on the street and asked, "Ooh, let me take your picture," I said okay. But that would draw another twelve people over, and that would draw some more people, and you stand there signing autographs while politely asking them about their mother and father.

If I could do that and didn't care, it would be terrific, I'd feel a lot better at the end of the day.

I wish I could, but I can't. But I also wish I could ski. And I wish I could play tennis well. I wish I could do lots of things, but I can't—and that doesn't make me a bad person.

JAMES GOLDSTONE DIRECTED *WINNING*, STARRING PAUL AND JOANNE.

Paul, Joanne, and I went to a "secret" restaurant near Westport on a Sunday night. They gave us a table in the corner, and some older woman at a nearby table notices Paul and Joanne—as likely everyone else did in this restaurant. All of a sudden, this woman pulls her chair over to our table, places it between the Newmans, and sits down.

Paul looks at her and did one of his wonderful takes, and for an eternity he just stared at her. And then he says: "Lady, you are the fucking rudest person that I've fucking ever met in this world. I'm sitting here with my wife and my friend, and you pull your chair over and put it right between me and my wife? What gives you the fucking right?"

The woman quickly retreated.

STEWART STERN

When we've been walking down a street, one of the things I've often said to Paul is how unfortunate it is that he won't look back at people who are looking at him. I get a glow by the time we've gone two blocks, and find myself smiling simply because of the pleasure in people's faces at seeing him. And it's something Paul won't see because he won't look.

When I first met Paul in 1954, he really had no sense then of his public self. People were still mistaking him for Marlon Brando, and asking him for Brando's autograph (which he sometimes signed!). He was more diffident at times, more garrulous at times, less abbreviated.

Over the years, Paul has become more cryptic. In communication, he has gone from being a Rubens to a Giacometti, a distillation, to the fewest possible words. He speaks in fortune cookies, and sometimes the beginning is the same as the end because there's a pause in between where an even more private process happens. Even in language, he stays beyond the moat of privacy.

Here are two stories that illustrate what I'm talking about. I had strongly supported Jimmy Carter's 1976 campaign, and in the early part of his presidency I was appointed one of the US representatives to the UN's disarmament conference.

One afternoon I was visiting at the White House with some acquaintances of mine from the National Security Council. I was walking down a hallway when I literally bumped into the president.

"Why don't you come up with me to the Oval Office?" Carter asked. I followed him upstairs, and let me tell you, what transpired

PAUL AT THE UNITED NATIONS CONFERENCE ON
NUCLEAR DISARMAMENT, 1978

was pretty uncomfortable. I'm not very at ease around people with power, never have been. But while I wanted to know why he'd recently decided not to address the UN himself on this issue, each time I raised the subject, all the president wanted to know was one thing: how movies were made.

Flash forward to around 1982. By then, I was deeply involved in car racing, truly loving that it was a world away from the film business and Hollywood.

I had flown out to the track in Brainerd, Minnesota, for a Trans Am race, one of my first professional competitions. It was still a novelty that a movie actor was racing, so not unexpectedly there were photographers everywhere. As we were all finally just about ready to begin, the track marshals began clearing everybody away from the cars and racers. But just as it was getting down to "Gentlemen, start your engines," there was one photographer who just kept clicking off shots of me, retreating for a minute, then darting back on the track like a bird.

Now, I don't want to blow this out of proportion, but this was the period before any race when you like to get rid of all the extraneous distractions and concentrate on what you have to do: thinking through your strategy, how you want to start, what car's in front of you, what's its horsepower, and where can you get an advantage—catch them in the first turn, say, sneak in a little late? This is when a driver really wants to center himself, and here's this photographer sticking his camera almost up my nose, clicking, running off, darting back on, and finally disappearing.

After the race was over and I was done being interviewed and everyone was packing up, I spotted the photographer and said, "I really want to ask you something. Why was it that you wanted to shoot me so badly that you had to keep coming back and irritate me, invade my space, and just do one more thing to make your presence felt?"

"You really want to know?" the photographer answered.

"Yes, I really want to know."

"Okay," he said. "Because I thought I might get the last picture of you alive."

———

PATTY NEWMAN WAS ARTHUR NEWMAN'S WIFE,
PAUL'S SISTER-IN-LAW.

Tress was near the end, and we'd all gathered at her bedside when the special nurse we hired called to tell us it was almost time. She was in a deep sleep, and after a time there were big pauses between her breaths. We all rushed to the side of her bed and soon it was clear she was gone.

Joanne called and wanted to speak with Paul. I asked her to hold on a minute.

"What is he doing?"

"If you can believe it," I told her, "he's signing a picture for the nurse."

———

By the time I began preproduction for *The Long, Hot Summer* near Baton Rouge in 1957, my divorce settlement was essentially finalized. That allowed Joanne and me to openly be together. But since the story of my marital split wouldn't hit the newspapers for some months, and since the press—in those days, at least—didn't just appear everywhere you went, we were able to avoid any frenzy.

It had been over four years ago that Joanne and I met backstage at *Picnic;* that we would finally get to work together again in *Long, Hot Summer* meant everything. The picture was loosely based on a William Faulkner story; I played the rakish drifter who goes to work for a rich, powerful family despot (played by Orson Welles). There's real chemistry between my drifter and Welles's daughter, played by Joanne. I know people have written that this was the first picture where I displayed sexiness—but if that was so, I attribute it completely to filming with Joanne. Before then, my sexuality was never there.

For the first time, Joanne and I could do what we longed for years to do in public, as well as put on the screen what had already been discovered between us. There was a glue that held us together then, and through the rest of our life together. And that glue was this: anything seemed possible. The good, the bad, and the wonderful. With all other people, *some* things were possible, but not everything. For us, the promise of everything was there from the beginning.

Making that movie was a lusty time together for us. The picture was hard work, a long schedule and shot on location in very hot weather because it was the end of Louisiana's summertime. But on Saturday nights, Joanne and I would drive to New Orleans and stroll into the French Quarter and we were really comfortable. It was a cornucopia of discovery. I was wide-eyed, because I'd never really been anywhere besides New York, Boston, and LA. She introduced me to the world of antiques and antique stores; we even bought ourselves a brass bed down there.

And a dog, too. Early one Sunday morning, we were walking through the Quarter and heard all this yapping in back of us. We turned around and there was this tiny little dog behind us being held by a length of yarn in some guy's hand. He was about the size of my fist.

"Good lord, what is that?" we asked.

"It's a chihuahua."

"Well, he's a fierce little bugger," I said.

"I raise 'em," the guy said.

"Is this little fellow for sale?"

He nodded yes, and I bought him for sixty dollars.

The guy handed me the dog and said, "You'll be able to keep him in your pocket for the rest of his life."

Needless to say, that dog grew up to be the size of a small truck. We called him El Toro.

El Toro was in reality some kind of mongrel, but I adored him. He was a cheeky dog. One of the most endearing things about him was the oft-repeated story of how he never liked my onetime business partner John Foreman. Whenever John came by my house, El Toro would just slink out of the room. And one time, John happened to leave his hat on the bed and El Toro took a crap in it.

What also made the shoot memorable was Orson Welles's presence. He was pretty standoffish and he seemed to feel uneasy around Actors Studio people; besides me, there was also our director, Marty Ritt (with whom I also later made *Hombre, Paris Blues, The Outrage, Hemingway's Adventures of a Young Man,* and *Hud*) and Tony Franciosa.

Orson couldn't understand screen generosity, where one actor allows another player in his scene to deservedly get the best camera shots. Screen generosity was not part of Orson's vocabulary. After a number of retakes on a scene he did with me, Orson asked Marty if he could have a private word with him. They stepped away together, and seemed to be discussing something rather serious. When they came back, we did another take, and afterwards, I asked Marty what was going on.

"Orson thought you were submarining him," he said; it was an actor's way of saying someone was stealing his screen time.

Orson had actually been dragging *his* part of the scene so I'd get less screen time than he would. At the Actors Studio, we believed that what the camera should create is a sense of community among a cast. When Ritt shot the big scene where Franciosa's character crazily keeps digging for a nonexistent buried treasure beside Welles's barn, Tony did it wonderfully; he was powerful, organic, and unpredictable. Orson went over to Marty afterwards and wearily said, "My God, I feel old, like I've been riding a tricycle in a barrel of molasses."

After the movie came out and was a big success, Marty became known in Hollywood as "the man who tamed Orson Welles." True or not, I know Marty helped me during rehearsals. He'd make me get rid of any extraneous shit in my performance. He'd make sure to give you a line, an intention, an active verb, to use in your moment.

Marty was very good with actors, gracious and gentle. He knew that what worked best for the actor was likely what also worked best for the character. He would flare his nostrils, make noises, and ask, "Well, what do you think, kid?" or "Isn't that funny?" Remarkable, too, is that Marty, who was once an all-state football tackle and a heavier guy, was the most graceful person on two feet. He clowned; he was whimsical; he'd do a fake waltz with some imaginary lady. He was like Zero Mostel—he could tiptoe across a floor and hardly cause a breeze.

The problem for me with a man like Marty, and especially later in my career with John Huston, was I thought I had to behave in a certain way to please them. So whatever I presented was artificial, because it wasn't really a response from my core. And that continues till today, because I'm still not sure about what my core really is. I am no good around people with power. Even as I think of it now, my hands start to perspire.

———

MARTIN RITT DIRECTED THEATER FOR MANY YEARS IN NEW YORK BECAUSE HE WAS BLACKLISTED FROM TV AND FILM DURING THE ANTICOMMUNIST RED SCARE. BY THE MID-1950S, HE WAS HIRED TO DO MOVIES AND DIRECTED PAUL AND JOANNE IN *THE LONG, HOT SUMMER*.

I believe there are two qualities that genuinely make a star, and neither of them has anything to do with acting: danger and sexuality. Paul, as a man, is a total sexual animal. That's why he is a star. When people see him, they feel it, whether they are aware of it or not.

Of all the women I've known in this town, Joanne is the most complete, a master woman. Onscreen, she doesn't have the sexuality Paul does, but she was a much better actor when we made *Long, Hot Summer;* they were not comparable. Joanne was as good an actress as existed at the time.

Paul knew that, and it was a driving factor in his whole life. He always felt guilty that he had become a big movie star and that Joanne never became quite as big a star as he did.

Only days after the *Long, Hot Summer* wrapped, Joanne and I had our Vegas wedding. We left for a quick honeymoon in London, then returned to take up residence in a rented house in Beverly Hills. We'd end up leasing many different homes in and around LA over the next decade. Jackie had decided to relocate with our kids to the San Fernando Valley, so when I was in California, they were often nearby.

I came home one evening to our new rental, drove up the driveway, and Joanne stepped outside wearing a bandanna and a paint-covered frock; I asked her what was up. She led me inside to a room off the master bedroom. When we'd first moved in, the room was filled with bicycle pumps, brooms, and all sorts of junk that Joanne had now shoved into the garage. Everything had been replaced by some thrift-shop double bed with a new Sealy mattress; next to it was a champagne stand, complete with an ice bucket in some raucous color. Joanne had been in the middle of painting the room.

"I call it the Fuck Hut," she said, proudly.

It was wonderful and had been done with such affection and delight. Even if my kids came over, we'd go in the Fuck Hut several nights a week and just be intimate, noisy, and ribald.

Joanne and I still drive each other crazy in different ways. There is a wonderful kind of balance. Like the arms race. Asymmetrical but equal. She had all of her heavy land-based equipment, and most of mine were submarines. But all of the misdemeanors, the betrayals, the difficulties have kind of evened themselves out and blended themselves over the years.

She was always so vulnerable, and she seemed to have no ego, and yet there is a towering ego there. We had that in common. One moment she would be filled with a sense of worth and the next it would simply shatter, and so when she would go off I would recognize it and hold her blameless, I would understand. Whatever it is, it's wonderfully equal.

JOANNE WOODWARD

I was always amazed that anybody could have liked me. How could they figure out what to like since I could not figure it out myself? That was always the problem. To think that I spent so much of my life feeling as though I was a not very important appendage. It's so silly when you realize that we put ourselves in those positions, we do it ourselves.

The commercial (and critical) success of *The Long, Hot Summer* didn't play much of a role in my being cast in another tale of the Deep South, the movie version of Tennessee Williams's *Cat on a Hot Tin Roof.* Don Murray, who'd just had a success in the movie of Bill Inge's *Bus Stop,* was considered for the lead; Robert Taylor, Van Johnson, and even Mickey Rooney were talked about, too. Though Dick Brooks, the director, had been greatly impressed by my performance on Broadway in *The Desperate Hours,* the studio executives at MGM had seen neither the play nor even my performance as Rocky Graziano. Still, with Brooks's support, I got hired.

Cat on a Hot Tin Roof began production only a week after *The Long, Hot Summer* hit the movie theaters. I was cast as Brick, Elizabeth Taylor's hard-drinking husband, and it was my job to make my character's refusal to have sex with Elizabeth seem believable—even though in our movie, unlike Tennessee's original play, we were barred from alluding to Brick's gayness as the reason for his marital abstinence.

Life imitated art about ten days after we began filming, when tragedy struck and an inadequate person—me—had to face a distraught woman.

Elizabeth had missed a couple of days on the set because of a virus. The illness also prevented her from accompanying her husband, the producer Mike Todd, on a quick trip to New York, where he was being honored by the Friars Club. Todd took off in his private plane from Burbank and died, along with another passenger and two pilots, when his Lockheed Lodestar crashed in the middle of a stormy night over New Mexico.

Elizabeth's doctor placed her under sedation. Our production was likewise in shock and also in jeopardy. I decided to stop by her home and offer what solace I could.

When I arrived, I was shown up to her boudoir, where I listened to Elizabeth sobbing, "Why him? Why now?" She was highly doped up. Not knowing what else to say, I started to offer her some well-worn clichés about how this was all God's will.

Elizabeth cut me off, looked up at me, and practically snarled: "Oh, shut up. Get the fuck out of here!"

I should have just said, "I love you and think you're a terrific lady," and admitted I was obviously unable to provide answers to the terrible questions she was asking. Instead, I just put my tail between my legs and silently left in a state of disarray. I was inadequate when I got to Elizabeth's bedroom, but I suppose I didn't really know that beforehand. My platitudes and discomfort in that situation have chased me through my whole life.

RICHARD BROOKS WAS AN EIGHT-TIME OSCAR
NOMINEE WHO ADAPTED AND DIRECTED *CAT ON A HOT TIN ROOF*
FOR THE SCREEN.

After the plane crash, Larry Weingarten, our producer, suggested, "Why don't we close down the show for now? Elizabeth is in practically every scene in the bedroom, and that's where you're shooting now." I argued that if they temporarily stopped, we might as well forget the whole movie, because we'd never get the company back to their current pitch.

"How can you shoot without her?" Weingarten asked.

"I'll get somebody to walk by very close to the lens wearing Elizabeth's slip, and if she does come back, we'll just spot her into the scenes. And if she doesn't, well, we can still spot her replacement later on."

So we began filming the bedroom scenes without her, and then, when Elizabeth hadn't yet returned, I wrote a new scene just between Paul and Burl Ives (Big Daddy) and I told the producers we had to shoot it then and there. Which we did—and that took another week. By then, I knew I was going to be in trouble.

But on maybe the next afternoon, a young Asian woman pops up on my closed set, walks up to me, and says: "Miss Taylor would like to speak with you. She's in a car outside the soundstage." I go to the car. I couldn't see her, because the windows were dark and there was also a curtain around them. I got inside.

"I'm going crazy," Elizabeth said. "I stay home. It's bad in the daytime and it's worse at night. Mike liked what he saw so far. If it's all right with you, maybe I ought to come back to work."

"It's up to you," I said. "When would you want to start?"

"Today."

We walked together onto the stage and into her dressing room.

"One other thing," she said. "I don't want to see that producer of ours here. If I see him, I'm going to leave. No newspapers, no Hedda Hopper. I can't take that now."

I assured her that only the other actors, the camera, and I would be there for the rest of the shoot.

Elizabeth worked for an hour that first day. The cast was terrific with her. Nobody came over and said "I'm sorry"; they just went about their business and played the scene. They were very careful about her, Paul particularly. I never had to say a word to him. He understood the situation completely, never even looking at her in a way that was too sympathetic. He was caringly professional.

The next day, Elizabeth worked for two or three hours. On the third day back, she stayed the full shift. And from then on, she never missed even an hour.

Cat on a Hot Tin Roof did tremendously at the box office, staying at number one for over a month. It also got me my first Oscar nomination; the movie itself was up for Best Picture while Elizabeth and Dick Brooks also received slots, for Best Actress and Best Director. (Burl Ives was nominated as well—and won—Best Supporting Actor that year, but it was for *Big Country,* not for our movie.)

By now, I'd become something of a movie star, I suppose, and I had the opportunity to go back to Broadway to work under Elia Kazan for his production of a new Tennessee Williams play, *Sweet Bird of Youth.* I'd play Chance Wayne, essentially a gigolo, who's attached himself to an aging, alcoholic actress, the Princess. One of the main prerequisites of Chance is that he is a person of external beauty, he'd gotten by on that, and now that personal beauty is beginning to fade.

Kazan, when I signed, was not a person to me at all, but a symbol of *The Director*. Kazan wanted to get acquainted with me, feel me out, get a sense of what I was like offstage, so we went for a walk in the city. I was quaking in my boots. He told me what he expected from certain sections of the play, especially Chance's soliloquy when he talks about seeing his true-love real girlfriend for the last time. Kazan wanted to create a great sense of personal grief for Chance. Because I felt obligated to tell him the truth (so that he wouldn't expect anything), I interrupted and told him that I was something of an "emotional Republican." Nevertheless, I said, I thought I could do it. I wasn't really worried whether I could deliver for an audience that wasn't as savvy as Kazan, but the test for me was whether I could get it by him. I wondered: how does a person who is anesthetized in real life tap a core of emotion that would be available for someone else to feel?

When we tried it on the stage, Kazan told me, "I want you to treat this soliloquy as an echo, a series of echoes that come back to you and that are so strong you can't control your emotions." As I began working on it, sometimes a trickle of emotion or a tear came, but I never knew when or if that would be there.

I had warned Kazan that sometimes it would hit me and it would be organic, but there'd be occasions that it didn't. Those times, I would stare at a light in the back of the auditorium long enough so it would make me tear up, since I have no light tolerance. Kazan would move around the auditorium, going from seat to seat, to find out which things I was doing seemed real, and which didn't. He wanted to check if he could hear you in the back of the house, and whether the size of what you were doing carried all the way to the last row—and whatever forceful motion you made that was visible in the first row could also be seen in the rear.

So one day we were running through the show and the light at the back of the auditorium went out. I realized Kazan must have wondered, "Is that what he's doing, staring at the light?" and was having his game with me. I was so enraged that I actually wept with frustration. Of course, I realized that fucked me over worse than anything I could have done. Yes, I had been discovered, but then I realized the emotion was now just sitting there waiting for me when I called it—light or no light.

Kazan also worked with me on something that could be called "the Kazan transition." It means that onstage, you don't sit around waiting for one emotional image to pop up, use it, and when it is finished, you just supplant it with a different one. Instead, you start with an image, and in the middle of that first image, you begin transitioning to seeing a second image and then to a third image and so on. Maybe Kazan did this with me because he wanted me to hurry moving from one feeling to the next, to make things more urgent for me, more hysterical and less in control.

What he was up to, on a subtler basis, I'm still not quite certain. I do suspect he wanted to mute or defuse any sort of assurance I could bring to the character of Chance Wayne, because it just would have been wrong for the part. A couple of weeks after we opened *Sweet Bird of Youth,* though, I might have unconsciously done that; Kazan came over to me and said, "You're balancing Chance and the Princess, you've made them characters of equal power. The play doesn't work now. You've fucked it up."

To tell you the truth, I never had a picture inside me of Chance Wayne. What people don't understand is that there's always some deep-seated aspect of your own personality that you can use—you don't have to go around looking and doing research. You simply tap those facets of yourself and you use them.

I remember being asked whether I ever found myself in a situation like Chance's. Where I needed to constantly scramble to keep a certain woman's opinion of me so positive (especially when my own opinion of myself could be so shitty). The answer is yes: Mommy, Mommy.

Who does one perform for? Who were you trying too hard to please? Mommy, Mommy—that kind of problem. There's half of me that says, "Oh, cut the shit." Because there's always a point where someone becomes master of their own destiny. And I'll be goddamned if I would give anybody the sense that they had much control over the way I behave now.

AN AUTOGRAPHED PHOTO FROM PAUL TO TRESS

ELIA KAZAN WAS ACCLAIMED AS ONE OF
THE MOST DEMANDING AND INNOVATIVE DIRECTORS
OF PLAYS AND FILMS.

When Paul first came up in *Picnic,* he was just a cute, good-looking boy. *Picnic* was almost like an audition for *Sweet Bird,* but corrupted—Tennessee Williams's scenes would provide the contrary, corrupting element.

When we did the play, Paul was a good actor, but not an exceptional actor—in a not exceptional role. He did the part right, but that part didn't permit him to be excellent or extraordinary. It's not what you would call a role you fall in love with, but Paul was honest in the part. He was always an honest actor.

Paul was very touching as Chance because he is touching as a man. He's really a soul. There's something in him that's masked but underneath it, there's a soul that wants to do many things.

I think what's most extraordinary about Paul is how he developed: what he puts on screen now is really quite a man, very strong. Most people spend their time saying things and doing things they hope will be liked. There's a lot less of that with Paul today.

RICHARD BROOKS DIRECTED PAUL
A SECOND TIME, IN HIS FILM ADAPTATION OF
SWEET BIRD OF YOUTH IN 1962.

This was not a natural part for Paul. He isn't naturally a hustler, and neither was Chance. Look, in the business we're in, all of us *may be* hustlers, but Paul has too much vanity, ego, and self-respect to hustle a woman by secretly taping her and blackmailing her later.

Paul played it so nervously, so full of a pond skater's activity. Paul was like a guy selling hot neckties on Forty-Second Street who thinks that any second he's going to be discovered, so he'd better get rid of them fast.

Look, many a sensitive actor has been disemboweled by the Hollywood system. Monty Clift couldn't function and it destroyed him in the end. This doesn't mean you have to submit to survive, but you need to know when it's time to reorganize, when to pull back in order to attack later.

Paul was like that, a very practical man, even about his own career. I remember years later running into him on a staircase at one of the goddamn studio offices; he was going up, I was going down.

"What are you working in now?" I asked.

"The Towering Inferno."

"Oh. That," I replied.

"Yeah, but I think it's got a chance," Paul explained. "I think it'll break even, maybe more."

== IX ==

Joanne gave birth to our first child together, Nell, in 1959 in California. The first time as an adult I remember crying—including when my father died—was when I saw Joanne in the hospital that day, ashen, with a dry mouth and lying on a gurney, headed into an elevator on her way to the delivery room. I was staggered.

When Lissy was born a couple of years later, I had my camera out and took billions of pictures. Joanne came back from the hospital wearing this bellhop hat and a very stylish dress; she looked like sixty or seventy million bucks. We brought Nellie in to meet her new baby sister; the first shot I have is of her leaning over the bassinet with a look of sheer hatred on her face. Next, I took a series of pictures where Joanne held the baby in her arms with Nell sitting next to her—with Nell putting on a gargoyle face. But then something happened; over the next few shots, Nell went from gargoyle to delighted mother-in-law, a grandma with a smile that stretched from one ear to the other. It was an incredible transformation. When I think of those pictures, it reminds me how Joanne handled our babies' introduction into our home with such class and foresight.

When Scott was born to Jackie and me in Shaker Heights a decade before, it was at a difficult time—between my father's death and my departing for Yale. It's all a hodgepodge in my head, muted grays that seemed to leave no mark in my mind; I don't really have any lasting memory of Jackie's pregnancy or her actually giving birth.

NELL IMPRESSES JOANNE WITH HER
FISHING SKILLS IN 1969

I do recall driving her to the Cleveland hospital in my family's '37 Packard for Scott's delivery, but I honestly have no recollection of bringing him home.

WARREN COWAN, THE COFOUNDER OF THE PR FIRM
ROGERS & COWAN, MANAGED PUBLICITY FOR PAUL AND JOANNE
FOR ALMOST FORTY YEARS.

For so many years Joanne would not go away on location or take a movie unless it was one with Paul. She did very few films after *The Three Faces of Eve,* after they got married, without him. And for many years, I believed that the marriage was working because Joanne was hanging in there. Because her husband was Paul Newman and she was doing everything to make that marriage work. Now I've come to believe that it's just the opposite. Now Paul hangs in there because of Joanne. I just think that he is so in love, and taken with her.

Over the next few years, Joanne and I made a conscious choice about taking the children with us when we went on location to make a film. In fact, for many years when the kids were little, we always just rented places in LA, then finally buying a place in Coldwater Canyon only after about five years together. Joanne and I sat down and counted recently, and came up with a total of twenty-four houses we'd all lived in either on the West Coast or in New York—and that doesn't even include the two houses we've had in Connecticut (sometimes when I look back on my career, the only reason I know I've made so many movies is that I have lived in so many houses). That was a lot of motion for a small family.

We didn't realize that living in so many different places could also have a negative effect on the kids. It may have given them strength in some areas, but they weren't able to maintain a stable group of friends.

When Nell was quite young, we took her around to some schools, and she wanted to go to the Montessori in Santa Monica. So we enrolled her there, and about a week later I decided to drive over to talk with the teachers and see what was going on. When I arrived, she was at recess, so I took a peek into the playground to watch. There were all these kids playing in groups of four or six, and then there was Nellie. She was standing alone up against a fence, pigeon-toed, hands in front of her, pulling on her fingernails like someone waiting to be asked to dance. There was something so brave and expectant and alert about her, just watching everybody else with such hope. I absolutely broke down and began crying.

With Nell, I know Joanne and I traveled around more than with the other kids. She came to Israel when I made *Exodus;* she was in Paris with us for a shoot immediately afterwards; even in London, too. But by the time Clea, our last child, was born in 1965, we'd decided they should spend their entire school year in California.

———

EVA MARIE SAINT WAS PAUL'S COSTAR IN THE OTTO PREMINGER FILM *EXODUS*, FILMED IN ISRAEL IN 1960.

I went to the location with my husband, my two babies, and my mother and father and mother-in-law. Joanne was there with Paul, and they brought little Nell, whom I loved. Nell always had on little white dresses and little white shoes and little white gloves. She was all in white. I was always throwing her up to my Laurette, who was then two: "Look how cute little Nell looks." So much like Joanne! Of course, once Laurette got into an Israeli blue hat and those little blue shorts, we couldn't get them off her.

Paul was not very comfortable. He was frustrated with the way the shoot was going. Preminger would promise script changes, then he'd shoot the scenes the way they'd originally been written.

So much effort was going into those damn crowd scenes, choreographing ships and such. Since it was really a story about relationships, much more time should have been spent working on the intimate scenes, but they were all done in one or two takes. Otto was busy making the picture at a price and had committed himself to United Artists to finish for a certain amount of money—and I think any overages came out of his pocket. There was so much pressure on him to finish on schedule, he couldn't deal with anything except getting those pages shot on time.

In the big love scene I play with Paul's character, there was something Otto didn't like about the way Paul was holding me or touching me. He decided to get in there and show Paul how to do it! I was really upset and embarrassed. I think Paul just took it, but I thought, "Oh my God, what are we talking about here?"

———

Did settling down with the children in one spot make everything right? I'm always anxious about admitting to failure. To not being good enough, to not being right. I am faced with the appalling fact that I don't know anything. I have great doubts about things. I have instincts about things even if I can't intellectually support them. And there are a lot of things I don't get about myself, either. But I am certain that nobody can always be responsible for what other people are. You can only be responsible for who *you* are. I'm afraid to get up in front of people. But I simply do it. If other people— one's children, say—don't do it, well, that's what they don't do, that is what they are. I realize, though, that in the area of being, of doing something in the arena, I am able to accomplish what should be the first order of a man—to provide food and clothing for his family.

PAUL WITH DAUGHTER NELL IN 1960

I could have been more consistent with my children. I could have been more understanding. I could have been more patient. I could have not gone away on location. I could have stopped working.

I could have done some things better. I might have done a lot worse.

I was delighted recently when Stephanie told me she remembered when she was little, she'd sometimes come to visit Joanne and me in our house on Long Island Sound. When the kids were tucked in, I'd come around to their beds, lean over, and say, "Oh, what's this? A bag of potatoes?" And I'd pick them up and walk them around like they were sacks over my shoulder. I hadn't remembered doing nice things like that, which were peculiarly mine, peculiarly physical.

DEDE ALLEN WAS A MUCH-CELEBRATED FILM EDITOR, WHO'D EARNED MULTIPLE OSCAR NOMINATIONS.

I remember Paul cooked. That always impressed me, that they did their own cooking. There were a lot of young children. Nell was the eldest of those three, very shy, very quiet, and I remember Lissy at six, who would sit in her father's lap with her arm around his head. I remember a lot of affection, a lot of tactile feeling.

MICHAEL BROCKMAN

I watch him with the girls now, with Lissy and Clea and Nell, and I remember when I first met them at the race track years ago when they were still little girls, how he seemed to really enjoy and get a great deal out of watching them do what they did and play and be themselves. He's a very loving, caring guy.

I would ultimately feel pained and stupid by not having realized my son, Scott, might not want to be like me and ride in a race car or on a horse. Thinking about it now, it is funny to recall that as a kid, I never really wanted to ride a horse *myself*; I was scared to death of them. Scott was a robust young man; he seemed to enjoy dangerous things and was delighted by horses and ponies. But I never did think to say to him: "Scott, would you *like* to go out on a horse? And it's no big deal if you don't want to do it."

It's the sort of mistake I'd made before. When Stephanie was about seven, Joanne and I threw a Fourth of July party at our Benedict Canyon home for the casts and crews of the two films we had both just finished shooting, *Hud* (for me) and Bill Inge's *The Stripper* (for her). I decided to try something a little special for all the kids who were there—a professionally performed ghost story. We set up the little cottage we had behind the pool as our stage, and I enlisted Brandon de Wilde, who had just played my nephew, Lonnie, in *Hud,* and our old friend the actor Bob Webber to help out. We'd turned down the lights, made the place spooky, and applied some pretty serious makeup to Brandon's and Bob's faces—and quite a bit of ketchup subbing for blood, too. The story I told was something about a dead skier coming back to haunt some friends and foes. And what we planned was that at the right moment in the story, Bob Webber, with blackened teeth, whitened face, and some wig from Joanne, would reach through an open window and grab Brandon and pull him away.

At Bob's cue, the kids were all squealing delightedly, but all of a sudden Stephanie shouted, "I'm really scared! I don't want to see this. I'm scared to death!" We immediately stopped, turned on the lights, and Brandon sat with Steffi and kept repeating, "I'm okay, look at me, I'm okay." It got to her. And I guess I'm dumb enough that I never know when the point is reached between delight and fright.

STEWART STERN

When Paul was directing *Rachel, Rachel* one of the issues was whether to do the scene or not, where little Rachel walks in and sees her father embalming the body of a little boy. Suddenly Paul didn't want to shoot it. He was concerned about Nell (who played the young Rachel) seeing it, and what it might do to her. She was only about eight, an age when you're not really sure how much she knew about death. . . . I remember that he had actually gotten the set up in that cellar when he quit. But we persuaded him to change his mind. Then he wanted to hang a lot of bicycles and things between where Nell would be and where the actual embalming was happening, whether for the aesthetics of the scene or to try and keep her protected, I don't know.

—————

I don't have a gift for fathering. And then there's the celebrity aspect; being a movie star means you start out with three strikes against you. The conditions are so strange, the adulation, the recognition in restaurants—these are completely unnatural. It isn't like being the owner of a baseball team, where you can take your kids out to the beach and 98 percent of the people don't have any idea who you are. You can go places with your children without anyone paying special attention.

Being a star throws everything out of whack for your kids.

There was a time, long before he died, that I thought the only way I could free Scott to go his own way would be to shoot myself. Then that pressure would be off his chest, and he could go someplace and maybe get rid of the affliction that was me and become a whole person.

He wouldn't have had to compete anymore; the competition would be over.

—————

Because I felt so detached from everything, I never had a sense of my children as people.

It is really just in the last few years that even Joanne finally, slowly, became not a wife, not an actress, not a sex object, but a person to me. And little by little, my kids have started to become people, too.

—————

THE NEWMAN–WOODWARD CLAN IN BEVERLY HILLS, 1965:
TOP ROW, LEFT TO RIGHT, NELL, SUSAN, SCOTT;
BOTTOM ROW, LEFT TO RIGHT, JOANNE, PAUL, CLEA,
LISSY, AND STEPHANIE

I feel like a person who has been doing prison time and is suddenly let out. He realizes he has only five or six or eight years left in his lifetime, and there's no way that'll be enough time to make amends. So he'll look at the mountain that is yet to be climbed and say to himself, "Well, I could've climbed that thirty years ago, or even just tried to attack it, but to try now with this little time and energy left is almost insurmountable."

Nevertheless, something *will* happen. The person will either be so delighted by his newfound freedom or otherwise suspect the damage is so beyond repair that any dent that can be made will be minor. One of those is going to win out, and it would be arrogant to assume that you know which one it is likely to be.

BY 1970, THE NEWMAN-WOODWARDS HAD RELOCATED TO WESTPORT, CONNECTICUT: *TOP ROW, LEFT TO RIGHT,* SCOTT, PAUL, SUSAN; *BOTTOM ROW, LEFT TO RIGHT,* LISSY, STEPHANIE, NELL, JOANNE, CLEA

Movies are a percentage business, and I try to allocate everything—success and blame and guilt—and I base how good I feel about myself on those percentage figures. With my children I think about their strengths, their individuality, their disappointments, their eccentricities—and I wonder how to allocate responsibility for all of that.

I especially wonder about Scott. What was savable, salvageable, what was in some ways the fault of the business I'm in, or of my divorce, and what does Jackie own of that, too? It's so hard to get any finite message. There's always "this, and on the other hand, that." One of the things that first drew me to auto racing was that it is so nice and clean about the results. If you come across the finish line first, you're first.

I never expected that I would be able to provide for my family the way my father did. I figured I would be a street cleaner or a gas-station attendant. What if I had really been a failure as an actor early on and been forced to keep selling encyclopedias or peddle insurance? Would my children be stronger, weaker, more individual? How much do children need to feel that they can surpass their parents? When that parent seems to them as way beyond anything that they accomplish, how does that affect their desire to quit or go on?

Children need plans. They need parents who have some sense and philosophy of what it is to raise children. We had no philosophy. We thought kids simply reached a certain age, they got married, had their own children, raised their children. They did their jobs, were successful or failures, they retired, and they died.

I see my children in terms of how they feel about themselves. I'm often uncertain about how they feel, but I know if they feel good I'll feel good, and if they don't feel good I'll feel bad.

I recognize things now that I didn't know when my kids were young. I know some people talk about the sound of attack in my voice. I was never aware of that, and if you'd told me that twenty years ago I would have told you to go stick it. The people who tell me that don't wish me ill, so I have to listen. I thought I gave off a very benign light.

I have this sense that I repeat my father's attitude; if my children are failing, I become sarcastic with them the same way my father became sarcastic with me. I wish I could catch myself. Joanne talks about the sound of my voice sometimes taking on a cutting kind of humor. It isn't a trait I would respect or honor in anyone else. And whether I got it from my father or didn't doesn't seem relevant to me. I just wish I didn't do it. I wish someone had defined the word "patience" for me; I was so impatient with myself, it isn't a surprise that I was impatient with everyone else. It's a terrible thing from which you never, ever recover. Was there some move I could have made with Scott? Some way I might have implanted a different set of values or aspirations, or told him he didn't have to be like me? That he didn't have to do macho things, and could just be himself? I wish I'd had that ability to explain that to him, to tell him that. And just to say, "It's okay, that's terrific."

I never figured any of that out until he was in his mid-twenties. I kept thinking he was going through a phase of adolescent bad judgment. It never seemed to go past the point of recovery. I never thought it would be fatal.

The same thing that happened to Scott certainly could have happened to me. That's a constant source of amazement to me.

———

He was really very much like me; he didn't get it, either. He didn't know how much danger he was in, and by the time he got it, it was too late.

There are people of good conscience who try to do the best they can given the information they have. I think I'm that sort of person. I have my strengths and there are some things I can take pride in. Friends have told me my eyes light up when I talk about my kids. But I wonder: is it genuine tenderness, or simply amazement at the process? It all seems doubly hard when you're an actor, because you make such an investment in other people's lives—the borrowing, the inventing, the stealing.

The one thing I've always admired is excellence. I recognize it in almost anything: plumbers, museum guides, limousine drivers, bank tellers—I delight in seeing it. Maybe we choose those arenas in which we have the best chance for excellence. For me, maybe that's acting, or being somehow connected to the theater, or capitalizing on the way I look, or fooling people. But I certainly didn't know what it was to be excellent as a parent.

SCOTT NEWMAN IN THE EARLY 1960S

In 1978, I was invited back to Kenyon to open their new theater by
directing a production of the Pulitzer Prize winner Michael Cris-
tofer's play *C.C. Pyle and the Bunion Derby,* casting some New York
actors in the lead parts and utilizing Kenyon students for all the
other roles and the stagecraft. It wasn't as if our production suddenly looked like a potential Broadway show, but everyone did all
right and it was a lot of fun.

I got the call from LA late one evening. Scott had died.

For six or seven years before that day, I'd been getting many phone
calls, every one of them saying, "It's just around the corner." Something terrible has happened. Something terrible is about to happen.
There's been a crash. He's missing. No one can find him. Calls from
his psychiatrists. From Susan. It just seemed that nothing was ever
going to stop that locomotive. At a certain point, it began to seem
like something inevitable. As if after so many close shaves, someday
the invitation would be accepted.

You kept waiting for The Call, and when you finally got it, you
almost didn't believe it. The voice on the phone—male, female,
old, young, professional, unprofessional—and the first words were
always "It's about Scott." And you'd be prepared for the worst, and
it turned out to be something less than that.

Not this time. It was his doctor, a fellow I'd met with just a few
weeks earlier, just before I headed out to Kenyon. He was putting
together a whole new program for Scott.

The day after I got The Call, I went to some kind of brunch and
didn't say anything to anybody. It wasn't until three days later that
I was able to travel back to Los Angeles, and be with my family. I
don't really know why, but I realize I did everything I could to try
and avoid recognizing that this had happened.

Many are the times I have gotten down on my knees and asked for
Scott's forgiveness. I ask for forgiveness for that part of me which

provided the impetus for his own destruction. I want to embrace the responsibility for that. What would it have taken to avert that? I'm not certain, but I don't think I could have gone into films and been a movie star. I couldn't have drunk. I couldn't have been a risk taker.

I realize that there is even something grotesque in saying "Forgive me." The energy up there that represents that kid will just give me the finger and say, "Well, what am I supposed to do with that?"

I think that's enough for me to say right now.

JIM MICHAEL, PAUL'S ONETIME DRAMA PROFESSOR AT KENYON, WAS INSTRUMENTAL IN ARRANGING HIS RETURN TO DIRECT *C.C. PYLE* ON CAMPUS.

Paul was scheduled to have lunch with the alumni secretary and his wife as well as a contemporary of Paul's who'd been through the 1949 Kenyon fire with him. That morning, he called me over to the house he was renting and said, "Something terrible has happened to Scott." He didn't specify what, just said, "I've been prepared for it. I always knew something like this could happen. I don't know what I can do."

Well, I never thought of death; I figured it was a drug thing or an accident.

"I've got to go to California, but I don't know just when, though I don't think it'll be for a few days . . . I don't know what to do about today's lunch."

"Maybe it would be good to keep the lunch date," I said. "Maybe you'll feel better if you just go through with this."

He agreed, and I drove him out to the country house where the alumni secretary lived. It turned out to be a good lunch, a good conversation. Paul was alert and talking about the things people always like to talk with him about. It wasn't until the next morning that I found out what had actually happened.

Within twenty-four hours everyone at Kenyon knew. But Paul stayed on rehearsing *C.C. Pyle* for quite a few more days; he kept up his schedule and ultimately personally thanked the students for their support.

Paul did eventually fly back to LA to see things through, but was soon back here again, picking up where he'd left off on the play. The remark by Paul I keep remembering from this whole period was this: "I would not want to have been one of my children." He was perfectly conscious of the strain.

———

JOHN CONSIDINE IS AN ACTOR WHO APPEARED IN NUMEROUS TELEVISION PROGRAMS AND FILMS AND WAS RECRUITED BY PAUL TO APPEAR IN *C.C. PYLE* AT KENYON COLLEGE.

When we arrived at Kenyon, I made it a habit to go over to Paul's place each evening. Either we'd drive over to the town of Mount Vernon, where Paul would order turkey with mashed potatoes and gravy, or we'd stay home and Paul would get us some soup, salad, and a couple of bottles of that expensive wine he liked.

He was worried about Scott, and he didn't know whether he was doing the right things to help him; this new psychologist he had just seen didn't seem to be doing anything. It was all preying on him.

"Have you ever wondered," he asked me, "if you could do it all over, would you have children again?"

The evening after we'd done the first read-through of the play, Paul's phone rang and I quickly knew something terrible had happened, since there was a lot of silence, nothing but a few monosyllabic things like "When?"

Paul hung up and I asked, "Is Scott okay?"

He looked very distracted and then answered, "He's not going to make it. I don't think he's going to make it."

Finally, after a long silence, Paul said he'd just been told that Scott had died.

We decided to go for a walk. Maybe half a dozen words were said, no tears. I remember wishing that Paul had been able to cry, to get something out. I put my arm around him. I wanted to hug him.

When it was almost dawn, Paul said something like "I need to have some time." He seemed okay, so much so that I was stunned. Because I knew he wasn't okay.

Later that morning there was a calling together at the theater of the play's cast and company to tell them what had happened and to discuss canceling the show. Paul came later, and announced that he'd decided that the best thing for him was to start our work. I kept watching him, keeping a close eye on him, afraid that he might burst. He never did.

I didn't know how he could stay, but I didn't question it. About three days later, he went back to Los Angeles.

<hr>

JOANNE WOODWARD

I knew there would be photographers and I couldn't stand that. I think that was one reason I wanted Paul to stay where he was. He was safe there and we knew that nobody in Gambier was going to take advantage of him, and they didn't. They were wonderful. He couldn't really make it real for himself until he came home some days later. He went straight to the mortuary and he said it was a totally complete experience. He said he really just had to go and be there with him, and he said, "I suddenly knew him, and was able to weep and look at him and love him."

JACKIE WITTE

Paul called me and told me what had happened. It was the first time we had spoken in years.

We chose to scatter Scott's ashes. Paul was there, I was there, and Susan was there, as well as a few of Scott's friends.

Did Paul and I come together over Scott's death? I don't think so. What I'm saying is that if both Paul and I had had a much greater understanding of Scott's situation and had worked in concert to help, it would have been a lot better for everybody. But we didn't.

When Scott was about eleven, we were at a friend's house one night and Scott came over to me and said: "I want to show you something, but I don't want you to say anything to Dad. You have to come with me outside." So we went out, and Scott reached into his pocket and pulled out a big .30 caliber armor-piercing bullet.

"Where'd you get that?" I asked.

"I can't tell you, but I wanted to show you. Should I keep it?"

"Do you want to keep it?"

"Yeah, I want to."

I told him it was a dangerous thing to keep, and explained how an accident could happen if it was dropped on a sharp object and hit the firing pin. And though he was afraid of the danger, I could tell he really wanted it. So somehow we got the shell apart, removed the bullet, dumped the powder, and dented the firing pin on a rock—and I gave him back the bullet.

Years later, when he was in terrible trouble in school back east and there was such a dance of death going on between Scott and his father, I wrote him and asked him to please try and communicate what he was feeling and not shut himself off from the people who might help him. And I reminded him about this story. I told him: "You have so much rage in you. You're so afraid of it. And at the same time you need whatever strength that anger gives you, because that's what the bullet was all about—you were asking someone else to take charge of the rage that let you feel so strong."

A. E. HOTCHNER WAS A NEIGHBOR AND FRIEND OF
THE NEWMANS IN CONNECTICUT. A BEST-SELLING BIOGRAPHER
AND WRITER, HE CREATED THE NEWMAN'S OWN CHARITABLE
FOOD LINE WITH PAUL.

Paul would say, "I'm having trouble with Scott," and then have to fly off to wherever the trouble was. I especially remember that terrible time when Scott was arrested and kicked in the head by a cop in the back of a squad car. Paul, of course, had to go.

It was a tough time for Paul; he was very anxious. We'd talk about the problem. "Gee, I don't understand what can be done, because I can't reach Scott." Then he'd try to get him into a film, distract him with employment, and be deluded into thinking, "Well, Scott is really acting, this is what he wants to do."

On one occasion, we gathered everyone for a party to watch Scott have a guest shot on *Marcus Welby, M.D.* Scott, who was also at the party, played someone dying in a hospital bed. Paul would show him off with great love and affection for his talents, as though Scott had just been nominated for an Academy Award.

When Scott was a boy, Paul had set up trampolines and target-practice gear in the yard. He fished with Scott, did all sorts of stuff. But for Scott, there was always the burden of being Paul Newman's offspring. Trying to be Paul Newman. The real tragedy was that he couldn't find some endeavors totally different than what his father had done. It would have been a saving grace for both of them.

DR. RHODA BURNHAM WAS A THERAPIST ENGAGED BY THE NEWMANS TO COUNSEL THEIR CHILDREN.

After Scott's death, Paul never discussed the situation with his girls, so they never really knew how much he grieved. I'm talking about the experience of his death; it was never talked about.

Paul is a very loving and caring father. He has tremendous respect and love for his kids. He will see the humor in Lissy, he'll see the dedication in Clea, and he can identify and relate to Nell's interests, which are similar to his own.

But Paul has had so many pulls on his time and energy, professionally, that it was not a consistent pattern of fathering. Paul would be very involved, very concerned, for several weeks, and then disappear. It wasn't that he was depriving his kids, it's just that there were other pressures. There was no follow-through.

The kids enjoy doing things with Paul on a one-on-one basis. But because of his presence and the reactions of the public, he couldn't take his kids to the zoo or to many of the other things fathers do with their children. When Paul would visit them at school, the girls used to be uptight because of the abnormal reaction all the people around them would have when they found out these were Paul Newman's kids. They've paid a price, and it is something they cannot change.

GEORGE ROY HILL WAS A FILMMAKER AND CLOSE FRIEND OF PAUL'S. HE DIRECTED THREE FILMS WITH NEWMAN: *BUTCH CASSIDY AND THE SUNDANCE KID, THE STING,* AND *SLAP SHOT;* HE ALSO DIRECTED SCOTT NEWMAN IN *THE GREAT WALDO PEPPER.*

Scott was a kid who was in over his head. Being the son of a star as famous as Paul and being wonderfully good-looking in your own right put a burden on him that he was just not equipped to carry.

Paul was much more indulgent with Scott than he would have been if their relationship had not been one marred by divorce; Paul always felt a certain amount of guilt, and he made a special place in his mind for Scott. He would tell me about the time he visited Scott at the Valley Forge Academy, where he'd attended boarding school; Scott came over to Paul and hugged him—it meant an enormous amount to him. Scott wasn't capable of faking a moment like that, but I do think he was capable of manipulating his father.

Scott, I think, was very disturbed, but Paul tried everything he could to straighten him out. Paul doesn't stint when he gives: he leaves himself very exposed to rejection, and I think he felt rejected by Scott's manner of life. He once told me he couldn't take it with Scott anymore, that he didn't know what to do, but that he couldn't spend the rest of his life making up to Scott what Scott demanded he make up to him.

PATTY NEWMAN

Scott was trying to get jobs and needed a car; Paul, we understood, was not about to buy him yet another one, especially because Scott by this time was in his mid-twenties.

When Scott explained his predicament to me, I said, "Look, I have an old little sports car which I'd be happy for you to drive for a while if that would help."

I felt terribly sorry for him and wished there was something more I could do for him besides loan him a car. Scott was a sweet kind of guy, very sensitive, likable, a pleasure to speak with. Scott always spoke to us as if something good was about to happen for him: he was about to find work, or go back to school, or have one of the acting things he was working on come through. He always had a reason for why he was without a job, but he was the eternal optimist, which is not uncommon with alcoholics or people with drug problems.

He'd been driving the car for quite a while when on a Thanksgiving weekend, Paul's family and my family went up to Santa Barbara, where Paul's girls were going to compete in a horse show. We decided to have dinner together in Ojai; it turned into a pretty big group. And of course everyone was drinking. Joanne and the girls headed out first so they could rest up for their competition; Paul left with Scott in the sports car, and Arthur and I were right behind them.

Arthur had just commented to me how fast Scott was driving, and how Paul was probably pushing him on, when we rounded a curve just as Scott's car slid across the road and rolled over. A complete rollover. The car seemed totaled and we were horrified.

I jumped out of our car, stared at the wreck, and must have had an awful expression on my face. Paul jumped at me, the only time he has done such a thing, and said: "What are you worried about? We can get you another car."

The car, of course, was the last thing I was worried about. He later apologized to me.

Paul wasn't hurt at all, but Scott had to get several stitches around one of his eyes. Arthur went with Paul and Scott to the hospital while I drove back to the hotel. We ended up having to drive Scott back to LA the next day, because now, of course, he again had no car.

Scott told us that he'd resisted going faster because the car's high beams were broken and he didn't want to outrun his headlights on the curvy road. But Paul had urged him on.

There was another aspect to the accident that bothered me but was never talked about. Paul had an elaborate mock-up done of my Opel GT—all banged up and wrecked. He gave it to Scott as a gift. That seemed odd to me; what happened that night was horrible, and it was miraculous that neither Scott nor Paul was really hurt. They could have been gone like that—and the possibility of their deaths was the last thing I would ever have joked about.

When Scott got the mock-up from Paul, though, even he laughed.

JOANNE WOODWARD

The night before I was planning to go to the mortuary to see Scott, I dreamed one of the most vivid dreams I ever had in my life: Clea and her friend Emily, who were little girls in the dream and not the ages they were at that time, were with me. We went up some stairs and into a room where Scott was lying. He sat up and sort of threw his legs over the edge of the coffin and was sitting on the side and we talked. And then

I don't know what happened with the girls, they seemed to disappear, and he and I talked, and it was very warm, very loving, and after we'd been talking for a while he began to glow, and he realized he was glowing, and he said, "I think you'd better go now." And I said, "But Susan and Lissy want a lock of your hair!" And he said, "All right, you can cut a lock of my hair." So with a pair of scissors I reached to cut a lock of his hair, and his hair turned into leaves, and I remember cutting it and thinking, "How strange! Now how am I going to put this in a locket, when it's leaves?" And he lay back down and smiled and waved, and I left, and that was the end of the dream.

I remember I used to tease Scott and say, "You really are from outer space, you don't belong here." But I wasn't really teasing, I always thought that if there is such a thing as a changeling, Scott was one.

X

CLEA AND JOANNE IN THE EARLY 1970S

During the 1960s Paul Newman made and released over twenty films. He received his first Oscar nomination of the new decade for playing Fast Eddie Felson in *The Hustler,* losing to Maximilian Schell for *Judgment at Nuremberg,* and the next one two years later for *Hud,* losing this time to Sidney Poitier for *Lilies of the Field.* (Melvyn Douglas and Patricia Neal, Newman's costars, each took home an Oscar that night.) In 1967 he was a nominee again for *Cool Hand Luke* (with costar George Kennedy, who received an Oscar for Best Supporting Actor). He closed out the sixties with one of the most commercially successful films ever, *Butch Cassidy and the Sundance Kid,* nominated for Best Picture (but losing to *Midnight Cowboy*). He racked up a lifetime total of ten Oscar nominations, finally winning in 1987 for *The Color of Money*.

He earned a nod for Best Picture in 1968 as the producer of the first film he ever directed, a passion project called *Rachel, Rachel,* which earned a total of four nominations, including Best Actress for its star, Joanne Woodward.

DEDE ALLEN

Paul called me as I was finishing up *Bonnie and Clyde*, and asked to see me about *Rachel, Rachel* (which was then called "A Jest of God"). I was very tired when I read the script; *Bonnie and Clyde* was an exciting but stressful experience. As when one has a child, you say, "Never again!"

There was something about *Rachel, Rachel* that made me very uncomfortable—maybe it dealt with things I was uncomfortable with. I met with Paul in Beverly Hills and I said, "I don't like this—I don't think it is the right thing for me to do."

"That's precisely why I want you to do it," he replied. "Joanne does not disagree with you about a lot of this, and that's why I want you—I want different points of view." One of Paul's great talents was to go right for the truth.

Paul said he wanted to direct the film, which was important to get made because it was "right for Joanne." Audiences, he said, were not getting the benefit of Joanne as an actress, so therefore, even though maybe I shouldn't direct, I'm going to.

JOHN FOREMAN

Paul thinks Joanne is a special creature endowed with magic that he has to work very hard to come close to. As a result, he has put up with lots of stuff from her over the years. Directing her in *The Effect of Gamma Rays on Man-in-the-Moon Marigolds,* she was as difficult as I have ever seen a star be in all the years I have been in this business. It was part of her work process, finding that difficult woman. Joanne had a hunch, I have always suspected, that to be considered seriously as an actor, you either had to be prettier than everybody, or better, and she chose better.

DEDE ALLEN

A picture like *Rachel, Rachel* would never have been made by anyone—a movie about a lonely thirty-seven-year-old woman who has never slept with a man? The studio let Paul make the film because they'd get an acting commitment out of him. And they left us alone, which was the greatest blessing that could have happened.

It was a watershed for me as not only one of my favorite films but one of my best work experiences. I feel the whole reason the picture worked was that it was loved into being—nobody was watching over us. The studio couldn't have cared less. They didn't give a shit about this little project. "Here's some film," they said. "Go play."

On the first day of shooting up in Bethel, Connecticut, Paul addressed the whole company: "I'm a virgin. Be gentle with me. I need your help!" Paul was so open, so honest, there was nothing that crew wouldn't do to embrace him.

———

ESTELLE PARSONS

I'd never rehearsed a film like that, on a marked-out floor, rehearsed a whole film as a play. It was very interesting. It gave the movie a very unusual depth. When we actually got to shoot the movie it didn't really have anything to do with what we rehearsed, but, having done it, the characters had a certain heavy relaxation, a certain depth that was not conscious, that you couldn't act. I thought of how really exquisite it was of Paul to do that, because whether we wanted it or not, we had a certain something that one does not usually see in a film.

———

SHIRLEY RICH WAS A CELEBRATED CASTING DIRECTOR FOR MANY BROADWAY SHOWS AND HOLLYWOOD FILMS, INCLUDING *RACHEL, RACHEL*.

When Paul made choices—maybe it is the actor in him—he would see things in someone. He could always tell the difference between the best and the not-so-good.

Actors remember Paul because he made casting a gentlemanly experience. They didn't have to go through: "What have you done lately?" He always had their pictures and resumes, but whatever happened at the moment of the reading made the determination.

His choices are marvelous—a real sense of what's right and good for what he's working on. He doesn't take weeks to decide—there was never any waste with Paul. And that discipline is true with his own acting, too.

TOM CRUISE

I auditioned for *Harry & Son* mostly because I wanted to meet Paul. I was nervous. Starting out as a young actor, you want people to like you, you want people to like your work, you want to be accepted. *Taps* had come out and I think *Risky Business*. I walked into the office. There's Joanne knitting, and Newman with a chain around his neck with a beer can opener on it. He was wearing an off-white sweater and jeans. He said, "Hey, killer. How's it going?" Very excited to see an actor coming in, very relaxed.

We started doing a scene and he was interested in my point of view and what I came up with and exploring it. I was really impressed. You think someone's one way and all of a sudden you meet him and see he can still be excited just by two actors doing a scene.

WARREN COWAN

My earliest recollection of *Rachel* is that I read the script on an airplane coming to New York and the next day went to meet with Paul at their apartment on Lexington Avenue.

I remember they had transformed the apartment into a production office. There were people working away at two or three desks in the foyer and actresses auditioning in the living room. Well, that very day Joanne had put an ad in *The New York Times* looking for a new nanny, so when the doorbell rang they said, "Are you here for the movie or to apply for the nanny?"

FRANK CORSARO WAS A RENOWNED DIRECTOR OF OPERA AND THEATER, AND AN ALUMNUS OF THE ACTORS STUDIO; HE HAD A LEAD ROLE IN *RACHEL, RACHEL*.

In many ways, Paul's best acting performance was as the director of *Rachel, Rachel.* I've never seen so much finesse, his extraordinary sensitivity came through. He was able to coalesce some of his most tender feelings and allow them expression through the film's actors.

As a director, Paul made very specific demands on the cast in areas of feeling and playfulness that very often were missing in his own work as an actor.

DEDE ALLEN

Paul's adoration of Joanne, not only as an actress but as a woman, was so overwhelming that when things were tense I think it was very disturbing to him and therefore the directing experience was harder than it might have been. It must be appalling to direct someone you love and live with when there's tension. Both of them were totally professional, but I do remember Paul's joking about "this directing situation is going to cost our marriage."

STEWART STERN

I remember filming *Rachel* he didn't want to shoot the love scene by the water. He didn't want to see Joanne in that position. His justification was, Let's play it on her face later, as she remembers it.

That night he saw a rehearsal of it and walked away into the woods, and I followed him. He said, "No, no! I'm not going to do it. It's a matter of taste! It's a matter of the actress!" I pleaded with him to shoot it anyway. I said, "You always have an option in the cutting room to throw it out, but this is not the time to make that kind of decision." He seemed pretty set, and I was almost in tears because I could feel the whole thing going.

DEDE ALLEN

I remember that discussion: I remember fighting very hard to get those love scenes. I felt that they were terribly important—and it's very interesting, because I do not recall, at the editing phase, our ever trying the film with that scene out. It was a great, tastefully shot scene, and I have no recollection of it ever not being in a cut.

ELIA KAZAN

Paul's an excellent director; he's sensitive, tough and strong. *Rachel, Rachel* was honorable, decent, and good. It would be very hard to resist being seduced by Paul. You'd do anything he wanted, which is part of the job of a director. It may even be his biggest talent. Maybe five years from now people will say, "Boy, Newman was a good actor, but when it comes to directing, he's better."

DEDE ALLEN

I was never convinced that Paul really realized how good he was, his talent was, and how almost in the way of someone who'd had years and years of managing groups of people, how well he worked with people. Kazan walks into a room a master psychiatrist in his own way, and knows exactly who you dump on and who you don't, when I'm vulnerable and when to send me roses. Kazan does it very well. I never get that feeling at all with Paul. I don't think there's any conscious manipulation.

SIDNEY LUMET WAS THE DIRECTOR OF *THE VERDICT*.

The reason I'm surprised Paul doesn't direct more is that it seems a great solution for him. If one is afraid of exposing one's vulnerability to the masses, it's clearly easier to confine the exposure to the very intimate circumstances of actors whom you'd get to know well during the process of directing them. It seems to fit in with his talent and fit in with what I've felt about him psychologically.

By the time *Cat on a Hot Tin Roof* was released in 1958, I had already grown incredibly frustrated by Hollywood's studio system. At the time of *Silver Chalice,* I had signed a contract with Warner Bros. that gave them tremendous power over what pictures I could make and how much I would get for them.

JOHN FOREMAN

Warners began to loan him, which really burned his ass because all his great successes were on loan-out, they got about a hundred and fifty thousand dollars for him when he worked at MGM, and by the time he was at Fox, five to six hundred thousand dollars. And he was still getting his two thousand a week salary.

Though Warners had promised me they'd never force me into making a movie I simply didn't want, they lied. Finally I called the studio directly. "Jack Warner," I said, "this is Paul Newman. Go fuck yourself." It took the finesse and nerve of the head of my talent agency, MCA's Lew Wasserman, to figure out a way to calm things down and set me free—sort of. Lew called Jack Warner and suggested I be allowed to buy my way out of their contract—for half a million dollars. The deal was frightening to me.

"Lew, this will make me an indentured servant for the next twenty years!"

"Let me worry about that," he replied.

I was still nervous, but the gamble ultimately paid off. Within a few years, I had paid back the $500,000 to Warners.

Jack Warner was very much of the "business is business" philosophy and let it be known he had no hard feelings. But not long afterwards, he was in New York and attended one of my performances of *Sweet Bird of Youth*; he asked to come by after the show and offer congratulations. I wouldn't allow him backstage.

I was determined to make my own choices—to decide what projects to do based on whether I really wanted to do them.

ROBERT J. WAGNER PLAYED PAUL'S RIVAL, THE RUTHLESS COMPETING RACE CAR DRIVER, IN *WINNING*, AND WITH PAUL'S HELP WAS CAST IN A KEY ROLE IN *HARPER*.

Paul was always rebellious about the studio contract system, about the kind of movies they wanted. He objected to that. He was always looking for more, for the edge, for values that were higher than he was asked to attain.

His thought processes as an actor were so bewildering and exciting. When Paul would think about a part or a character, his interests were so extraordinary, his depth of investiga-

tion about life and behavior were always so much more than
I would ever think about. I'd never been around someone
who works so goddamn hard to get where he goes and to get
the strength he's got.

***

It is probably no coincidence that as I entered the 1960s, my
political awareness and activities were increasing.

Perhaps it began with Gore Vidal. We'd met in 1955 when I played
the lead in his *The Death of Billy the Kid*. When Joanne and I were on
our honeymoon in Europe, Gore and his partner, Howard Austen,
had a wonderful celebratory dinner for us; when we settled back in
LA afterwards, we actually shared a rented house with them for a
time.

We all became close friends, and when we came back east, we'd
often stay at Gore's country estate, Edgewater, near Red Hook,
New York. Gore held a real salon there, attended by literary types,
theater people, and even some military folks. Also, more than a few
political figures, as Gore, of course, was very politically astute and
active. We'd stay up late and drink formidable amounts of liquor,
wine, and beer. It didn't matter whether Gore went to bed at four
a.m., he'd be at his typewriter working at nine in the morning. I was
always a bit concerned that I was difficult to talk with because I
wasn't educated in the same way as Gore and his guests.

Gore, of course, was part of a distinguished family; his grandfather
was a US senator, and Gore grew up in Washington, DC. In 1960,
Gore received a Democratic nomination for election to Congress,
gaining Eleanor Roosevelt's endorsement for the Hudson Valley
House seat long held by Republicans. Joanne and I were impressed by
Gore's liberalism, and offered to help. In what was my first political
experience, I made many a trip to Gore's upstate New York district
to campaign for him. We went door-to-door, and I made speeches on
his behalf. Gore ultimately lost the election, but that began my long-

term involvement with Democratic candidates, surprising, perhaps, for an "emotional Republican" from Shaker Heights.

About three years later, at the height of the civil rights movement and a burgeoning resistance to Governor George Wallace's rabid racism in the South, Marlon Brando phoned me and asked if I would go down to Gadsden, Alabama, with him to help bring attention to and mediate a confrontation between the Black community and the big white-run steel makers in town. Tensions were high, and there had hardly been any conversations happening between Gadsden's white business class and the Black population.

Besides me, Marlon had also asked Tony Franciosa and Virgil Frye, the boxer and actor, to fly down. So we did, and soon after landing near Birmingham, we realized our vans from the airport were being followed. We were being tracked, and the people chaperoning us made us switch cars for our own security. I don't think there was any real physical danger, but we sure didn't make a lot of friends down there.

While we got together with members of the African-American religious community, at least one business leader and Gadsden's mayor, Lesley Gilliland, refused even to see us. "They are serving no purpose in Gadsden except to create trouble and chaos," the mayor said of our group.

We visited several Black churches, met the parishioners, shook hands, asked for advice on who we should meet and what we should say to help them with their voting rights and employment issues. We were all staying for two or three days at a motel run by one of the local ministers. I was speaking to one of the Black activists who was also based there, and he was telling me about the violent tactics the police and troopers used on the protesters.

"Would you like to see what we get on a regular basis?" he asked me.

I told him I was interested, and he brought over a cattle prod that was used by the cops on Blacks. I said I was willing to see how it felt. And with that, he touched it to the muscle that runs down along my backbone and I jumped about ten feet across the room. It had an incredible jolt, and all I could imagine was what would happen if someone got shocked in their chest or stomach.

I'm not sure of any tangible results that came from our trip, but we did our best to reassure the community that they had support from us and our colleagues. Most important, though, was the national media coverage we received. As a result of the wire photographs and stories, many theater owners in the South decided to pull my films from their screens.

By 1964, I'd been asked by the national Democratic Party to attend its presidential convention in Atlantic City. Though LBJ was enormously popular and had no real competition for the nomination, they wanted me to address the Young Democrats, juice them up for the general election and calm any fears they might be having about LBJ's foreign policy. I was brought into a huge auditorium, with several thousand people there, and my subject was the slow-simmering war in Vietnam. Johnson's position, his very effective position, was that he would contain our involvement in Southeast Asia, while his GOP opponent, Arizona's conservative Senator Barry Goldwater, would escalate the US role. I gladly—and very unfortunately in retrospect—gave my speech supporting his stated plans.

Years later, when the Pentagon Papers came out, it was clear that the decision to escalate the war had already been made by the White House in May 1964. Goldwater, being a member of the Armed Services Committee, would have been conversant with the decision—but could reveal nothing, because it was a matter of national security. So here were two guys with plans to escalate in Vietnam, but with only one admitting he wanted to do just that while the incumbent claimed he had no such intention. Goldwater couldn't get up and say, "Look, on this issue, it's going to be the same no matter who is elected—don't think for a minute that won't be the case!"

I'd always believed that on some minor issues there was chicanery in government, but I'd never really imagined a president of the United States actively getting up and lying to the people. Actively asking me to put my status and reputation on the line to support someone who had already torpedoed us.

It was a terrible feeling to realize the extent to which we'd all been taken by LBJ. Four years later, during the next national election, I did all I could to try and repair the damage.

━━

HAROLD WILLENS WAS A COFOUNDER OF THE CENTER FOR DEFENSE INFORMATION AND A MAJOR SUPPORTER OF PROGRESSIVE CAUSES, INCLUDING THE ANTIWAR MOVEMENT AND NUCLEAR DISARMAMENT. HE RECRUITED NEWMAN TO DONATE AND PARTICIPATE IN THESE AND OTHER CAUSES.

Paul was then and has always remained someone who made no pretensions about having more knowledge than he did or being more profound than he is. He has always tended to downplay himself. But there was a willingness, even eagerness, to learn, and this has gone on for all the years I've known him.

━━

It wasn't easy finding a candidate who'd take on his own party's incumbent president in a primary. But while many on the Left were urging some well-known antiwar national politicians to challenge LBJ and put a stop to the Vietnam madness, only the relatively obscure Senator Gene McCarthy, Democrat of Minnesota, rose to the moment. When McCarthy first began campaigning as the antiwar candidate against Johnson in early '68, virtually no voters knew who he was. He could literally walk through his hotel lobby in New Hampshire, site of the first battle, and not a single head would turn.

I'd been in New York, cutting my film *Rachel, Rachel,* so I had a relatively large amount of time on my hands. I'd work on the movie three days a week and then spend the rest of my time campaigning for McCarthy in New Hampshire.

When I first volunteered, I'd never met the man. But when we finally had lunch together, I found him to be someone of great political and intellectual charisma. He was incisive, a senator of great integrity. There was a joke going around that if McCarthy was elected, he'd leave diplomatic pouches hanging on the wall while he'd go off in a corner composing poetry. I ended up spending much of the next forty-five or fifty days doing everything I could on the trail to help McCarthy defeat the president.

At the beginning, what I did was pure grassroots stuff—canvassing, speaking in conjunction with others at Rotary and Kiwanis clubs, churches, high schools, even from the back of some flatbeds. McCarthy was often there, and I'd introduce him, but there were more than a couple of times that I'd have to hold the fort because he was running late. I was fairly well prepared, pretty well read on Vietnam, and got better as I went along (like everything else in life). Though we lost New Hampshire, the whole country was shocked by how narrow a victory LBJ had eked out—50 percent to 42 percent.

I went on to Wisconsin to help with McCarthy's run there. After a few days on the hustings, we felt the momentum turning McCarthy's way; one late poll had us up by more than fifteen points. When I landed back in New York shortly before the voting, I turned on my car radio just in time to hear Lyndon Johnson declare, "I shall not seek and I will not accept the nomination of my party for another term as your president."

God, I felt angry: Johnson wouldn't give us the satisfaction of licking him. Bobby Kennedy, of course, decided then to jump into the race, which I felt was not cricket. I stuck with McCarthy.

A couple of months later, while campaigning in Chicago before the Illinois primary, McCarthy had to abruptly bow out of an event and left me alone to the wolves. The appearance was scheduled in a poor Black neighborhood, and I was on my own in front of a pretty big crowd. With the horror and trauma of Bobby Kennedy's murder just a week earlier, minority voters were now giving McCarthy a second look, and as his surrogate, I was asked about race relations, equal opportunity, and so forth. It all came down to one key question that someone in the crowd shouted out: "What are you going to do for us?"

"Let me be clear," I improvised. "There's going to be nothing for the Black community as long as the Vietnam War is going on. Only if we stop the war will the government have the energy and money to do things about racial equality. But if we stay in Vietnam, you're going to get nothing."

I really didn't know what else to say, but my answer scared the hell out of me. It had just appeared in my mouth while I was standing before the crowd, and it was really exciting to say it out loud.

Oddly enough, the scene I most sharply remember from that campaign came when I got in late one night to one of the midwestern primary states, and the kid who met me at the airport asked if I could boost the morale of the young campaign volunteers who were working their butts off for McCarthy. Even though it was already eleven p.m., I agreed to go over, say hello, clap them on the back and offer something encouraging. When we arrived at the church basement office, there were still about a half dozen people hard at work—and a suspicious odor of marijuana wafting through the air. I thanked everyone, and began to chat with one guy, maybe nineteen, with a beard and big bushy hair.

"Are all of you college kids?" I asked him.

"Yeah," he replied.

"And where were you going to school?"

"Princeton."

"And you gave up a whole semester of Princeton to volunteer in McCarthy's campaign?"

"Yeah, that's what I'm giving up."

"And what do you get out of it?"

"I get to be known as a revolutionary."

"A revolutionary," I said. "What's the benefit of being a revolutionary?"

"Revolutionaries," he explained, "get laid a lot."

So much for the joy of democracy.

HAROLD WILLENS

When Paul would spend weekends in New Hampshire in 1968 campaigning for McCarthy, there was a rental agency which made a fancy car available for his use. Paul learned that Richard Nixon was coming to the state to campaign and he was to receive use of this same car.

Paul wrote a note and left it in the car for Nixon: "You'll find this car very suitable for you. It has a crooked clutch."

My bottom line take on Paul is that he is the quintessential citizen who pays a high price with much more than money for the things he considers to be important.

He cares about things larger than himself. Macrocosmic problems concern him and evoke a response.

He also has the ability to accept that human enterprise, whether it's directing a film or trying to save the world from extinction, requires a process, a process that shouldn't be measured in terms of "Will the ten thousand dollars I contribute bring some specific result by next Monday?"

To my amazement and delight, this guy turned out to be profoundly aware that history is a stream of events that precedes us and lies ahead of us. He understands it is worthwhile doing anything that can point the process in the right direction.

GEORGE ROY HILL AND STEWART STERN

GEORGE ROY HILL: I hate when Paul gets in his political mood, because it's soporific for me. As soon as he talks about Washington and what's going on down there, he can't say the first two words when I click it off, don't pay any attention to it at all, because it's the most boring subject in the world. But he really gets off on it. You know that's something that always interested me about Paul is why he never got into politics.

STEWART STERN: The reason he gives me is that—I think the drinking, the opposition might seize on that.

GH: The drinking?

SS: Yeah. In the past.

GH: Oh, come on! He's full of shit.

SS: The other thing is that—

GH: He never had a problem with drinking.

SS: Well . . .

GH: I mean, my god, when you think of the lushes they have in the Senate and the Congress.

SS: But also, the main overriding thing is that he's not able to show the kind of enthusiasm for things that he has no sincere interest in. He's very, very uncomfortable selling a product, and you have to sell products.

Let me get back to Gore for a moment and a story that started without a shred of politics, but ended up with almost more than we could handle.

By the mid-sixties, Gore and Howard had pretty much moved full-time to Italy. Long-distance relationships can be hard to maintain, so when Gore invited Joanne and me to take a sailing cruise together around Greece, it seemed like a wonderful chance to escape our hectic home lives and be reunited with one of our long-time friends.

Gore had chartered a four-stateroom launch (with crew) and we were to sail from Piraeus in May, always said to be the best month for traveling the Adriatic's Greek islands. If you're headed through places of historical or political significance, there is no one better to travel with than Gore; he's a living encyclopedia, and for an illiterate person like me, it's like having your own twenty-four-hour-a-day guide. Still, things started terribly.

On the day Joanne and I flew into Athens, I lost my passport. All the embassy could do for a temporary replacement was to hand me a slip of paper that identified me (in Greek) as Paul Newman, US Citizen. When we eventually took our bags over to Gore's yacht, we met the captain and first mate—and made some unsettling discoveries. While we'd known the skipper was Greek, we'd been assured his first mate spoke French, so he could communicate with any of us and act as our liaison to the captain. Problem was, this mate actually couldn't speak a word of French; he didn't even know what *potage* meant. I thought, "Well, there's going to be trouble."

Besides our captain's language issues, he also worried us by bumping into everything while leaving the dock. We literally ricocheted off other yachts. Whatever direction we were headed, the captain alertly and aggressively looked the opposite way. (The captain reminded me of myself in a way: wherever there was knowledge or experience or understanding and you had to point yourself in that direction to embrace all that good stuff, I looked in the other direction.)

Within a day of setting out, we also encountered what was said to be the worst May weather in the Adriatic for fifty years. Joanne had laid out one of her Gucci dresses on the top bunk in our stateroom, and the ship's maid had forgotten to tie down the porthole as the weather kicked in; the water gushed right through and got sucked up into the dress, which now looked like a child's bathing suit.

When we pulled into the first island on our itinerary, our captain was unable to dock our boat, because there was another sixty-five-foot launch blocking our way to the marina; he couldn't figure out what to do. Though we all wanted to go into town to explore, the only way to head ashore was in a tiny three-person dinghy. (We did have a Boston Whaler tethered to our ship, but its motor, of course, conked out.) So a mate rowed two of us in, turned around, and then shuttled the other two of us in to shore. We ate the best fish imaginable, and were finally rowed back the same way we came. But the next morning, with the sea increasingly rough, our captain decided it was too risky to sail on, so we had the mate row us back to land again. We walked all around this wonderful little island, and on our way back to the dock, we stopped and bought some bread, sliced meat, vegetables, and other provisions.

By this time, word must have gotten around that there was an American movie star onboard this launch anchored just three hundred feet from the dock. So as we prepared to reboard our dinghy, fifty or sixty people had gathered at the water's edge, observing us with curiosity. I grabbed our leeks, lettuce, and bread and got into the dinghy while Howard quickly followed, stepping down on the outside gunnel—and flipping over the rowboat. I surfaced to polite applause from the natives, who kept yelling "El comandante!" and "Il capitano!" and "Bravo!" and "Ole!" or whatever. So besides my humiliation, we were also out of bread and leeks. But I must admit, it was hysterical.

When we sailed on the next morning, we again were wallowing in a roiling sea. Joanne was sitting on the deck atop a heavy sea chest—which suddenly broke loose and skidded across the entire boat. Joanne was riding it like a colt and was finally stopped by hitting the gunnel. It was amazing she didn't go overboard.

Joanne turned to me and in her sweetest Southern drawl said: "Get me off this fucking boat!"

We managed to tell the skipper to tack south and at least get the wind at our backs. He took us into the lee of another small island, where we suddenly heard gunshots and saw another vessel speeding our way with an armed crew.

I thought we were being hijacked. Gore was asleep downstairs, and I told Joanne to get down below and lock herself in the bathroom. All I had on was a pair of shorts, no weapons, and when the boat pulled alongside us, two young kids with submachine guns hopped onboard and pointed their guns at us.

The other boat's skipper then came onboard and demanded everyone's papers. When he got to the handwritten temporary passport I'd received from the American embassy, the skipper looked up at me, then back at the paper, then looked at us all again. He motioned for the gunmen to quickly get off the boat, but explained we needed to follow their vessel for the next three or four hours.

Greece, it turns out, was in the middle of a coup d'état, and our moron captain had sailed us into the lee of the little island where all the political prisoners were being detained. When we followed their vessel to a different port, our captain was led away for questioning. Joanne looked around the harbor and asked a local policeman what was the large boat that just docked at the next quay. "That's the ferry to Athens," he told her.

Joanne packed in four minutes flat. Weeping copiously, she bought a ticket and ran onto the ferry. "I'll see you later, guys" were her parting words.

She flew right back to the US from Athens, and I wasn't far behind.

———

I've always been impressed by Gore; he even reminds me of myself in some ways—he's a real inner-outer type, different layers of personality for different situations. He could write *Julian*, a great, brilliant book, publish a terrific novel like *Washington, D.C.*—and then the next day he'll do something dumb. Gore had a rather inflated sense of where he stood in the literary world. He has a sense of being truly powerful, but while he is a power, he was never truly powerful.

Over the next few decades, it was more Joanne than me who kept up our friendship with Howard and Gore; they loved her. In fact, when my courtship of Joanne was still secret, there was the occasional gossip-column item that said Joanne and Gore (who, of course, was gay), who occasionally dined or went to the theater together, were a couple.

My mother had somehow become suspicious of them, too. When Joanne invited Tress to the premiere of *Ben-Hur*—which Gore co-wrote—she noticed Joanne and Gore chatting and casually holding hands. A couple of years later, Tress came to visit us in New York when I was on Broadway. We were driving one evening in my Volkswagen, when suddenly my mother said to me: "I know why your wife hates me! It's because she is having an affair with Gore Vidal."

I slammed on the brakes.

"Get out of the fucking car."

There were tears and apologies, but I still dropped her at the corner of Eighteenth Street and Fifth Avenue. Joanne was absolutely aghast that I would throw a sick woman out of my car. Joanne has always wondered why I didn't just roar with laughter and say, "Mom, honestly, an affair? Such a thing is manifestly impossible." I didn't see it that way; she insulted my wife.

My mother was quite a dame. She had an internal drummer and that drummer was not affected by any other rhythms; there was a song going on with her and she stuck to it. If she thought something was going on in a certain way, then that's the way it was. It didn't make any difference what actually happened; to her, it wouldn't change. And I didn't speak to my mother again for fifteen years.

Was it all because of what she said about Joanne? No, not really, but it was such a relief to use that as an excuse to escape from her. She represented all my leaden luggage, the parts of myself that I didn't like. That sense of subservience, uncertainty, not knowing where the next attack was coming from or what the reason for it might be.

After that night in Manhattan, it took a decade and a half for my brother, Arthur, to engineer an armistice. He booked her on a flight to LA, picked her up at LAX, and drove her up to our beach house in Malibu. And since she figured this was going to be uncomfortable, she made it uncomfortable for everyone. Not surprising that the first moments of our truce began with an attack on my flank.

"Hello," she said when she walked in.

"Hi, Mom," I said, "it's been a long time." I kissed her on both cheeks.

"What a wonderful house!" she went on. "Is that the beach out there? You can just sit there and watch the waves come in? Wonderful."

I told her she was right on all counts.

"Are you working? Is the work good? How terrible it must be to be involved in a rotten industry that settles itself in violence and profanity and sex and gore. Oh, what you could do if you only tried!"

And this was all in the first five minutes.

I don't know if she had decided to say that in advance, but I'm sure images of Sodom and Gomorrah were running through her mind. She acted oblivious to what was going on around her with her family, her two grown children engineering a rapprochement, struggling to find something affirmative in this meeting. Tress was not about to let that happen.

We'd never see each other again on a regular basis until my mom became quite ill and I'd visit her a few times. It was important for me to show up, though there was never any change of feelings.

When I think about it, I never really spoke to my mother for not just fifteen years, but for fifty years. I was too wary. I didn't respect her perceptions of things—although I didn't necessarily respect my own.

We never discussed our rift and she never apologized.

JOANNE WOODWARD

Tress absolutely adored Paul and was probably never comfortable with the fact that he got married, either to Jackie or me. I don't recall her being affectionate with any of the grandchildren, but the funny thing was, when we finally went to her house, there were all sorts of pictures of us all over the place. That rupture must have been terribly painful for her because it was just at the time of Paul's greatest success and he hated the fact that she basked in the limelight. I don't know why. It's so sad. Why shouldn't she?

LUCILLE AND BABETTE NEWMAN

LUCILLE: In all those years that Paul wasn't talking to Tress, he took care of her. He did it through Arthur or more directly in some way. She didn't need financial support.

BABETTE: She always claimed she was a millionaire.

LUCILLE: She was. She was a marvel at stocks. But Paul was still helping. Through Arthur, he was always conscious of what was going on with her every minute, and would try to get her to move to California.

Whenever anyone used to ask me to describe how specific parts I played came into being, I gave the same answer: I simply followed instructions. The screenwriters have a guy leaning against a fence post, being sexy and saying sexy things? It's all from the character on the page and the actor's ability to interpret that character. There's

TRESS NEWMAN IN MALIBU, IN AN UNDATED PHOTO

nothing organic about it. If someone writes about a ne'er-do-well who drinks, fights guys, and is really successful with women, with a lot of scalps on his pole, it's not because the actor has these things. Someone wrote about the scalps; only the character has them.

Newman as a sexual image is something invented and is in the mind of the writer, which I simply interpret. It's like the accountant who goes to work in the morning and doesn't see his job as glamorous. It's possible for an actor to have a job that seems very glamorous to someone on the outside, and even be excited about the machinery he went through to create the part, but the work to the actor is sometimes no more interesting than the interesting parts of accounting. It's all just a process.

———

WALON GREEN WAS A NOTED SCREENWRITER
AND CLOSE FRIEND OF PAUL'S.

I remember Paul said he always had misgivings about taking on any part, doubts about his ability to find the role, mold it and craft it. Except for Fast Eddie Felson in *The Hustler*. It was the only script in his life where he read the first five pages and knew it was dead right for him. He knew he had to play it and felt it immediately—he was the guy.

———

WARREN COWAN

Shortly after *The Hustler* had opened, Paul phoned me one night and asked me to meet him for a beer at the Daisy, which was then the hottest see-and-be-seen restaurant in Beverly Hills. When I got there, Paul was in back shooting pool, which he truly enjoyed playing. We met at the bar and after we ordered, some guy came staggering over, a little smashed. "Mr. Newman," he said, "I saw *The Hustler* three times. And I just watched you play in the other room. And I have to tell you, Mr. Newman, it's one of the great disappointments in my life."

———

FRANCES WOODWARD WAS JOANNE WOODWARD'S
STEPMOTHER. JOANNE'S FATHER, WADE WOODWARD, WORKED AS AN
EXECUTIVE FOR CHARLES SCRIBNER'S SONS FOR TWENTY YEARS.

Just before *The Hustler* was made, we went to Paul and
Joanne's Park Avenue apartment, the one that had a pool
table in the dining room. Wade was very good at pool,
because when you're a book man, all the publisher men
would go to the local pool hall and play until it was time to
meet with the local board of education.

So Wade and Paul had some Scotch, then dinner, and afterwards played pool for two dollars on the corner. When Wade
won Paul's two-dollar bill, Paul would complain, "Dad, that's
a dirty thing to do—drink my whiskey, eat my food, and then
take my money!" There was a lovely flow between them; Paul
was very dear to Wade.

They once took a train together from New York to California. They each had a bottle of Scotch when they left Pennsylvania Station; they drank Wade's Scotch first, then they
drank Paul's. And then the conductor found them another
bottle somewhere. Joanne, who was on the train with them,
got disgusted and went to bed.

The next day, everyone had to change trains in Chicago;
Wade and Paul were feeling pretty bad, and Joanne made her
daddy go shopping with her while they waited for the connection. Meanwhile, Paul also went out and bought Wade
a gift, one of those face masks you freeze to help relieve a
hangover. Wade loved it.

PIPER LAURIE WAS NOMINATED FOR AN ACADEMY AWARD FOR BEST ACTRESS FOR HER ROLE AS PAUL NEWMAN'S DOOMED LOVER IN *THE HUSTLER*.

Paul always used to say: "What am I doing this for? I don't know why I'm acting. I really want to be a carpenter." I have no idea whether he was actually good at making things with his hands or not, but this was his regular refrain.

Of course, I had a crush on him at a certain level (even though I was in love with someone else then). It was a crush I could never act on; he was supposedly happily married and Joanne, who I'd met, was carrying their second child. The first time Paul and I shook hands—it was in our rehearsal hall on the first day—I couldn't look at him. I went through that thing that a lot of women go through when they meet Paul. The eyes, those brilliant clear eyes, the beautiful face. There is a kind of openness, some sort of special quality he projects. It took about two weeks, and only then, out of his generosity and naturalness, was I able to deal with him as just another actor.

Paul was also unfazed by our nude scene which happened before people were doing nude scenes. We were supposed to wake up in my bed, and I had it in my head that I was supposed to be naked, and if I wore some sort of contraption to keep myself modest, it would interfere with the work; it would make me feel dishonest. I went to our director, Bob Rossen, and told him I was going to play it with nothing on from the waist up—and, of course, I forewarned Paul so he wouldn't be surprised. Rossen was upset about it. What we finally did was shoot the scene two ways—naked for the European market, and with me wearing a slip for America.

Years later, after moving out of New York, I phoned Paul

and Joanne to tell them I was getting married. He said some-thing to me on the phone, and I still don't know whether he was joking. "Enjoy it," he said, "because it may not last."

I remember the words precisely because I didn't know how to take it.

MARTIN RITT FORMED A PRODUCTION COMPANY
WITH PAUL AND DIRECTED *HUD* IN 1962.

When the screenwriters Irving Ravetch and his wife, Har-riet Frank, first worked at MGM, Clark Gable had been in several films in which for the first half of the film he was an incredible shitheel and in the second half some girl, or Spen-cer Tracy, or God, converted him. The Ravetches had the notion that they'd like to take a character like that, a man of unbridled appetites, and carry him through to his logical conclusion. We philosophically all agreed that we should make a serious film about that kind of man rather than one of those silly fucking movies that always used to get made.

When I got their script for *Hud* (which they'd adapted from a Larry McMurtry novel), I loved it. Hud is a man deter-mined to win, even at the expense of everyone else in his life. I knew I had to get an actor so attractive that I could hook the audience regardless. And so I took it to Paul, who had really then just become a star. He was noncommittal. And his agents at MCA took the position "The part's a shitheel; why do you want to use a star for *that*?" In those days, it was considered ridiculous to think that an actor like Paul New-man, just emerging into stardom, would ever play a shitheel.

I liked Paul from our time making *The Long, Hot Summer,* and thought if I went into business with him, I could get *Hud* financed. Without Paul, I wouldn't have gotten it made.

And then I had to fight to get *Paul* to even do the picture.

Paul had flown to Israel to shoot *Exodus* for Otto Preminger, and I literally followed him there. I persisted. He wasn't as sure of the material as I was. I think he may have also had some doubts about me—I was never an "in" director with the intellectuals.

Paul finally agreed, and we ended up making three-picture deals with both Paramount and Columbia—we each would do two pictures out of the three, including at least one together (though we never did make any for Columbia).

We shot *Hud* in Texas in a small town called Claude, and based ourselves near Amarillo (a town where they'd recently been burning books from the local library). But the next thing we knew, all these young girls started pouring into our motel, camping out at Paul's door. It was incredible to watch and it became clear then that that's what it was all about with him. Paul finally just kept his door locked. He's always been a very private man.

When we made *Long, Hot Summer,* Paul wasn't aware of his impact. He still looked at himself as Little Paul Newman from Shaker Heights. After *Hud* opened, Paul became this incredible sex object; it hit him like a ton of bricks. When we took *Hud* to the Venice Film Festival, we were all invited to a big reception. Though I was the director and Paul was the star, it didn't take twenty seconds before we were separated and everyone there, man and woman alike, descended on Paul. It was entirely sexual. I was left alone standing in the corner.

How did Paul come to have that shambling walk, that iconic pose on all the *Hud* posters of him staring straight ahead, one hand on a cocked hip, the other one holding a cigarette? He actually worked all those things out by himself. These were the kind of details that he was always so concerned with in every picture he made. All I had to do was let him find it.

———

ROBERT WEBBER WAS A VETERAN TELEVISION AND MOVIE CHARACTER ACTOR WHO MADE FILMS WITH JOANNE AND PAUL, BOTH OF WHOM HE FIRST BEFRIENDED IN THE EARLY 1950S.

Paul turned *Hud* around so that the audience loved him. He became the God of the piece instead of the devil. Paul was unable then to let an audience dislike him because of his image of himself. Something Marty Ritt taught me: "The moment you get a set image of yourself, you're finished as an actor, because you're protecting that image, not playing the character." One could say, "Well, a director is the person who should shape a performance." True, but not when the actor is a superstar.

———

PATRICIA NEAL HAD AN ILLUSTRIOUS HOLLYWOOD CAREER FOR MORE THAN THREE DECADES; SHE WON THE OSCAR FOR BEST ACTRESS IN *HUD*.

I think I was at the Actors Studio the first day Lee Strasberg taught; I sat listening to him, looked to my right, and all of a sudden here was this fabulous boy and he was all I could look at. I'd never heard of him, never seen him before, never anything. I could only stare at this beautiful boy with those blue eyes and that great profile. I mean, he was staggering.

That was my first impression of Paul Newman: the beauty of the world.

Paul was a very good man to work with; he was busy being that character, Hud, who is a horror. I don't know if Paul still does that, becoming the character he plays when he works, but he was hysterical during the shooting. In the script, Hud and his young nephew, who was played by Brandon de Wilde, go to town and do things. And Paul's relationship offscreen with Brandon was just like in the film. Now don't take my word for it, but I think I'm right: they'd go out every night, get drunk, take women. Really. He was making it work, and he's a very clever man.

———

I was riding my exercise bike this morning, just running the channels, and there was *Hombre,* a film I made with Marty Ritt, based on an Elmore Leonard novel, that attempted to depict anti-Indian racism in the Old West. I watched about fifteen minutes on the TV— but I can't look at my work in that picture without disparaging it.

There on the screen is this goddamn movie star with blue eyes playing a half Apache. And I remembered how when we started the film, it just wouldn't come together for me. I went out alone to a reservation in New Mexico, and I hired this Indian bureau agent to show me around. We drove out for breakfast, and on the way we passed a little general store; on the porch was a man from a local tribe with his arms crossed, standing on one foot, with his other heel hooked over the top of the windowsill.

A couple hours later, after we finished our meal with a local family, we headed back and drove past that general store again. The man on the porch hadn't moved an inch, still on one leg, heel still hooked over the ledge. I ended up taking my whole character from that man—the sense that there was no reason for him to move, so he didn't. A sense of surety and no use of motion. Maybe it worked on the screen when *Hombre* first came out, though it certainly didn't do very much for me.

If I was playing that part now, I'd approach it differently. I think I'd make that immovable presence the core of the character, but not in such an obvious way. And I would desperately fight to wear brown contact lenses. The blue eyes just destroyed everything.

We filmed most of *Hombre* in southern Arizona, but while we were there, the winds blew so strong, there were times you could barely walk. We often couldn't shoot on our mountain-reservation location, and we ended up going forty-two days over schedule. I spent most of my time waiting around, reading about thirty books and taking tennis lessons at a nearby club; there was a pretty good pro there—but just as important, he was an incredible beer drinker.

To break up the routine, I convinced my film-crew driver to let me get behind the wheel of our rented Cadillac. There was this wonderful, undulating gravel road from our actual location back to town. I drove it rather fast, and ended up cruising along many of the back roads. It didn't hurt that the crew driver had installed an ice case filled with beer in the trunk.

The day I flew home, my very even-tempered, gentlemanly driver shook my hand at the airport and said, "Mr. Newman, I'd like to thank you for one thing."

"What's that?"

"Before you got here, my reflexes were set for fifty miles per hour, and now they're set for a hundred and five. And I feel really terrific."

There was a lot of camaraderie on that set. Richard Boone, who played the villain, would race me every day to our cars parked just off the set and try to leave first—not because we were anxious to get out of there, but because whoever left second was literally left in the swirling dust that the first car would kick up and leave behind. So much of it, in fact, that it sometimes took four or five minutes before you could see well enough to drive out. I wasn't going to let that happen; I started to spike Boone's car to the ground, tie it to a hook, even steal his keys. In all the weeks we were on location, he never beat me, not once.

Sean Connery, then at the peak of his 007 fame, came out to visit his wife, Diane Cilento, who was cast as the female lead. We decided to have a dinner for them at the Tack Room, which back then was a very famous restaurant in Tucson. It had these long wooden tables, and they'd put out these plates of terribly hot peppers that would put a flame in your mouth. Even if you bit off just a sliver, it would bring tears to your eyes and clear out your sinuses for a month.

Sean was at one end of the table, I was at the other, when I saw him grab a big handful of these peppers, pop them in his mouth, and start to chew. It all happened so quickly that I was immobilized. I waited for the top of his head to lift off his neck two or three inches, separate from his ears, and for his chair to fall over backwards while he ran for a swimming pool to submerge the fire.

But nothing happened.

Sean just kept speaking normally through this onslaught of heat. And I stared at him with the sort of reverence and admiration that I might reserve for a bullfighter or kamikaze pilot. I'd never been so awed; it was spiritual. I don't remember whether I ever had the chance to tell Sean, but I came to regard him as one of the toughest men on the face of the earth.

———

STUART ROSENBERG WAS A HIGHLY REGARDED TELEVISION DIRECTOR WHEN HE PITCHED THE *COOL HAND LUKE* SCRIPT TO PAUL; IT WOULD BE THE FIRST OF FOUR FEATURES THEY MADE, THE OTHERS BEING *WUSA*, *POCKET MONEY*, AND *THE DROWNING POOL*.

Back in 1967, there were basically two movie stars in the world: Steve McQueen and Paul Newman. And I decided Paul would be perfect to play Luke.

I called his agent, arranged a meeting, and next thing I knew, we were talking in Paul's yard on Whittier here in Beverly Hills. I was very impressed because he'd read the script, read the original novel, and his intelligence was very impressive. There was no bullshit. And although I had no real track record as a feature film director, he committed to the film because he liked the character.

We put together a company that was like a kind of Group Theatre. Every one of those kids we cast in the chain gang—Dennis Hopper, Joe Don Baker, Ralph Waite, Harry Dean Stanton, Wayne Rogers—eventually made it. And Paul was everyone's favorite. Not a superstar, but a guy in the trenches working. It was a very physical picture; the actors had to get out on the road, cut grass, lay tar.

The way it was written, the other prisoners show their respect for Luke by giving him space and moving to the other side of the barracks when he discovers that his mother has died. Luke was not the sort of character who would make a speech in her honor, but we were worried the audience would feel cheated if he didn't pay some sort of tribute.

It was never in the script. It came up during a rehearsal. A few days earlier, I'd heard Harry Dean Stanton, with his long, bony face, singing this irreverent song around the campfire one night. Stuart heard it, too. "Get yourself a plastic Jesus," was the lyric I remembered.

STUART ROSENBERG

The problem was Paul's not a musician. And he had to quickly learn three things: how to play the chords on the banjo, sing the song, and do the scene. I also wanted it to be the first time on film that people really saw Paul Newman weep. But Paul is such an incredible professional, and on the afternoon we were going to shoot, he invited me into his dressing room and played the song for me. I said to myself, "He's doing it too well!" I wanted more ragged edges from him.

Just as we were ready to go, I thought I needed to upset Paul a little to get what I wanted. Before he hit the first chord, I stopped everything and said, "Paul, sorry, we've got a copyright problem with the song. You're going to have to reverse the first and second lines."

"Oh, Christ, after all this fucking work—goddamn!"

I told the camera operator to start rolling, we hit the clapper, and Paul just began. I let him go on a little but then yelled "Cut!"—though I'd prearranged with the operator to keep going.

"Paul, I think moving things around is really screwing things up, I think maybe you should—" He cut me off and just started to sing. I motioned to him to just keep going. He stopped, started again, and the tears started to come down. It was fucking brilliant.

I know people felt it was very emotional, very moving. But I would have done the whole thing much better in the privacy of my bathroom. I don't mind standing up and singing in front of people, but if you heard me sing, you wouldn't ask me to do it. I was really unhappy with the first takes, and I asked Stuart to try a few more.

"No," he said. "We've got it, let's go."

I practically begged him. "Jesus Christ, please don't do that!"

Finally, we maybe tried it three or four more times under terrible pressure of time; it wasn't getting any better.

I really don't know about that weeping.

STUART ROSENBERG

For a lot of performers, acting is a way of dealing with some sort of severe problem, mastering personal demons. Paul is an exceedingly inhibited person, and painfully shy. When he'd walk away from a spot on the soundstage, it was wet. I've never seen anyone perspire so much. He fights all the time, fights all of his nervous qualities. But a strange thing happens when you fight like that and win. There's an intensity that comes out, even in the throwaway moments, because you're working so hard against the barrier for control.

What makes Paul so terribly interesting as an actor is there is always this desperation to win that battle. Whenever I used to talk with him about what sensation he gets from his auto racing, it was never about the breaking loose, the soaring feeling, freedom, any of that. It's the balance between a machine that is on the edge of being out of control and the mastery in controlling it at its extreme.

GEORGE ROY HILL

The sultry, hip-slinging, brooding American male had always been Paul's persona onscreen. But that wasn't Paul. And when he finally had a chance to shed it, he found such joy.

He started out wanting to play Sundance, not Butch. In fact, he was signed to play Sundance; Steve McQueen was going to play Butch. Paul and John Foreman [Paul's producing partner] came over to my house and started talking about the movie. Later that day, Freddie Fields, Paul's agent, called.

"Gee, you made quite an impression on Paul," he said. "Now, who do we get to play Butch?"

"Paul."

There was a long silence on the other end of the phone.

"You've got it wrong," Freddie said. "You mean Sundance."

"No, I mean Butch."

"Did Paul agree to that?"

"Unless I just had the most fucked-up conversation I ever had, I think he agreed to it."

Paul eventually did agree, but he kept saying how very uncomfortable he was playing "comedy." He thought he'd only be comfortable in Sundance-type roles—the silent, glowering, sexual male who was quick on the trigger. McQueen, who was a much more dour character than Paul, would've been a good Sundance, but he only wanted to play Butch.

Paul was very, very nervous when we started shooting. The very first day, we did the scene where the train was stopped by Paul and Redford's gang, and Paul was supposed to cajole the Wells Fargo agent out of the mail car before they blew up the safe. Paul called out the character's name a couple

PAUL AND STEVE MCQUEEN PLAYING POOL IN THE EARLY 1960S

of times and suddenly—I don't know whether he lost confidence in me or himself or in the script—but Paul was trying to make it funny. I kept telling him he had no responsibility to make it funny, that was up to Bill Goldman, the screenwriter; the screenwriter writes funny situations and if you play it straight, it can strike us as humorous. It's not a joke, (and Paul tells terrible jokes, they're really a put-off), and the minute you try for comedy, you're going to lose it.

Once he saw it in rushes—and saw he actually didn't have to make it funny—Paul seemed relieved. And I was relieved, too, because I wasn't going to have to fight with him during the whole course of the picture (though fighting with Paul is kind of fun, anyway). He never said another word about it and played it beautifully.

During the whole shooting, I kept trying to keep the laughs out of it. When we had our first preview in San Francisco, I was actually very upset because the audience laughed so hard. I guess I had done a kind of con job on myself.

LINDA FOREMAN, ACTRESS, AND WIFE
OF PAUL'S BUSINESS PARTNER AT NEWMAN-FOREMAN,
JOHN FOREMAN.

John, Paul, Joanne, and I went to see a rough cut of *Butch Cassidy* at Fox. Paul made popcorn, brought some beer, and we all marched into the screening room. George Hill is already there, as are the producers, Dick Zanuck and David Brown.

We're sitting there, hooting, laughing, and popping the tops off beer bottles. At the end of the picture, we turn around and everyone else is gone. John runs down the hallway to find them; they were angry, and one of them says, "When there is a screening, I come to work, I don't come to hear people eat popcorn, laugh, and drink beer."

Well, the next day, Joanne calls Dick Zanuck, who immediately picks up the phone because it's Joanne Woodward. "When my husband and John Foreman make a film," she says, "they can come to a screening and do whatever they want. And if you don't like it, you can go fuck yourself."

Paul thought that was just terrific.

STEWART STERN AND
GEORGE ROY HILL

ss: In *Butch,* when you first see Paul on the bicycle saying, "You're mine, you're mine, you're mine"—was that in the script?

GRH: It was in the script, and I remember it very well because that's my voice.

ss: It is?

GRH: Yeah, Paul couldn't do it. "You're mine!" You needed the vibrato in it. Finally we were in dubbing and he said, "Look, I can't do that—I can't do it. Why don't you do it?"

JOHN FOREMAN

Every director Paul had worked with turned down *Butch Cassidy:* Marty Ritt, Stuart Rosenberg, Bobby Wise—everyone. I was desperate. I suggested George Roy Hill, who hadn't gotten another job since he made *Thoroughly Modern Millie* with Julie Andrews a couple years before.

Paul, at first, turned down George; he said George had once treated Joanne badly, firing her off some Kraft cheese TV program two decades ago. Paul had hated him ever since. I told Paul we had to go see him anyway, that I didn't know who else to get.

So it is arranged. We're in New York and we go to George Roy Hill's house in the snow. No taxis anywhere. (This is as compared to a George Roy Hill coming to see the star.) We get there, pick the snow off our coats, and before those coats are even hung up, Paul says to George, "Well, how do you see this picture?"

"It's a love affair between two men," he replies. And Paul and George fall into each other's arms and have loved each other ever since.

Incidentally, 20th Century–Fox, in the person of Dick Zanuck—who now lists *Butch Cassidy and the Sundance Kid* as one of his credits—wanted Warren Beatty to play opposite Paul. Beatty said he wouldn't meet with George Roy Hill until he received a firm offer for the role. And George said he would not meet with Warren Beatty if there *was* a firm offer. No meeting ever occurred.

PAUL ADJUSTS HIS BROTHER ARTHUR'S WIG ON THE SET
OF *THE OUTRAGE* IN 1963

GEORGE ROY HILL

Redford always hated to talk through a scene before shooting. His eyes would roll back in his head, because Paul wanted to discuss everything. Redford's there saying, "Can we do it? Can we just do it?" while Paul's going, "Wait a minute—I've got to get this straight." Then what Paul would do with the scene would have no relationship to what we'd been talking about for the last half hour.

I likened Paul to a Chinese puzzle, the type where there's that one last piece you had to slip in somewhere in its own mysterious way. I'd just keep talking in the hopes that something would come out of my mouth that he could latch on to. And then he would suddenly say, "Ahh, that's right! That's what I mean," and he'd go play the scene. Of course, there was no connection between what I said and what he did. But it was as if the last piece of the Chinese puzzle just somehow slid into place.

JOHN FOREMAN

I remember Joanne once saying to me: "When you're trying to imagine what's in Paul's head—if you think he's thinking something, he's not always thinking something."

GEORGE ROY HILL

I think there was an opportunity for Redford and Paul to form a close relationship, but it never came about. They did friendly things together, but there's a quality of reserve in both men that has them basically uncomfortable with each other, except in a work situation where they obviously get along very well. They respect each other enormously.

One of the things that irritated Paul about Bob was his being late. Years later, in fact, when we were making *The Sting*, Paul and I sat down with Bob and told him his being late to the set was upsetting all of us. He was on time from that point onwards.

As far as I'm concerned, punctuality is the courtesy of kings.

Back when we were filming *Cat on a Hot Tin Roof*, Elizabeth Taylor was half an hour late to the set; I got terrified that her behavior was going to lead the picture—and my whole career—out the window. As we were sitting there waiting for her, I looked at my watch and announced, "I'll be back in half an hour." So I left and it's really the most important thing I did on that movie—I had plucked up courage enough in a protest of conscience to show that what Liz had done was not professional. You don't, because you're a star, keep people just sitting around a table waiting for you to show up. It was like Iraq—you don't come in and invade a country without having to pay some kind of penalty.

One of the prerequisites for anybody who is going to be friendly with me is that they always have to be dependable.

Redford and I decided we were really going to get some time

together. We'd do some fishing, really talk about ourselves, the movie business, whatever. We went out on Bob's houseboat on Lake Powell, south of Provo, and started exploring.

Now, Powell is a pretty lake with thousands of miles of beautiful coastline and all these endless canyons that branch off the periphery of the lake. We anchored at one of these out-of-the-way coves and then set out in the Boston Whaler we had tethered to catch some dinner. The plan was to hook the fish, cook the fish, have some corn on the cob and beefsteak tomatoes, sit around over a six-pack and shoot the shit.

Well, the fact is we didn't catch much of anything. We had to sail over to the commissary, buy some fish to cook from them—which was pretty funny. Still, dusk was happening, the sun was starting to set, and it would be just perfect for us. But as we approached the cove where Bob's houseboat was anchored, we started to hear music. And as we approached, we saw there was another houseboat anchored right next to ours; it was blasting "Raindrops Keep Falling on My Head" from outdoor speakers, just blaring across this idyllic spot. We could see these four or five beatific faces leaning over the gunnel, smiling, just ready to party. They were ready to sing songs for us, bring us comfort and solace, keep the music going until midnight. These people didn't get it. If we wanted company, we would have docked in the marina.

Redford and I just looked at each other. We thought maybe if we just acted rude or disinterested, they'd simply go away. Well, they didn't. So we had to lift anchor, tie the Whaler back onto the houseboat, and find someplace to hide. We stopped at another cove about forty-five minutes later.

By that time, both Bob and I were in foul moods.

ROBERT ALTMAN

I invited Paul to lunch in Westwood. I sent down and got a six-pack of beer, two-hundred-dollar tins of beluga caviar, a can opener, and a spoon, and I said, "Here's your lunch." He said, "Altman, I don't understand your movie at all but you've sure got class. Let's do it."

Quintet was a fairy tale. What it required was Paul's persona, so the audience could imbue it with its attitudes. And Paul embraced that. He didn't say, "Well, I'd better have a piece of gum to chew" or "I should have a funnier line." He just played that straight cipher and accepted everything I asked of him.

Newman never asked questions that I had to answer. He asked questions that I couldn't answer. He perfectly accepted my nonanswer. I'd say, "I don't know," and he knew I had given him all the information I had. I think Paul believed me, that's all. Some actors are a pain in the ass to work with. They say, "What are you directing the picture for? Aren't you supposed to know?" Paul never did that.

There's an approach to this kind of collaborative art, and Paul—generously and with anticipation—fit right into it. He just gave himself to it completely.

Unfortunately, the picture didn't work—I don't think it would have worked under any circumstances. It's a very specialized film. A mass audience is not going to sit through it. Princess Grace said to the board at Fox, "How dare you allow my good friend and wonderful actor Paul Newman to be in such an atrocious Robert Altman film?" And Allan Ladd Jr., who had heard a lot of complaints about the film, just jumped up and said "Oh, fuck you," and walked out.

I really liked that film.

Sometimes you don't know who to root for when you're reading a screenplay. In *The Color of Money* maybe the actual progression of the people from point A to B isn't that strong, but I'll tell you these are pretty interesting people, and they use language and images in a different way than I've seen before. That's the hook. That's what's going to keep people interested. So fuck the plot. You hope the audience won't be concerned about what's going to happen they'll be so fascinated by the how of it. That's why *The Glass Menagerie* works, because the emotion of it works, not the story, not the logic, not the people going from one point to another.

As an actor, *The Verdict*, of course was one of the best for me. I never had to ask myself to do anything in that picture, never had to call upon any reserves. It was always right there. I never prepared for anything, never had to go off in a corner, it was there immediately. It was wonderful.

It's just been a slow evolution. I started out as an emotional republican, and now I've turned into someone who's always amazed at how available the emotion is. I have to sit on it more than I have to really work to get at it. It's like an open sore now.

———

TOM CRUISE PLAYED NEWMAN'S BRASH PROTÉGÉ
IN *THE COLOR OF MONEY*.

The Verdict. I've never seen him work the way he did in *The Verdict.* The low-angle shot on the phone when he'd lost a witness, the vulnerability and the fear, and the trying to control it was so rich.

———

STEWART STERN

The Verdict was absolutely his essence. When he's working on a scene or even just reading around the coffee table and starts feeling his way into a role and I see one experience after another crowding themselves into his eyes, I don't know how he does it. I don't know how any actor does it, when it really happens that far inside.

ROBERT ALTMAN

I like the exposure that he gave of himself in *The Verdict*. That's what I liked. As an actor, when he does that certain thing, he's very, very good. When he opens up, when he shows you his pink places, that's when you can say, "There's a real soul, a real flesh-and-blood somebody throbbing in there."

XI

In 1969 Paul Newman appeared in a film called *Winning* with Joanne Woodward and Robert Wagner. It would ignite a serious passion for auto racing that would last the rest of his life. He became an accomplished driver who won his final race at Lime Rock Park in September of 2007.

I think the IRS has audited me every year since 1972, and the biggest bone of contention has to do with my automobile racing and whether it is a vocation or an avocation. My longtime lawyer, Irving Axelrod (also known as Irving the Ax), had to go down to the IRS on many occasions to argue the case, that it was anything but an avocation for me.

"You don't understand the psychology of racing," Irving told them. "Mr. Newman's career had hit the skids. He was a down-and-outer. And it was determined by his battlefield management plan organization that he needed to improve his image. At which point it was decided, in concert with his management crew, that Mr. Newman should take up auto racing and become one of those macho guys that get behind the wheel and risk their lives. So he did it and it worked.

"Mr. Newman is now on the front page of many newspapers. He has become known as a racer and won four national championships. He was this elderly fellow in a young man's sport—and got a lot of mileage out of that."

But this still did not convince the IRS that it was an accurate portrayal. So Irving added one other key piece of evidence.

"You know those big seat belts they use in race cars? Those are actually to keep Mr. Newman from leaving the car, no matter what. Even if he wants to desperately claw his way out, the reason they strap him in is so he can't escape." And I guess to some extent they finally bought it.

―――――

JIM "FITZY" FITZGERALD WAS A CHAMPION AUTO RACER AND MEMBER OF THE NEWMAN-SHARP RACING TEAM.

I met Paul in 1972 at Road Atlanta. Paul was going to race in a Datsun 510, and I was asked to show him the track. I took him around in a Nissan 240B and we went around and around. He couldn't get enough. "Show me more," he kept saying. "Do it again!" And when we were done he says to me, "Do you have a cooler?"

"Oddly enough, yeah."

"Well, if you have the cooler, I have the beer."

We ended up at the Holiday Inn across from the track, with connecting rooms, and stayed for ten days. We'd come back from the track, open the beers, make some popcorn, and collect some newspapers to keep the smell from getting out from under the door. Finally, Paul said he'd just have to call it a night so he could do some script study.

But wouldn't you know it, it wasn't long before I'd hear a scratching noise on my door. It would be Paul.

"Screw the script study. Let's get on with it!"

So that sort of started the development of our friendship.

The night before one of our races at the Mid-Ohio track, Paul and I had a couple of beers, ate dinner, and went strolling afterwards around our motel. You could tell what kind of mood he was in, because he wanted to walk arm in arm. "You're a pretty lucky guy," Paul said to me. "Everybody likes you."

"Well, I'm not sure about everybody, but I do get along with folks."

"There are people who wouldn't mind putting a spear right through me," Paul said. "Most people don't like me."

I told him he was full of shit, but he wouldn't take it any further. I thought to myself: Is this why Paul isn't more outgoing? Is this why I never see him let anyone get really close to him? We all go through depressive cycles, I know, thinking the world doesn't like us, but I wondered, Jesus! Does Paul really feel this way?

I would very often stay at his house in Westport, and spent a lot of time there with his family. I'd kid him about Joanne, about what a lucky mucker he really was.

"She's not perfect all the time. We've had our problems. It hasn't all been a bed of roses."

Again, that's as far as Paul wanted to go.

———

Since the time I was a kid, getting a straight story has been difficult for me, and it keeps getting increasingly difficult. I've been suspicious all my life.

My team was at the 1986 SCCA runoffs in Atlanta, and I think I qualified over Fitzy by over a second, and I had a twelve- or thirteen-second lead over him for the championship. But coming out of the seven turn, my car just lugged. I started to lose second gear and I couldn't get it to hold. Fitzy kept eating my lead. We came out of the five, and he was right on my tail and stayed there, but he didn't go around me. I knew he had me, but he didn't pass. Coming down the straightaway, I realized and said to myself: "That fucker has instructions."

If someone had just said, "Hey, Paul, don't worry about the win. Fitzy won't beat you no matter what happens as long as your car's still running." Then I would have said okay, fine. I paid for the team. Since I had unqualified Fitzy and outrun him, and this was simply a gear-box failure, I would have said, "Well, I'll take this. I won't like it very much, but I understand."

═══

JIM FITZGERALD

There weren't instructions. But the understanding on our team is that Paul is our flagship.

═══

Afterwards, some of my folks denied what happened, waffled, and actually told me, "Well, you could have just pulled ahead." But I said, "No, I couldn't even shift the fucking car."

Fitzy was a top driver, the winningest in SCCA history, a member of my racing team, and one of my dearest friends. And while no one pays much attention to superstition these days, it's worth noting that the night before his death, Fitzy ordered a glass of sambuca to go with his after-dinner coffee. When it came to the table, there were four coffee beans floating on top. Problem is, it's supposed to be bad luck to drink sambuca that contains an even number of coffee beans. It's like walking under a ladder.

We were in St. Petersburg in 1987 for the final Trans Am SCCA race of the season. At sixty-five, Fitzy was the oldest racer on the circuit. His mood, the next day, at the time of the race, was festive.

I saw the wreck. It happened on the third lap. He'd backed into a wall. There wasn't any fire, there wasn't even the kind of damage that would give a driver a bad headache. He should've been able to get out of the car and walk away. So when one of the crew came over to the pit and told us Fitzy was hurt, that an ambulance was coming, and that we should all get over to the wreck, I had no idea what was going on.

One of our team said to me, "I'm not sure he wasn't hurt before he hit the wall, because his head seemed down."

"What do you mean?"

"When I saw him come around that last turn, his head was slumping forward." Another crew member told me Fitzy wasn't moving and it wasn't looking good. He wasn't alive by the time he reached the hospital.

All that I could figure was that Fitzy must have had a stroke in the instant he came around that last turn. At that point, he became just a passenger in an automobile. Since his body would have already been limp when he hit the wall, he offered no resistance to the crash and broke his neck.

The race, of course, had stopped. There was much discussion about what to do, particularly among my crew. All the drivers sat in their cars waiting for a decision, myself included. When the officials decided to restart, our crew wanted to pull our car off the track.

"I don't think that's what Fitzy would have wanted," I told them. "He'd want me to finish this race."

You feel a lot of things at a time like that, including mad and angry. You can actually drive very well when you're angry, as long as you don't make any mistakes. But when all the racers got ready to get going again, I couldn't fire up my car. I must have done something stupid, left one fuel pump on when I thought I'd turned everything off, and one of the cylinders must have flooded with gasoline.

The ignominy of not being able to start the car! We tried to give it a push, but it just locked up completely. To the crowd, it must have looked as though I was putting on some kind of act.

Fitzy represented to me all that's best about racing. He had a fierceness of attack in an automobile that I envied, and he offered the kind of camaraderie that racing should be about. It's not just all engine and speed, it's not a business for me, not a career. It takes me away from people in film, takes me outside that fictional experience into something real and quite primitive. And it speaks to whatever competitive feeling I have that I can't afford as an actor.

Fitzy was the best of all because he broke through my fastidious reserve. He laughed a lot, had a sense of humor and was very open and outgoing. He was the fun side of racing, and we were buddies well met.

When I won the President's Cup, the highest award SCCA awards to its drivers, I had two important races pretty much back-to-back. In the first one, I started out conservatively, was involved in a shoving accident that I probably bore a lot of responsibility for. Well, it was not a great race. I finished third. I was disgusted with my performance.

But in the next one, I just took off. I was clicking a second a lap on everyone, and no one could catch me. I won by an incredible margin. It was a great race. The trouble is that if you're a racer, you can't just have one great race. That's what separates the great racers from the amateurs. Mario Andretti, who later raced for my team, doesn't have bad races. He may have races where the car doesn't work or a tire goes bad, but there's no such thing when he'll say, "Oh god, I drove badly." The great driver's excellence is always there, can be tapped each and every day. Someone like me has had some pretty good days but also some desperately bad ones.

It's never a matter of getting pissed off or not being cool. The best races that I drive, that a lot of racers drive, are the ones where you spin out early, you lose your position, and you have to go back and meticulously knock the other guys off, one by one. There's nothing to lose at that point, nothing at stake, nothing to protect. It all becomes a lark. Your mind is freed, your muscles are loose. You just don't give a shit.

I should say that I own the best racing team there is in the U.S. Mario is the most prestigious, revered, and legendary of all racers. But while I always thought it would be satisfying to replace driving with owning a team, well, it's just not the same as being in the car yourself.

———

ROBERT WAGNER

During the filming of *Winning,* Paul and I lived together at the Indianapolis Athletic Club. We were learning race-car driving together; he loved it, you couldn't keep him out of a car. He'd be driving on the track all day.

Me, I couldn't wait to get out of those cars. I was scared, really frightened, by the goddamn things. I was glad to do it for the film, but wanted no further involvement, ever. Paul was really feeling something, getting something out of it. I thought, "Here's a man whose livelihood is himself and he's putting that at such great risk." He's out there—and he kept pushing it a little bit more each day. I don't know whether it was some sort of leveler for him, a way of dealing with thoughts of death that he never talked about. For these racing guys, it's always "the car" or "the element" or "the fuel" or "the mistake"—they never mention death. Yet in a split second, by someone else's error, a mechanical failure, nothing you have any control over, it can happen.

It seemed like a fucking ridiculous thing to do, but if you said "Don't drive" to Paul, he would have just done more of it. He didn't race because it made him more of a man; it was really just the speed, the risk, and all that. He was able to feel it—and I never got it.

———

I got into one of our stock cars for some practice laps just as it was starting to rain. As I'm going around, it started to rain harder,

PAUL AND JOANNE IN AN UNDATED PHOTO

and I was sort of not paying attention, and I wasn't easing up the way I always do coming out of a turn. Suddenly I realized, "Boy, it's really coming down now, isn't it?" And as I go into the next turn, I go "Oops!" because the car doesn't do a thing. It doesn't shift direction at all when I steer, not a degree! Next thing I know, I'm looking at a fence. I busted a couple of ribs.

There's a wonderful expression on the track: "What's the most frightening sound a driver can hear when he's racing a car? The sound of his own voice as he says "Oh, shit!"

GEORGE ROY HILL

Paul tries to give himself challenges. He wants to be alive, and the only way to stay alive is by defying death—literally in terms of the racing and figuratively in terms of his profession.

JAMES GOLDSTONE WAS HIRED BY UNIVERSAL IN 1968
TO DIRECT *WINNING*, ABOUT TWO RIVAL INDY 500 DRIVERS;
HE LATER DIRECTED PAUL IN *WHEN TIME RAN OUT . . . ,*
A BIG-BUDGET DISASTER FILM.

When I was filming the racing shots for *Winning,* I'd put fourteen to eighteen cars on the track along with Paul. All the moves we wanted to do would be laid out in advance, and I would signal Paul with flags—one flag might mean pass the guy on the right, a different flag would mean pass the guy on the left, and so on. It was all well choreographed, but with the exception of a couple of responsible adults, we were working with ding-a-ling kids who drove their cars very fast. And Paul was falling in love with going fast and the personal challenge of coming out ahead.

I needed to get a series of shots of all the cars passing Paul for one segment of the race, so we started with Paul in the first position and all the kids behind him. By the time I got my footage from the camera car, Paul was where the script said he was supposed to be—in last place. So I put up a green flag indicating the shot was done, and Paul immediately put his foot into it. These kids were driving with a big star, and it had been impressed upon them, "We can't kill him—he's an amateur and you're pros."

But Paul kept going faster, passing each one of those cars, and our safety guy is yelling at me, "I'm gonna put on the light to get them off the track—everyone's driving too fast." Paul obeyed the stoplight and rolled into the pits in second position—he'd passed fourteen drivers. He had this wonderful sheepish grin on his face. He knew he wasn't supposed to have done it, but he felt good—just like a little kid.

Maybe he was proving that it wasn't how much you got paid or whether you got an Academy Award, but was about who was in control and who has balls.

And now I will reveal a secret to the world.

After I was finished with the picture and was putting it together, I needed a couple of inserts to go into a montage just of Paul's eyes inside his racing goggles. Though I had very good close-ups of Paul driving at 120 miles per hour, I just had to get forty more seconds of the bridge of his nose and the eyes.

The problem was, Paul couldn't get out to LA from Connecticut right away. But I had an idea—why not use Paul's brother, Arthur, who was working as our production manager, for the shot? I'd gotten to know Arthur well during the shoot. I had him come over to my office and we put Paul's goggles on him. "Yeah, I think we can get away with that; we don't have to wait for Paul."

So we shot his eyes, and they get maybe three cuts in the final sequence. But those are Arthur Newman's eyes in *Winning*, not Paul Newman's famous blue eyes. The brothers don't really look alike, but they have the same eyes. We pulled it off.

MICHAEL BROCKMAN

Before I started acting class, Newman said to me, "You want to do something? Go prepare a scene for me." So I get a copy of *Sweet Bird of Youth,* and practice the monologue where Paul's character talks about his youth.

Not long afterwards, we were packing up after an event at the Orange County International track, when Paul asks me to jump in a race car and he just shoots down the straightaway. We jump out and Paul says, "Do the scene." So, stiff as a board, I deliver the monologue at the end of the Orange County straightaway.

Paul laughs and says, "Too much Beethoven, and not enough Stravinsky." I knew Beethoven, but not the other guy, so Paul went on. "You're all in one key—get some life in it. Do it how you feel. Just be you. Like this!"

And wham, he knocks off fifteen lines of the monologue. He hadn't done it for twenty years. It was incredible, so real, so believable. And then he stopped and said, "Or, you could try it this way." And wham, he does a hundred-and-eighty-degree different approach. Then he does three more versions. All standing at the end of this drag strip. I couldn't believe it, and it still gives me chills thinking about it. It's the kind of friend he's been to me.

JOHN FOREMAN

Elizabeth Taylor and Richard Burton were the first two actors to get a million dollars a picture. I was always proud Paul was the third. That's what I got him for *Winning*.

I was up at the Portland International Speedway when I got a call from John Huston. He had recently directed me in *The Life and Times of Judge Roy Bean,* one of my happiest movie experiences. He was one of maybe half a dozen people I've known with whom I wish I'd been more comfortable; I regret it. I could always share things with him in a creative sense, but I wasn't loose enough or natural enough to be fun for him socially; we'd run out of things to say.

Anyway, I answer the phone in my Portland hotel room, and I'm thrilled to hear John's voice.

"You're racing this weekend? I'm going to come and see you!"

"That'll be wonderful, John, but it's a pretty long trip up here."

"Where are you?" he asked.

"Well, you dialed, don't you know?"

"My girl did that," he replied. "Now, where are you?"

I told him, and he quickly responded, "I'll be right there."

And he hopped on a plane in LA and flew up from California.

John arrived on a Saturday, when I was driving this big Datsun, one with over nine hundred horsepower. He was awestruck by the cars.

He ended up not staying for all of Sunday to see the race itself.

"Take care of yourself, kid," he said. With that, he got on his plane and left.

———

When Huston invited Joanne and me to stay with him at his manor in Ireland, Clarens House, as we were starting production on *The Mackintosh Man,* I politely declined; we ended up at a little hotel in town that was closer to the set. To be honest, though, I don't like to stay in people's homes, and neither does Joanne.

I don't know how I talked Huston into directing that terrible movie, *The Mackintosh Man;* I guess I was feeling my oats and I thought it would be fun to play an Australian; unfortunately, the story wasn't very good, and Huston never was comfortable with the script. But filming *Judge Roy Bean* with him the year before, in 1972, that was simply special. It was completely original. He let us discover things in rehearsal; he had great faith in the actors. There was a sense of real appeal for me, a different aroma around it, beyond description. An atmosphere. What was the essence of John Huston? When he directed *Roy Bean,* he'd have his director's chair stuck out in the desert, about a hundred yards from where everybody else was. After he rehearsed the actors, he'd take out one of his cigars, light it, and just sit out there and mull. I always laughed and said I was certain that the seat of John Huston's inspiration was in his cigar.

I don't think Huston ever thought of me as a great actor, but as a good actor; there was such patience. I was actually tongue-tied around him, maybe because he had such a strong aura of expectancy. He was mystical, magical, something undefinable.

We'd put together a great company for *Judge Roy Bean,* lots of interesting people on the set and others who would fly in from LA just to visit John. Each afternoon, about a dozen people might be sitting in John's trailer for lunch, and all of a sudden a lion, unleashed, would stroll in and stretch out across the width of this mobile home. The lion was apparently there to keep the bear company.

Because, of course, we also had a massive bear on the set; it was the same bear that had been on TV playing Gentle Ben. In the film, she dies saving Roy Bean's life, and I cradle her lifeless body. Before that shot, I'd done something stupid. We were shooting a scene where I was supposed to be angry at the bear—and I belted him three or four times. It just happened, really—one of those unconscious moments; it had nothing to do with having guts. The trainer was standing just off camera and he was without voice, speechless. Apparently, the bear's backhand is very real and pulverizing, like a six-hundred-pound heavyweight boxer's. They are so fast, and I'm very lucky.

People have also asked me about the scene where the bad guys get rid of the young Roy Bean by tying him with a rope to a horse, shooing the horse to a run, and then shooting at Roy's dragged body.

I wanted to do the stunt myself. Huston and the production crew were both very uncomfortable with me doing it, especially with blanks being fired at the horses—you never really know what they're going to do. But I insisted.

I actually wasn't even in a harness or on a platform. Instead, I was placed on a soft-leather skimboard and was dragged over the rocky terrain by the camera truck. I just raked the ground.

JOHN FOREMAN

I got a call one day from Paul Kohner, John Huston's agent, saying John wanted to come see me. How can I say no? Huston, years before, had moved heaven and earth for Paul to do *The Night of the Iguana;* Paul turned it down; he just didn't want to do that part.

Anyway, the door opens at our production office at Universal, John walks in and drops John Milius's script for *Roy Bean* on my desk. "I love this," he says, "and I want to do this movie."

"I'll talk to Paul."

"Where is he?"

"In Connecticut."

"Good. I'll go see him there."

I call Paul and he immediately lists all the John Huston movies he didn't like. "I don't know if he'd be right for something like this."

"He's coming to see you, Paul."

"Don't you dare tell him to!"

As soon as I hang up, I call Huston and give him Paul's address. When Huston heads east, I phone Paul again and say, "Gird your loins, Huston is on his way."

"I won't be at home. I'm going to lock the gate."

My phone rings that evening. Huston has been in Westport for four hours and he owns Paul's soul; he "got" him, the essential Paul Newman, the real, real, real, honorable, caring Paul.

The last night of filming was two days before Christmas. We were outside of Tucson and it had snowed, so we already lost a day and were really pressed for time. John Huston decided as part of the final scene, the whole frontier town should burn down. My feeling was that if John Huston wanted to burn down the set, we burn the town!

John had an awful cold when he came out to the set that evening. This was the big shot, one chance only, with everybody pursuing everybody through the flames, with Judge Roy on his horse.

And during the shot, John Huston passed out sitting in the director's chair.

With the cleanest, best communication I ever had with Paul, there was an instant recognition of what was required—Paul went ahead and directed the rest of the scene. No one knew. He did it with the old man passed out, and when the moment came to say "Cut!" John lifted his head up and yelled "Cut!"

We carried him back to his trailer and called an ambulance. When he emerged to head to the hospital, the entire company serenaded him as he was driven away.

Judge Roy Bean never fully caught the public's fancy, but it still made a profit. It wasn't *Butch Cassidy,* which is what Paul would have liked to be in—*Butch Cassidy I, II, III, IV, V,* and so on.

Paul really liked the Roy Bean character, and I think he really liked John's appreciation for his performance. There's something about John that makes you know that if he expresses appreciation, it is a valuable gift.

JOHN HUSTON

The last night on *Roy Bean* was one of my first real contests with emphysema. I'd had a coughing thing that went on and on; I had pneumonia. I was sick. I drank to keep even with it. I didn't get drunk, but that was the only way I could keep going all that night, that night that it just suddenly hit. It was a bad time.

Paul, of course, is incomparable. I find no flaw, no fault in him, as an actor or as a man. He's a moral and ethical man, superb in every way; I so admire the way he has lived his life.

This is a business where others of his accomplishments cover themselves with the honey of self-importance, as though they'd just come back from the hive. Not Paul. He's never dramatized himself the way others in his league have done. Marlon, whom I admire tremendously, does dramatize himself, perhaps consciously. Paul and Jack Nicholson live on the same street, but they have different addresses.

After we'd finished the film, Huston asked me if I would accept an award on his behalf in New York. So I wrote this little thing, and I was very moved standing in for him; I got terribly choked up as I delivered it.

Somebody apparently recorded it and sent it to Huston. I got a call from him. "I don't know whether I'm more touched by the sound of my own voice," he said, "or by the richness of my writing." I felt it was from the bottom of his heart.

GEORGE ROY HILL

At first, I didn't offer *The Sting* to Paul; I didn't think the part was big enough for him. Paul's role as Henry was quite different when originally written by David Ward. We added a lot and changed it from Henry's being a real slob into a very slick dandy.

The famous card game with Bob Shaw was really just Paul doing things I had seen him do—all I did was remind him and he fell right into it. I think it is one of the best scenes ever done by an actor, anywhere. Paul was gleeful—he'd never had a chance to play that sort of part before, to play his own humor.

WARREN COWAN

I think Paul loved doing *The Sting* even though he worked less in it than in almost any other film he's ever done.

GEORGE ROY HILL

We did have a problem with facial hair. When Paul first tried on the mustache for his character in *The Sting,* he was not happy.

"Look at this ridiculous thing!" he said.

"I love it, Paul. I want it."

I was going for a very 1920s look, so we also had him part his hair down the middle—Paul had a hell of a time getting used to that. But he did it. And when I told him again he looked great, his answer was a quiet, "Okay, fine."

He kept saying he thought he looked like that actor from the silent pictures and early talkies, the one with the trademark mustache with each end set into a little curl—Edmund Lowe.

One of the great things about working with Paul is that after a take, you can always say "That's terrible" to him. He'll just shrug and laugh—believe me, you can't do that with every actor. But Paul has a carapace of indifference, which may be just that—a way of shielding his inner self. But it works with him, and it is a nice relationship to have with an actor.

I don't actually remember Paul ever working with the writers while filming. If he had an issue, he would come to me. I prefer to have the writers on the set every day because there are constant little things that I want their opinions on.

About halfway through our rehearsals, I had a fight with David Ward, who wrote *The Sting* (and won an Oscar for Best Original Screenplay); I asked for some changes, and he didn't give them to me. So I made them myself, and David was very upset. He was also upset about how I was directing the picture—he had envisioned a much more serious film than I was making. I wanted the feel of a period film—using a double image to introduce the characters, turning over a page onscreen to announce new segments. That made David more upset. After the first two days of shooting, the Writers Guild went on strike, and fortunately David couldn't show up anymore.

Ultimately, when the movie was released, David was approached by the press; he was gracious and said the result came out far better than if he had directed the film himself.

The next picture I made with George Hill was *Slap Shot;* it was absolutely magical, totally original, a subject that had never been touched before—hockey, which I loved as a kid. Getting it made, not surprisingly, was an adventure in and of itself.

A couple of years after *The Sting* hit, George sent me a script and called to say, "Read it quickly. We have a preproduction that we have to start on right away—this picture has to go like a rocket." The biggest issue was our having an actual hockey team as extras and more; it was essential to the film—we had to catch players out of their season, same with getting the use of some pro hockey rinks for sets.

I read the script right away, and, to everyone's surprise, I said yes—I loved that it was foulmouthed and profane. It was really a new way of attacking an athlete's story—and the side characters, mainly the gang of hockey players, were written wonderfully.

My lawyer, Irving Axelrod, called me about it a week later, saying that he still had not finalized a deal for me. "These guys at Universal are such jerks," he said. "They're putting roadblocks in the way of everything. I think we're at an impasse."

"How can that be?"

"Don't worry, it's just them blustering. We'll settle after the weekend."

A couple of days later, one of George's daughters comes by our house to go horseback riding with Nell. When she's leaving, I tell her, "Say hello to your father for me."

"I can't right now," she replies. "He went down to Palm Springs."

"Well, say hello tomorrow when he comes back."

"I don't think he's coming back."

"What do you mean? We've got to go to work; we're really up against a deadline here."

"Oh, well," she said, "that's off. He got fed up with the *Slap Shot* negotiations. That's why he went down to Palm Springs—so he could just get drunk and excise himself from the project. From his system."

I immediately got in touch with George's assistant, and she wouldn't tell me where he was. He'll call in, she tried to assure me.

"Well, I have a feeling he won't."

I tried back at his office at four p.m. the next day, and—still no contact.

"What's his license plate?" I asked her.

"Oh, I can't tell you that."

So I called the garage at Universal. "Paul Newman here. I have to go down and pick up George Hill's car. I know it's a four-door maroon Mercedes, but I don't remember his plate number and I don't want to make a mistake." The garage attendant politely obliged.

I then called Robert Wagner, who lived down in Palm Springs, and asked him to get me the name of a good private detective. He rang me back a few hours later saying he couldn't find anyone who was trustworthy.

"Hey, this has nothing to do with a woman or some corruption scandal," I told him. "There's just been a little misunderstanding and I've got to find this guy."

Wagner called me again to say he found a PI who used to work in corporate surveillance, Westinghouse or something, and had also once been a detective on the local force. I scheduled a call for eight o'clock that night.

"George is not the kind of guy who'd stay in the center of town," I told the private eye. "And he's very cheap, so he wouldn't be in an expensive place, either—figure something moderately priced on the outskirts." With a thousand hotels and motels in Palm Springs, I figured this could take two days.

The detective called me back at nine that evening. "I got the car," he said.

Next morning, five a.m., I drove down to Palm Springs in my Porsche. I hit the hotel an hour and four minutes later, saw the Mercedes, stormed into the manager's office, and demanded, "What room is George Hill in?" He was so rattled, he told me I just needed to cut across the patio and he'd be right there, in room 12.

Just as I get outside, I see the curtains pull open in room 12, and there's George, his back to me, stretching, with a bottle of Scotch on his table. I tapped on the window, he turned around, opened his patio door, and said to me, "Get out of here."

He'd had it with everyone; they'd all taken a big piece of his pie. "Shit, what am I in this for? There'll be nothing left for you or for me."

The problem was that though George was actually producing *Slap Shot,* there were two additional guys who were also "producers" on the film and had nothing to do with it other than having fronted the option money and gearing up to go to the premieres. They were just on the gravy train. Maybe that's unfair, because without them *Slap Shot* would probably never have gotten done. But we were both still pretty unhappy with the state of play.

George and I went outside, sat on a curbstone, drank some Budweisers, and settled our own deal in no time. "George, what do you want?" I asked him. "I'll split everything with you."

"Look, I'm not in it to screw you out of anything," I went on. "But I'm going to make sure that Universal doesn't get out there and suck on my bones, either." We'd make sure that we could create the overall package for the movie; we wouldn't need anyone else to put it together for us and take another 10 percent from George's share and off the top of whatever the movie costs to make.

Have I been screwed a lot? Yes. And while I always say the price of not being screwed is eternal vigilance, eternal vigilance is a very time-consuming and detailed business—going through receipts, checking out every little thing. It can actually be less painful to be screwed than to look after things—at least sometimes.

There are some people you meet who you know will never betray you for their own advantage, things are just as they appear to be. There are others who you are 95 percent certain about—that while they won't usually take advantage of you, they would in a pinch. I could never sort some people out in my head and have never been certain of their allegiances. I've never been certain what constitutes

JOANNE AND STEWART STERN

loyalty—it is a very hard thing to find out. You grow aware of the people who are anxious to climb up with you and those who are anxious to climb up *on* you.

Anyway, George and I settled our arrangements, got out of Palm Springs, and had our business guys get right to work on drawing up the contracts.

━━━

GEORGE ROY HILL

Paul has a habit of pulling practical jokes, and the one he pulled in Johnstown, Pennsylvania, when we were filming *Slap Shot*, upset me very, very much. I'm not immune to practical jokes, but this was absolutely insane.

There was a guy on our crew, a focus puller, he was right

there on the camera all the time. I don't know whether Paul knew it or not, but he had a heart condition.

There was a shot where Paul had to drive his car into a space, park there, then walk into a nearby house. About two or three car lengths around the corner from the house was a garage where we were having all our vehicles in the film serviced. Well, Paul drove up to his mark very fast, put on the brakes, then literally slid into his spot. He came over to me and said, "Listen, I'm worried; the brakes on this car just aren't very good."

"Take it easy, Paul, and don't take any chances. We'll just do it a couple more times to see if it is safe."

He agreed, I called "Action!" and Paul came barreling up the road again, faster than before. He went straight through our shot, out of sight and around the corner to where that garage was—when suddenly we heard a tremendous crash. There was dust everywhere, a stray wheel rolled out into the street; I goddamn near died, and our focus puller was so shaken, he began clutching his chest and we had to get him home.

I ran over to investigate and saw and heard our crew members laughing. The whole accident had been a fake, staged. I wanted to fire everyone, including Paul, though I couldn't do the picture without him.

I was furious and resented terribly that the guys would pull a stunt like this—though I realized that Paul, being who he is, likely talked them into it. I was ready to bring in a whole new crew, but Paul pleaded: "You can't do that; I can't be responsible for all these guys losing their jobs. I couldn't take that, it would just undo me."

I finally saw his logic and came around. I told him all right, and the moment I said it, Paul cried. He wiped his eyes and said, "Jesus God, tears yet!" In just a moment, he was trying to make a joke out of the whole thing.

I know they all thought it was hilarious and funny, but I don't see the humor in destroying things, ever. And this caused pain, real pain. Paul finally realized it had been a stupid thing to do.

If I wanted to psychoanalyze practical jokes, you could say they are just hidden, though not really well-hidden, hostilities. You don't put people into bad situations where they get anxiety-filled and shocked, where someone nearly has a heart attack. It's just real anger. When Paul and I talked about it later, I made the point to him that this was really his hostility showing, and he's since told me the incident was a turning point; he hasn't staged a practical joke since then. Of course, it is very difficult to think of Paul as a hostile man in any respect. It's just his humor, and frankly, some of Paul's humor is pretty terrible—usually on the raunchy side, too. He does come up with some very funny things, but as Paul himself says, his humor comes right out of the toilet.

Beginning with *Butch,* Paul finally learned to relax. He didn't have to push anymore and that role really eased him into what he was able to become for the remainder of his career—the easygoing actor he was in the very beginning. He settled down and came into a style of his own. Paul's getting to be like Walter Huston, who didn't do a damn thing onscreen, you never saw him act—he just *was.* Paul has some of that quality now—he couldn't make a false move if he tried.

***

STEWART STERN

One of the engaging things about Paul is his enthusiasm. You know, his discoveries, things he wants you to share. And the lengths he will go to get you to share them: the size of the black olives that have to go into your drink, or some new invention—like the padded wire crown he made to hold his eyeglasses off of his nose in the sauna.

ROBERT ALTMAN

He threw a great party up here at the end of *Buffalo Bill*. Had two hundred lobsters flown in. Had beer, baseball, go-karts, all the things that he likes to play with. We both tend to have the same kind of extroverted, juvenile behavior in groups. Before we started to eat, he had my favorite hat thrown up in the air and they shot holes in it. He took my good Indian doeskin gloves and had them french-fried and served them to me for lunch. I kinda hated losing the gloves, but I didn't mind losing them as much as I enjoyed the affection that went into the joke.

HAROLD WILLENS

Paul and I were driving to our first board meeting with the Center for the Study of Democratic Institutions in his Volkswagen. He had some wonderful music on—he liked to listen to classical music—and he would turn it down and say, "Listen to this, listen to this!" Then turn it up like an excited little boy. At a certain point he poked me and said, "Watch this." We were driving on the freeway, and ahead of us was a massive, powerful Cadillac. "Be sure to catch the guy's expression!" he said, and then he gunned it. I thought we were going to take off and fly! He didn't tell me that his VW had a Porsche engine in it. That's a lasting vision of him, this little boy having fun, roaring with laughter.

MICHAEL BROCKMAN

I remember how late we were to Paul's birthday party at Malibu. Joanne left the go-kart track before we did and she said later that was a mistake, because Paul and Elliot and I were all within a couple of hundredths of a second, trying to beat fast times, so we stayed and stayed while all the party guests were waiting. Paul didn't want to leave until he was the fastest.

XII

It's an interesting challenge, how far you can take the drinking without really self-destructing. In the early 1970s, I think I took it as far as it could go, before realizing I had taken it that far. It was like climbing Mount Everest; at least you can say, "Okay, I've done that—now let's quit and move on to something else."

Alcohol seemed to focus my mind a lot better—when I didn't take it to really extraordinary excess. From reading about Jackson Pollock, it seems he might have been the same way. With people who were otherwise impossible to communicate with, the first four beers would open a window for him—for about twenty minutes. By his seventh beer, he'd really have some profound and interesting things to say about art and about himself. But by then the window would shut and stay shut thereafter.

There was a time when booze unlocked a lot of things I couldn't have done without it. It was the key—but not necessarily the room. It allowed me to explore some things in my head in the privacy of the bathroom or the basement. Things that I otherwise couldn't unleash, and wouldn't have recognized or even seen.

In the early part of my career, when I was doing a lot of television, I'd get a room at the old Emerson Hotel and just lock myself inside with a script. I don't mean I'd go on a four-day drunk. I'd sit there, work on the script, make notes to myself, and around dinnertime I'd have a beer. And then I'd have two more beers, then five beers—though all the time I'd be cutting, editing, and making notes to myself.

Next morning, I'd wake up and 95 percent of the notes I'd made were terrible, I crossed them out so no one could ever see them. They were just alcoholic garbage. But five percent were physicalizations, mannerisms, pieces of stage business that could be interesting—and they all seemed too eccentric for me to have thought of in a normal state.

Gore Vidal always justified his attachment to alcohol on that basis: creative benefits. And I know there are certain break-throughs that I was able to accomplish in my head that I could later use onstage. For someone as controlled as I am, to experience the delight, the luxury, of being out of control, not to have an inkling of what's around the next corner and to keep yourself constantly at risk, is simply pleasurable.

There are terrible, bad things that happen with booze, dangerous things. I marvel that I survived them.

TOM CRUISE

Paul constantly hurts himself. He'll torture himself by drink-ing a case of beer, then sit in the sauna for hours. He laughs about it—what alcohol does to your body and what a sauna does to your body is like constantly pulling yourself from one extreme to the next.

He's a volatile man, and yet he really keeps himself in check, really controls himself. He seems to handle his pain in a certain way and is not as self-destructive as he used to be. He has always reached for stabilizing forces in his life: choosing to be an actor, Joanne, sticking with those things.

ROBERT WEBBER

Paul told me his drinking was like his character Brick's drinking in *Cat on a Hot Tin Roof.* He'd be drinking a certain amount, then suddenly, *click*, you'd turn off and couldn't remember anymore.

To black out and keep functioning is fascinating. My best friend was a Catholic who didn't live up to the strictures of the church. So he'd go out, black out, do whatever he wanted, and didn't feel guilty because he didn't remember. Does that hold true with Paul? There's definitely a trigger at work: "This is as far as I want to go now. I'm going to turn and I don't want to know what I'm doing."

I remember a time Paul had forsworn hard liquor. "I only drink beer," he'd say. Yeah, but he was drinking a case a day. We were at a party where I kept noticing all the beer was disappearing. I wondered how anyone could drink that much: how long he kept it up, I don't know. He was never an obnoxious drunk. As I said, he would just click off.

MORT SAHL WAS A CONTROVERSIAL POLITICAL SATIRIST AND STAND-UP COMEDIAN WHO FIRST BEFRIENDED PAUL IN THE MID-1950S.

How many movies have you seen where Paul Newman comes in in the morning and puts his head into a sink full of ice? I think he's done it in thirty-eight pictures. Dreams die hard.

Paul loved taking those long saunas. We'd go into one, and he'd take a big brandy snifter and fill it full of ice cubes and

Scotch. He would tell me about his mother, and he would cry. She used to bait him. If there was anything bad in the newspapers about him—reviews, say—she'd clip and mail them to him just for torture.

Paul could be very morose. "Why can't people be tolerant?" he'd say. "Maybe it's impossible to get through the night without three bottles of Scotch. If anybody can get through the night with a *snake,* you should leave them alone—because at least they got through the night."

Paul used to drink through the night.

I don't know what it was all about, unless it's people not being equal to the task. Every actor I've ever known thought he was getting a pass. And I'm sure down deep Paul thought he was stealing the money and wondering when it's all going to catch up with him. People who don't feel good about themselves will do anything to feel better. Philanthropy is supposed to make them feel better, but it only works a few minutes at a time.

He had so much going for him of course—marriage, stardom; but even with work there were always challenges. In the days when Paul was constantly said to be working in the shadow of Marlon Brando, even after Paul had really emerged, he never won the awards. Steve McQueen bothered him for a time, too; he felt McQueen was the rise of the illiterate in acting. Paul wanted to be seen as an intellectual: "You don't know how lucky you are," he'd say to me. "All I get is applause, but you get respect."

PAUL ENTERTAINS PRINCESS MARGARET ON THE SET OF *TORN CURTAIN*
IN 1965 WHILE DIRECTOR ALFRED HITCHCOCK LOOKS ON.

ARTHUR NEWMAN, PAUL'S OLDER BROTHER,
WAS A PRODUCTION MANAGER ON MANY OF HIS FILMS.

Paul was a great admirer of Fredric March. When Freddie
was filming *Hombre* with Paul, he said to me: "Arthur, you
have to watch Paul on the drinking thing. I have seen more
great actors go down the tubes from drinking than from anything else."

Personally, I don't think it affected his work or there was
ever a day of bad performance because of the drinking. After
a day of shooting, Paul would just go back to his motel room

and drink there, but you never saw him hanging around the local bars getting drunk.

I think Paul's addiction to physical fitness and the sauna may have boiled some of that damned stuff out of his system before it would've finished him. Alcohol kills nerve cells, and the nervous system's cells don't replace themselves. So with Paul, instead of the booze killing off twenty-eight cells, it only killed thirteen.

Look, all human beings are constructed with self-destruct systems. And people run around all their lives trying to push that button and self-destruct. Every time they push the button, it does damage, and it builds up. The damage is minimal at the beginning, but it affects you later and just gets bigger and bigger.

That I was predisposed to addiction or alcohol could have been better for me, it could have been worse. That I could have drunk *more* is a reflection on the fact I couldn't be persuaded to do that. That I could have drunk less is also an indication that I wasn't able to be persuaded to do that. Whatever level I seek is like water seeking its own level. The individual seeks the level at which it will be persuaded to be one thing or the other.

That I didn't reach for a kilo of cocaine is, I suppose, better than if I had reached for it. That I didn't was uniquely me—and obviously, to some other people's discomfort, was uniquely not them. They did, I didn't. Now, there are some people who don't reach for alcohol, don't reach for cocaine, don't reach for anything. Well, that's them. I applaud them. It's also not their mother, or father, or their uncle—it's always a mixture of things that go into someone.

What I know about nature and nurture is that it's divided somehow depending on the individual. But what that individual does to the extent they were un-nurtured or natured improperly ultimately belongs to them. People have to take responsibility for what they do.

If I had to define "Newman" in the dictionary, I'd say: "One who tries too hard." An incredible part of me believes you're a free agent inside of your genetics. And that complaining that "Mommy never kissed me" is a bunch of shit. But somehow I got a pretty shitty opinion of myself that had to come from somewhere.

CHRIS HUNTER, SON OF ACTORS JEFFREY HUNTER AND BARBARA RUSH, WAS A CLOSE FRIEND OF SCOTT NEWMAN'S.

Scott told me about some adventures with his dad. Paul and Scott would go out cruising in that racing machine of Paul's and get very, very fucked up. Get a lot of beer, get drunk, and go joyriding. One time they crashed through the back of their garage into a refrigerator.

Maybe one of the relationships they had, sort of a kinship, was to get drunk together. You share some sort of alcoholic netherworld experience where you get outrageous—I think he was impressed he had shared that with his dad and had even gone through a wall. (He told me not to tell anyone.)

JOHN FOREMAN

When Paul and Joanne first got the house in Connecticut, Paul and I would sit far into the night and drink steadily. But many times, I'd go off to bed and Paul would just be passed out. Many times as he got drunker, it was nice, but many

PAUL IN THE EARLY 1960S

nights would take a turn and Paul would get exceedingly ugly and bad. He often talked about "the click," and suddenly all you'd hear would be "cocksucker" this or "fucking" that. He'd attack the business, everything he had done, all his work, his failures as a husband and as a father, on and on until finally, he'd just be making slurred animal noises. Paul would stay in his leather chair, and I felt it was somehow part of my job as his agent, my obligation, my love, to take the evening to its end. Then he'd pass out. Or call me dirty names or tell me how much he hated me.

In the early years of their marriage, Joanne would sit up into the night, too. Eventually, she'd just get out of her chair, go into their bedroom, and close the door. And that was that. She simply couldn't have anything more to do with it.

JOANNE WOODWARD

While Paul was directing *Sometimes a Great Notion* out in Oregon in 1971, he really almost killed himself. One night he fell out of bed. I found him on the floor with his head bleeding, and I came as close as I ever had to saying, "This is it, I just can't stand it." After that film was done, Paul gave up hard liquor.

I used to think the only peace Paul ever found was that peace he used to find in being dead drunk. Now he finds it in racing cars. Peace and grace, the comfort of knowing he has done something well.

The time when I was doing *Sometimes a Great Notion* was a kind of unhinged period for me. I felt unsettled, I was warring with everybody. There were even some difficult times with Joanne. The Newman-Foreman Company was producing the picture, I was starring, and our director, Richard Colla, had to be replaced. I ended up having to direct the film myself—and then the production had to be briefly shut down because I'd had a nasty motorcycle accident near our set in Oregon. I had too much pressure on me from every direction, and I didn't ask for it.

Even with getting bombed, I felt I did a tremendous amount of work on this film. The alcohol helped fuel a sense that you'd accomplished something. Maybe it was a very false sense of accomplishment.

GEORGE ROY HILL

Paul called me and asked if I could come out to the Oregon set and give him a hand. He was floundering. I got into my plane and flew out there, spent maybe a week looking at the footage that had been shot both by Paul and by Colla, did a little work on the script. I think my presence gave him more psychological help than professional, some extra confidence more than anything else.

When I'd first worked with Paul on *Butch Cassidy,* he'd just directed a film, *Rachel, Rachel*—and he'd won the New York Film Critics Award for directing, and got nominated for the Directors Guild prize. Though Paul never said a peep about it, in my mind I had to contend with it. But it was like there was this big sign always behind him with large letters saying: "I just won the director's award!"

He was always enormously grateful I'd come out to Oregon, though to be honest, I think he got more out of it than I gave.

JOHN FOREMAN

We went right from *Sometimes a Great Notion* to start *Judge Roy Bean*. You know what the difference was for Paul? With John Huston directing, Paul didn't have the responsibility of both directing the film and making it succeed. And between those two pictures, Paul, more or less, made a decision to stop drinking.

JOANNE WOODWARD

Drinking used to be the anguish of our lives. Now he drinks less and less. I told him recently: "That tiny glass of wine you're now drinking is just a pacifier—it's not that you need it, it's just you're afraid to let it go."

SIDNEY LUMET WAS ONE OF AMERICA'S MOST CELEBRATED DIRECTORS, BEST KNOWN FOR SUCH FILMS AS *12 ANGRY MEN, SERPICO, DOG DAY AFTERNOON,* AND *THE VERDICT,* STARRING PAUL.

Paul and I were talking about his character's, Frank Galvin's, drinking.

"I know about that," he said. I had the feeling that at one point, Paul had a problem, too, though I never asked further.

We discussed the concept of "playing the denial," which was one of the acting coach Sanford Meisner's great insights.

JOANNE AND PAUL ON THE SET OF *SOMETIMES A GREAT NOTION*
IN OREGON, 1970

How do you play a drunk? As someone who says, "I'm not drunk, I'm sober." You play the sobriety, put all the effort into being sober. Paul was very concerned with self-pity, because a drunk is, by nature, self-pitying. There was no way Paul was going to be crying in his cups.

Paul thought up these physicalizations that may be unpleasant but revealed Galvin's problem. The first time we see him he's going to a funeral and spraying his mouth with Binaca; that was Paul's idea, as was Galvin's always putting in eyedrops.

To stay sober, Galvin had to keep moving; stillness means he'd lift a glass—when he's working he has to stay in motion. For Galvin/Paul, you see the resolution in his final address to the jury—he doesn't move at all.

———

I don't think I ever reached any comfortable emotional moment in any picture until I did *The Verdict*. In fact, I can only remember a couple of moments that really worked in my films.

Lumet gives you the script, you go in on a Monday morning and read it around the table, then you start blocking. It really took me time to button up that character; I'd been behind with those huge long scenes with the judge, with the jury. I went home and really worked on those lines.

———

SIDNEY LUMET

There was a critical moment in *The Verdict* rehearsals. Paul had subtly let me know that he preferred to work on a character's externals first: What's the voice like? What's the body like? It doesn't matter to me where the acting comes from, I'll work any way an actor wants to work.

We had a run-through at the end of our second week; Paul still had the book in his hands, he had memorized maybe only a third of the script. He gave a very good performance but there was no life to it. After I made some comments to the cast, I sent them home, though I asked Paul to stay on. In so many words I said to him: "What's the matter? It's not working."

"Oh, it's just the lines, Sidney, I'm having so much trouble with the fucking lines. I'll be all right."

262 · THE EXTRAORDINARY LIFE OF AN ORDINARY MAN

"No, Paul. It isn't the lines."

He blinked, sort of, very rapidly, and said, "What do you think the problem is?"

"I think you have to make a decision," I said. "You have to decide how much of *you* you're going to let us see. It's you that's missing, the heartbeat."

Paul didn't say anything. We broke for the weekend. When he came in Monday, he was a different actor. It was all there, and there was very little to work on after that. I think Paul was waiting for someone to make a demand on his talent. He knows what good acting is, and good acting is about self-revelation.

In the summer of 1948, I had my first exposure to drunk performers. And by "drunk," I mean when they were offstage and onstage. I don't know how I made it through.

I was an intern at the Priscilla Beach Theatre in Plymouth, Massachusetts, and I had the honor, as a first-timer there, to stage-manage some productions. The theater was famous for doing a lot of current shows for short runs, often pulling audiences with big-name Hollywood or Broadway stars taking the leads while the interns did the rest. We also took these productions for brief tours elsewhere on Cape Cod.

Diana Barrymore and her third husband, Robert Wilcox, were the draws for the suspense drama *Laura*. Diana Barrymore was the legendary John Barrymore's daughter, and Wilcox was a regular leading man, mainly in B movies. We were set to go on at a theater in Woods Hole, on a very oddly configured stage; when I walked in, I thought we absolutely needed to have some sort of rehearsal before we opened there. So I, apprentice stage manager, called one for four o'clock in the afternoon of opening night. This was unheard-of for an apprentice stage manager. And as soon as Diana and Bob came in at four o'clock and saw the layout, they bolted to the bar across the street and got drunk. And when they returned near our eight o'clock curtain, they were just fractured.

There was a big sofa dominating downstage that was literally ten inches or so from the apron; Diana had to make several crosses in front of it, and the audience kept laughing because it looked like she was just going to fall into the house. They were fumbling their lines, and when one of the other actors (as per the script) pushed Diana into the sofa, the whole sofa fell backwards, and Diana wasn't wearing any panties; she exposed her entire crotch to the audience. It was a hoot.

After one of the Woods Hole shows, another intern, Charlie North, and I were designated to accompany Bob and Diana back to their company-provided cottage, a drive of about half an hour. Charlie drove, and in the spirit of our passengers we made the drive in only about eighteen minutes, running stop signs and red lights, rolling over curbs, everything. We'd actually bought a case of beer to take back to our dorms nearby; I think we had finished most of it by the time we got there. I guess we figured that if we were going to get hit, we may as well all be rubbery at the moment of impact.

The stars' cottage had a large lantern out front that illuminated the porch and made it highly visible from the female apprentices' dormitory. Just as we were letting off Bob and Diana, they started arguing. As it escalated, Wilcox grabbed the front of her sundress and just pulled it down, yelling, "How do you like that!" Both of them screaming. And you could hear one window after another in the dorm having the decency to slam shut.

For me, things were once again identified by really hard work and really hard partying.

And there's a coda to this. . . .

MEADE ROBERTS

I had gone to Philadelphia to see Paul, who was doing a pre-Broadway tour of *The Desperate Hours*. We went to dinner at the Variety, a private club for show people on the road at the Bellevue-Stratford Hotel. In staggered Diana Barrymore; this was maybe 1955, practically the lowest point of her career—schlepping around the country in a dreadful French farce called *Pajama Tops*. She was an alcoholic, bloated beyond belief, and she was with her husband, Bob Wilcox, also in the *Pajama Top* play and also an alcoholic.

"There's Diana Barrymore," Paul whispered to me. He told me how he'd known her at Cape Cod well enough to say "Good evening, Miss Barrymore."

"Do you think I should go over and pay my respects?"

"I'm sure she'd like that very much. It's just seven years since summer stock and you're the star of *Desperate Hours* and she's here doing some turkey."

So Paul got up from the table and walked to her table and said, "Miss Barrymore"—which is all he *could* say before she looked up at him and screamed out, "Marlon! Marlon!" She grabbed Paul, bent him over backwards, and kissed him on the mouth to the point where Wilcox and some other guy had to pull her off. Paul's face was the color of a beet; I'm sure she never remembered she'd ever met Paul Newman.

He came back to our table and said just one word: "Jesus."

When I'd gone over to Diana's table, I saw this little old face on this little old woman who was then not out of her thirties. She was just unrecognizable.

It was the same thing that happened in Beverly Hills not too many years later. I walked into La Scala restaurant, and I heard a voice call "Paul?" I looked around, but it was sort of dark and I couldn't see very well. And the "Paul?" was repeated and I realized it was coming from someone sitting alone in a booth. I went over and couldn't recognize this ravaged face with black-circled eyes.

She said, "Paul, it's me—Pier Angeli," and I was stunned. Pier was my costar in *The Silver Chalice* (when she was dating Jimmy Dean, who was shooting *East of Eden* on the next soundstage) and in *Somebody Up There Likes Me*. It hadn't been that long ago. And here was this lady now who'd once been so attractive, who'd had a modest gift but a great sense of physical style. Her head was the size of a pumpkin, no feature to identify it, even to remind you of what she had once looked like. It was appalling and frightening.

Neither Diana nor Pier lived to age forty. Wilcox made it to forty-five.

———

One of the reasons I used to get in so much trouble with booze was that I always drank so quickly. I was, after all, the chugalugging champion of the Seventh Fleet.

The way those chugalugging contests worked was the opponents each got a twelve-ounce glass of beer, one guy did a countdown, and you drank the beer. First guy to finish the glass won the round. I don't know where the gift came from, but I was able to do the same thing with whiskey, just down it like beer. And when I finally said, "Geez, I'd better go to bed," so I did, but then something happened. You have to remember that your body has to take the temperature of all the liquid you drink and get it up to blood temperature so it can be absorbed. I'd lie down, and try to sleep, while my body was warming up this ice-cold fluid and I'd actually be getting drunk and drunker as I dozed.

This whole effect was one of the reasons the British never used to get as drunk as we did. They'd drink their beer warm and never put ice in their whiskey.

My whole system, though, was based on catching up with all those ice cubes.

STEWART STERN

There was a certain wonder to it. Paul would get quite sloshed just sitting talking and say, "Well, I'm heading to bed now," and he'd shamble up to his room. And not so long afterwards, he'd shamble back down in his pajamas and start a whole new conversation. And again Paul would say, "Well, now I'm gonna go to bed." But each time he did that he'd be a bit more sloshed.

I would wake up and not know where I was. And sometimes I would wake up in strange places under strange circumstances. But I don't know if this is the time to talk about that; I mean, it's not exactly going to bounce off the page . . .

PAUL ESCORTS DAUGHTER CLEA
DOWN THE AISLE IN 2004.

XIII

I'm in the pool hall at the Hole in the Wall Gang Camp when this little child with wonderful pigtails walks over to me using a walker. One of the counselors says she has to go downstairs, so I pick her up. As I carry her, I realize that both her legs are plastic; I can feel the rivets against my arms. When I get her downstairs, I set her back on her feet and ask, "Are you okay?"

"Yeah," she says, "I'm fine," and she goes off and plays.

———————

I've always questioned my charitable impulses. I don't know how altruistic they really are. Or how generous, or Christian, or anything, really. The only thing I can readily say in my defense is that I do them, and that's better than not doing them.

The reason I'm suspicious of my charity is that I'm not sure what came first, the urge and then the theory or the theory and then the urge. The theory is, of course, having the luck of the draw, living in a democracy, being of the majority color, having an opportunity for education, enjoying the Bill of Rights, the Four Freedoms, and everything else. And that it must be regarded as a privilege that carries the unspoken obligation to hold out your hand to people who have less than you.

But isn't it easy to be hypocritical about this? To say, "The greatest enjoyment I've had is when I've given back to the community even as I've taken from it"? I got it for myself first, so I can afford to be charitable; I'm not going to be materially affected. What will

I suffer when I give away ten million dollars? That won't change the way I live. I won't eat less well. I can still stick a Buick engine in a Volvo.

The easiest thing I can do, frankly, is to give away money. It does not represent the kind of sacrifice that, it seems to me, might enhance the magnificence of the gift. Am I actually a philanthropist, the way so many in the media have come to describe me? As far as I'm concerned, a philanthropist is someone who gives up an entirely comfortable way of life, goes out into the populace, gets his hands dirty, and dedicates himself to whatever keeps them dirty. The grace of that person is formidable.

What's hard to give is time. To offer hands-on relationships to people who are less privileged. That's a big reason I question myself.

I remember, when I was a kid, taking bushel baskets of food and hand-me-downs to my aunt's church at Thanksgiving; we were also given the addresses of poor homes for my mother to drive to and drop things off then, and again at Christmas. There were kids with no shoes. I was appalled by the poverty. It felt like a threat of future pain, and it so immobilized me, I was overwhelmed. I'd been raised in that supersanitary home where anything unsterilized or that had the slightest smell of mustiness or decay was to be devoutly avoided.

I sometimes suspect the root of my charity came from having no civic impulses at all, just inventing them the way I invented everything else. Paul Newman, the inventor of Newman the Football Player, Newman the Actor, Newman the Citizen, Newman the Lover—all of it. You can exercise charity simply from the perception that you lack it and it really is something you should have. You ladle it out of a pot, like soup, but it's nothing you cooked yourself. I'm terribly concerned about the appearance of things, and charitable is a nice thing to be. It's easy to be charitable if it actually doesn't cost you anything; it's not like the people who get out there and take care of people at some cost to their own lives.

My instinct? I'm aware that in some ways it's my nature to deprecate everything I do—deprecate effort, deprecate friendship, until I cannot sort out the truth of things anymore. I weigh things meticulously, trying to be fair about everything—to my motivations, to myself, to everyone else. I set all this stuff on a scale so it doesn't tip, because the second it looks like it might, I put something on the other side.

STEWART STERN

I used to suffer with the mystery of what Paul thought of me, how he felt about me, because you can do a multiple-choice test about what feelings are going on behind that still face, that silence. But then, when I was sick, I overheard him talking to the doctors about me in intensive care. I realized that underneath the silence is his caring.

GEORGE ROY HILL

If I ever get depressed he's always very supportive and calls and makes sure I get out of the house, and will get me out for dinner or something. He isn't just giving me a phone call and saying, "how are you today?" He's saying, "meet me at Louie's for a drink" and we'll go on and have dinner and then we'll meet Joanne and we'll go to a movie or something like that. He's very active in that way. That's something that's been very important to me. I don't have any other friends that really take that kind of effort and time to support me.

When things come too easily, it seems you're never really aware of the effect they'll have. That a salad dressing that was begun so frivolously makes $19 million a year seems ridiculous. If the profits are $3.5 million—which is probably the highest margin of any food company in the US—well, to give that much away otherwise without being taxed, I'd have to earn $3.5 million from my own investments and acting jobs. I can't give away more Newman's Own profits than the equivalent of 100 percent of what I make. Unless I'm dead, in which case I can give away more than I make.

That the salad-dressing money goes to charity isn't really that interesting; it goes there because it would have been tacky to do anything else with it. The whole venture started as a lark when two old friends, A. E. Hotchner and I, were having some fun pouring homemade salad dressing into old wine bottles and selling it in tea shops and the like in Connecticut. It just developed a life of its own. The more people said "This isn't going to work," the greater my compulsion to make it work, including putting my name and picture on the labels, an act I'd never believe I'd see in my life (certainly not with my blessing).

But to watch it take off like *Six Characters in Search of an Author*—to see this little bottle running around looking for a home, bump into closed doors, then turn around and look for another path till the answer it found was charity, then find a rich uncle who helped it find its own life without asking unexpected favors—allowed me to say "Why not?"

As I said: that the money went to charity is no big surprise. That it can make $6 million or $7 million in profit a year but remains absolutely pure and untampered—and that I don't siphon something off for myself—well, that's the surprise.

I know a lot of people that have been involved with charities, people who raise a lot of money—they do appearances, they go on

TV, whatever, and get paid exorbitant fees for their efforts. People think they do it for nothing? They don't.

I don't know why I'm changing. I don't think it has to do with the imminence of death; I don't understand the impetus. I think our starting the camps in the mid-eighties had something to do with it, because setting that up was no more calculated than a change was in me. It was simply an idea I stumbled upon along with the where-withal to accomplish it. There was a real sense of providence.

Part of the inspiration was definitely the death of my friend Bruce Falconer in 1987. He was an architect in Connecticut, a man with a real sense of life. He had lost a leg in an accident as a kid, but still went out and pursued boating in a way that almost landed him on the Olympic team; I remember him flying to Italy one year for the trials. When his life got cut short by cancer at age fifty-two, I just kept thinking: "What a tragedy!" But then I realized that if what happened to Bruce was a tragedy, what must it be like for eight- or ten- or twelve-year-olds with cancer, who don't even get the short shot at life Bruce had? And shouldn't these kids get a crack at having some of the same kind of sense of accomplishment Bruce had? Shouldn't these kids get cared for, and in a way that gives them that chance?

So I just jumped in. I may have questioned my motives, but not what had to be done. It was an act that developed an emotional life and compassion of its own. I just woke up one morning and said, "Well, that's what I'm going to do." Knowing providence would take care of an idea that good, there was no way it wouldn't get completed. And so it was built. And became a source of great inspiration to a lot of people. And I'm inspired by it, too.

Not that providence would have necessarily changed me, but suddenly you discover you've committed $14 million to a children's camp and you only have $7 million on hand. Unless the salad-dressing business suddenly went kaput—the biggest risk I actually had was that I might have to borrow money against my future earn-ings. And even that jeopardy disappeared when one day a young kid from Saudi Arabia comes to Connecticut and you play Ping-Pong with him.

The kid tells you he happens to have a usually fatal blood disease and that he's currently living in Washington, D.C. And that he also happens to have connections with the Saudi royal family whose crown prince just happens to be their ambassador to the US and lives in Washington, too. And as a Muslim and a Saudi, the kid happens to have the right to petition the king himself through the crown prince. Then all of a sudden you're flying back to Connecticut from DC with a check for five million dollars for the camp and a letter that says the money is a gift from the king and the people of Saudi Arabia.

Now who can explain that? Who's going to know how the recognition of the pluck those camp kids have, and how they deal with their lives, simply triggered an unknown and previously unresponsive mechanism in me? A mechanism that opens a door into myself and lets me see what actually might be lurking there. Then you simply change? The answer may just be: "It was time." Suddenly, here I am, an atheist, a nonmetaphysicalist, who finds himself stuck right in the middle of God.

It's weird. It's human. And it's inexplicable.

It wasn't too long ago I met an eight-year-old kid at the camp who wasn't very mobile; his legs and hands were terribly weakened. His own immune system had somehow attacked his body, and now his body was rejecting itself. He was sitting on one of the big rocks near the camp entrance, talking to one of our counselors about God. The kid said he really didn't know much about God, but he did know about the big bang theory, and he understood that there was incredible energy expended in that concept and likened it to an atomic blast. The kid said he understood, though, that you couldn't get more energy out of anything than had been put in to create it.

"Well," the counselor said, "I think I get back more energy from the camp than I put into it."

The eight-year-old looked back at the counselor and said: "Well, you see, maybe that's what God is."

I think about the fact that I have been privileged to stay alive so long that anything I accomplish after this is gravy, and it seems to me that kids who don't even get the beginning of that privilege before it's threatened, they deserve something. Whatever you can do to give them an experience they can treasure, you should, if you have the capacity to, do it. What could be more meaningful?

STEWART STERN

The camp is about a personal drama as any that has ever been played out inside of him. Sometimes people are really congruent with themselves, where the impulse and what comes out of it are exactly in line. That camp is the purest expression of him, it's exactly him. Paul loves that camp and the truth of that connection helps to pull everyone in. It's amazing.

I did quite a lot of asking on behalf of the Hole in the Wall Gang Camp. You go out and do fourteen benefits. You have your picture snapped six thousand times. You host dinners in Boston and Hartford and New Haven and Stamford—you just raise the money. It was worth it. I flew out to St. Louis to see August Busch, who then owned Budweiser. I walked into his conference room and said, "August, I want you to be responsible for the crown jewel of our camp, the mess hall."

"How much do you want?" he replied.

"I need $866,000. And we'll match it."

"Deal," he said, and I left. It all took about eight minutes.

I wrote Busch a letter afterwards in which I thanked him for being the first corporate donor to give us the kind of support we hoped to get from the business community. His was a lavish gift, I wrote, and I had thought about it a great deal. "In all the years since I was in the Navy, starting at age eighteen," I explained, "I have consumed approximately two hundred thousand cans of Budweiser beer. So, if you really look closely at the figures, your contribution comes to just about a four-dollars-a-bottle rebate. And since you've had use of the money since 1944, it isn't really all that much. Still, I'm grateful."

I guess it hasn't hurt that in most things, money-wise at least, I'm actually a pretty easy touch. There was a time in recent years when I added everything up and it turned out I was responsible for forty-two people. Maybe that doesn't sound like much to an executive at a General Motors, but for someone like me, it really seemed frightening. It wasn't like I could just oversee the manufacture of forty cars and then sell them to earn the investment back. Plus, with the people on my payroll, I'll admit that maybe only half of them were serving a legitimate purpose.

Of course, once you find yourself responsible for so many people, it's very hard to cut them loose. How did I finally reduce the head count? Well, the good Lord cut them loose. Maybe I felt a sort of obligation to help others in order to make my own success bearable to me.

I think there is probably a large element of truth in that. I felt so much of my success was based on appearance and not really on what I did. I felt less reason to be proud of my accomplishments, less deserving, so I felt I had to give it away. I don't feel that way anymore. There is real poignancy for me with the camp and what happens there—and what has been happening at home, what is happening with this memoir project. It isn't there yet, but slowly, my insulation is beginning to break down.

XIV

PAUL AT HIS EIGHTIETH-BIRTHDAY PARTY WITH HIS BROTHER,
ARTHUR, AND GRANDSON HENRY

I have a feeling that you start out your life with a certain number and certain kind of people you are friendly with. If you become older and more successful, then you start having more friends for the wrong reasons. On the one hand, I hope I'm not as paranoid as my mother was, though on the other hand, I know there are people who have taken advantage of our acquaintance so that I feel used, and I am always very wary about it.

I wonder what my old age is going to be like, because I really don't have many friends. It's hard to feel lonely in New York, but I do sometimes. When Joanne is out of town, or I've been by myself for longer than I'm accustomed to, I realize there aren't a lot of people I can count on, and the ones I can count on are few and far between. If I wanted company, I wouldn't know who to call. Most of the people I know well are not around, so I just walk around the house and bump into things. I don't know if I'd have it any other way, because I don't seem anxious to do much about it; so it can't be all bad. Or maybe I'm just too proud to be seen making the effort.

PAUL AND HIS GRANDSONS, HENRY AND PETER, IN 2005

JOANNE WOODWARD

It takes such a long time to grow up and by the time you really get there the people usually you're growing up for are gone.

There are two parts of me out there, the ornament and the orphan. The ornament keeps doing all these things, and the orphan, the core, tries desperately to catch up, to seek an opening so he can raise his hand, speak forcibly, and say: "Let me be part of you again!"

When they do connect, we'll discover what kind of human being they make together. It's like the reunification of Germany—will it be a noble country this time, or are all the doubts that the cynical part asks really true?

When the orphan and the ornament become one person, will the question still be "Where is the compassion?" Will the answer be "Holy shit, there isn't any"?

Will you have struggled through a whole book, a whole life, to find decency underneath the ornament, to see these parts together and ask "Who's really home?" and have the answer come back: "A serial killer, that's all." The completion, the merging—it was hopeless, and all the impressive attributes you were looking to find in the blending of the halves were simply wiped out, your worst fears realized.

Me, I'm still wondering. And I dread the terror of discovering that the emotional anesthetic I've lived with will never be able to let the orphan get out front and have a life of its own. I've often thought what a terrible liability it would be for someone to become an actor who, like me, is somehow detached and anesthetized.

I've always had a sense of being an observer of my own life. Whether that's been heightened by the Budweisers, I don't know.

I have a sense of watching something, but not of living something. It's like looking at a photograph that's out of focus, because the camera was shaken and the head is blurry. In fact, you can almost see three or four separate distinct images, depending on how it's been vibrating. It's spacey; I guess I always feel spaced out.

PAUL AND JOANNE, SOMETIME IN THE MID-2000S

The times I have felt most together, without different parts of me splattered everywhere, are when I'm working. I might be trying to sort something out that's inventive or imaginative or original for my role. Whether I'm working alone or on my feet with people working together in a script, I feel trust, which is not a common experience for me.

Still, for me, acting gave me a sanctuary where I was able to create emotions without being penalized for having them; I could always giggle and say, "Oh, that's not me, that's just the character." It was so important to me to find a release, even in a fictional way—even if I couldn't reach those emotions in my real experience.

What shuts down a person? That's what I want to find out. Isn't it that a person wants to be anesthetized because he doesn't want to feel whatever sensation might be available? It isn't that you don't care, but that you're always observing and so detached you can never get inside. The core has never had an opportunity to fly, to discover its own curiosity. It was usurped, outranked by the decoration.

The core never had a chance.

The thing that's always fascinated me is that you think you emanate a certain color of light. You are convinced that you are a nice guy, or convinced you're a bad guy, you're convinced that you're terribly complicated, whatever it is, the light that people are looking at is not the same light that you think you are emanating. They see something entirely different. To have one thing on one side of the page completely contradict something that's on the other side of the page is interesting. It's good theater. It presents a very clear picture that there is no clear picture. There is not a statement, or a series of statements, that simply define a person. The thing that defines a person is, I think, a set of serious contradictions that you get from splashes of color. Out of that, you have a painting. Out of that painting, you find parts that are worth looking at or not worth looking at.

The uncertainties have always been there for me. I've always been in pain, always needed help. And one of the reasons I decided to enter therapy (on more than one occasion) was that there were a lot of things that I was painfully unperceptive and irresponsible about. I thought I could learn to perform in a more adult way.

My therapy was about my children, marriage, drinking, acting, politics—anything you can look at. You'd examine every single action you make, and if you think it is either not well thought through or done without a plan or immature, you work to correct it in some way.

I always had the sense I cater to appearances, that I drink too much, that I don't know how to define myself, so that I can't define my children, either—all of these negatives in my life. I've always been a private man who needs all these people around me all the time. The damage for me has come when I've realized what people were clamoring for was not me. It was characters invented by writers. It was the wit and ability of the authors, the wit and ability of the people who did the exploitation and selling, that had the appeal. What the public was demanding in no way resembled the decoration, let alone the orphan. Do people think that I'm William Faulkner's Ben Quick? Or Hud? Or Butch Cassidy? Or Frank Galvin in *The Verdict*? Or any of the other parts I've played? It's a shell that's photographed onscreen, chased by the fans and garnering all the glory. While whoever is really inside me, the core, stays unexplored, uncomfortable, and unknown.

STEWART STERN: Are you angry now, at anything?

PAUL: I think I'm angry at getting old. I'm not going to age gracefully.

I only have a few firm convictions. I don't believe in a hereafter. I don't believe in resurrection. I'm not a mystic or a supernaturalist.

But I am convinced that this is only a dress rehearsal. And when I die and they put me in that box down into the ground, someone is going to yell, "Cut!" Then a director will say, "Okay, let's go back to the number-one position, let's get the cameras back there and shoot that scene all over again." And my box will open up again and some other life will be continued or pursued. I actually think I'll die seven or eight times.

It will all turn out to be some kind of joke.

JOANNE IN THE EARLY 1980S.
PHOTO BY ALOMA GRUSKOFF

PAUL, 1976

AFTERWORD

STEWART STERN: Joanne, who do you think understands Paul?

JOANNE WOODWARD NEWMAN: The girls understand him better than he thinks they do.

The interviews in this book took place from 1986 to 1991. Dad was in his early sixties when they started and seemed to want to put it all out there. To hear and be heard by his family and friends with no holds barred. Ultimately, it was a snapshot in time—and for sure a pivotal one of realization and reflection. It wasn't the end of the story, though; in some ways, it was the beginning. He evolved immensely in the last quarter of his life; he became more present and reveled in giving back. It was an incredible gift to our family, and the world benefited from it.

Although he didn't focus on awards, he won a lot of them later in life. After ten nominations, he won an Oscar for *The Color of Money*. He also was given the Jean Hersholt Humanitarian Award (which was probably more important to him), the FDR Freedom from Want Medal (with Mom), as well as the Kennedy Center Honor (with Mom as well). The brilliant film editor Dede Allen said, "I was so shocked that the Academy would give him a lifetime achievement award. They usually seem to do it when they either expect someone might not be working again or someone to die. He was so graceful the way he handled it. He did it with humor, and yet I sensed an edge to his voice, particularly when he said, 'I hope my best work is ahead of me.'"

It was. He continued to choose roles that inspired him and delighted in working with Mom again to make *Mr. and Mrs. Bridge*. He did his best to surround himself with wonderful cast members who wanted to spend time rehearsing and enjoying their craft. He had such fun making *Nobody's Fool*, *Road to Perdition*, and especially *CARS* (for his grandchildren). He continued to search for another great script to make with Bob Redford, but they could never find a project to follow *The Sting* and *Butch Cassidy and the Sundance Kid*. That was a big disappointment to both, I believe. Remarkably, after a dare from Mom, and at the ripe old age of seventy-seven (his words, not mine), Dad went back to the stage after a thirty-eight year hiatus. He played the Stage Manager in a production of *Our Town* at the Westport Country Playhouse, our hometown theater. After a short run, the show went straight to Broadway! After seeing Mom go back to her roots many times, it was a treat to see Pop do the same.

Dad also got incredible joy from being behind the wheel of a race car. He was a very competitive person and had finally found a sport he excelled at—some would say, very much so! He began driving while making the film *Winning*, and never stopped. He raced in the Sports Car Club of America (SCCA) as well as professionally and won numerous championships. At the age of seventy, he even finished first at the Rolex 24 Hours of Daytona, landing him in the *Guinness Book of World Records* as the oldest winner of a professionally sanctioned race. He also teamed up with Carl Haas to form Newman-Haas Racing, one of the most successful teams in CART (Championship Auto Racing Teams) and IndyCar history, winning eight championships with Mario and Michael Andretti, Nigel Mansell, and Sebastien Bourdais. He rarely missed a race and loved being at the track to help in any way he could, even just cheering the drivers on. They were his "peeps." He loved everything about the racing community, and many of the drivers and team owners became his closest friends. He won his last race at Lime Rock Park, one of his favorite courses, at eighty-two, about a year before he passed away.

Dad had a lot of reasons to consider himself extremely lucky. He talked about that all the time. With the success of his charitable food company (including one of the first dedicated lines of organics), he went full throttle (pardon the pun) into philanthropy. Dad was always generous beyond words. Even his accountant used to say, "Paul is the most financially generous man that I know. He doesn't discuss why he's giving—I just see the end result of what he's done, and it's done very often anonymously, which to me is the true test of a philanthropist. I've never seen anything quite like it." His obituary in *The Economist* noted he was "the most generous individual, relative to his income, in the twentieth-century history of the United States." He was also incredibly loyal to his friends and would help beyond what most people would do. I know of a few times he gave up part of his salary to his costars and directors to level the playing field. He strove for fairness in all things.

When visiting an ailing friend in the hospital, Dad met many families with seriously ill children, and he thought this too wasn't fair, so it came to him—he would create a place where these children could get back to being kids again and, as he said, "raise a little hell." That idea, over thirty years ago, launched the Hole in the Wall Gang Camp, where kids could escape the fear and isolation of their illness. After realizing no one camp could serve all the children who needed it, he created what is now known as the SeriousFun Children's Network, which has grown to thirty camps and programs around the world, free to all who participate. That is what he was like: when he saw a problem, he wouldn't just talk about it, he would do something. In 2005, at eighty, he engaged in another important issue: water. Building on a lifelong commitment to environmental issues, he cofounded Safe Water Network, which collaborates with others to bring safe water to the two billion people around the world who lack this most basic need. He was never idle, forever finding ways to make a difference in people's lives.

He passed this philosophy along to his family: when you are lucky enough to have a good life, then you should give back. One of my favorite quotes from Dad is, "I'm not looking for sainthood. I just happen to think that in life we need to be a little like the farmer who puts back into the soil more than he takes out." There are few people who knew Dad who weren't inspired by that simple idea. He put it into practice with grace and humility. Ultimately, he saw philanthropy as his greatest legacy.

A final thought . . .

Dad was certainly one of a kind. What a silly expression, but it's so true. He never stopped learning or trying to better himself and the world around him. His family, friends, work, and passions are what fed his soul and made him better. He never stopped reaching for that elusive "excellence" he always spoke about—in his acting, his racing, his philanthropy . . . not to mention the burgers he made on the grill. We were so fortunate to have him in our lives and are doing our best to learn from his successes and failures, as children do. Even now, so many years after he passed, we can still hear him in our heads: all the good advice, the bad jokes, and unwavering encouragement.

It was often a blessing—and sometimes a bit of a curse—to have a father so revered by so many, but in the end, he was surrounded by his family as we said our final goodbyes. It will never be enough, though: there is always so much more to be said, to be argued over, to be understood on both sides, and we miss him terribly every day. He was the glue that held us together. So again, this offering is for all of us—his family, friends, and anyone who takes the time to read this book. The process of putting it together has certainly been an education, and I hope it will help inspire all of us into the future. You can't ask for more than that.

Clea Newman Soderlund

Paul Newman's first-person memoir is based on the numerous recorded conversations that were taped between him and Stewart Stern in 1986 and 1991.

In adapting this dialogue into this text, careful attention has been paid to accurately reflecting Newman's side of these conversations. Though Paul and Stewart's talks followed no obvious chronology, the material here has been largely restructured in a chronological fashion. While some quotes have been conflated and reorganized for narrative effect, and while some language has been added for the sake of clarity, this account represents an accurate if condensed adaptation of the Newman/Stern transcripts.

Newman left no specific instructions about how he'd eventually want this material to be constructed. Nevertheless, the spirit and tenor of his conversations has been preserved.

INDEX

Page numbers in *italics* refer to illustrations.

PHOTOGRAPHIC CREDITS

A NOTE ABOUT THE AUTHORS

PAUL NEWMAN was an actor, film director, race car driver, and entrepreneur. A ten-time Oscar nominee, Newman won an Academy Award for Best Actor for *The Color of Money*. He was also the recipient of numerous other awards, including a BAFTA Award, three Golden Globe Awards, a Screen Actors Guild Award, an Emmy Award, the Cecil B. de Mille Award, and the Jean Hersholt Humanitarian Award. His films include *The Hustler, Hud, Harper, Cool Hand Luke, Butch Cassidy and the Sundance Kid, The Sting, The Verdict, Mr. and Mrs. Bridge, Nobody's Fool, Road to Perdition,* and Disney-Pixar's *Cars,* where he was both a consultant on the film and the voice of Doc Hudson. As a race car driver, Newman won several national championships; he is listed in *The Guinness Book of World Records* as the oldest winner of a professionally sanctioned race at seventy years old, finishing first in his class at the Rolex 24 at Daytona Beach. As a political activist and humanitarian, he raised and donated nearly $1 billion to many charities. Newman had six children and was married to Oscar-winning actress Joanne Woodward for fifty years. He died in 2008 at the age of eighty-three.

STEWART STERN was a screenwriter and a longtime friend of Paul Newman's. He is best known for writing the screenplay for the films *Rebel Without a Cause, The Rack,* and *Rachel, Rachel.*

A NOTE ABOUT THE EDITOR/COMPILER

DAVID ROSENTHAL is a former publisher of Simon & Schuster, as well as of Villard Books and the Blue Rider Press, which he founded. He has worked as a journalist, magazine editor, and publishing executive for more than forty years.